MASTERING ITALIAN

N. MESSORA

EDITORIAL CONSULTANT
BETTY PARR

First published 1983
Reprinted 1984, 1985, 1986, 1987, 1988

Published by
MACMILLAN EDUCATION LTD
Houndmills, Basingstoke, Hampshire RG21 2XS
and London
Companies and representatives
throughout the world

Printed in Hong Kong

ISBN 0–333–34310–7 (hardcover)
ISBN 0–333–34311–5 (paperback, home)
ISBN 0–333–35461–3 (paperback, export)

Cassette ISBN 0–333–34057–4

The cassette which accompanies this book can be ordered from your local bookseller or, in case of difficulty, from Globe Education, Houndmills, Basingstoke, Hampshire, RG21 2XS (telephone 0256 29242).

CONTENTS

CONTENTS

CONTENTS

II REFERENCE MATERIAL

SERIES EDITOR'S PREFACE

Mastering Italian is the fourth of the language books in this series, intended primarily for adult beginners working without a teacher. The publishers make no promises of instant mastery and recognise that a small volume such as this cannot contain more than the basic essentials of any living language. It is believed, however, that these initial books fill a notable gap in an otherwise well-cultivated field.

In the first place, they provide a carefully planned introduction to the language and a secure foundation for further study, for which it is hoped that this series will ultimately give additional help. Furthermore, they differ from existing publications, which seem either to concentrate on teaching 'how to survive abroad', or else to adopt a mainly academic approach. The distinctive feature of the language-books is their dual aim: to assist not only those studying for practical —usually tourist or commercial—purposes, but also those wishing to acquire a more formal knowledge of the language, with the intention of extending their skills by subsequent study.

The twofold objectives of these books are made clear from the start, so that students may determine their own learning strategy and work in ways best suited to their needs and capacity. The main emphasis is placed on understanding and speaking the language of everyday life, but the importance of reading and writing is not overlooked. Each chapter starts with lively dialogues, presenting useful words and phrases in a realistic context and providing the basis for all the associated teaching material. Specific indications enable the student to distinguish between essential basic language and the more difficult items needed for deeper study. The exercises, necessary for practice, consolidation and self-assessment, are arranged at two levels, so that students with different linguistic aims may choose their own programmes.

The table of contents is detailed and informative. The author's introduction explains the nature and sequence of the material and suggests various ways of working with it; this section will replay close attention, so that the best use may be made of the well-constructed dialogues, the comprehensive vocabulary lists, the explanations of background information and grammar, as well as the numerous and varied exercises.

Mastery of the spoken language presents one of the greatest difficulties for the student working alone. Without considerable linguistic experience, it is impossible to develop an ear for the sounds and intonation of a language by reading the printed page. All the language books in this series contain a helpful guide to pronunciation, and there is also a most valuable adjunct in the form of a cassette, in which all the dialogues are recorded by native speakers. As Italian is a phonetic language, with generally consistent rules for pronunciation and stress, it is relatively easy to pronounce individual words with fair accuracy. However, in order to speak good Italian, with authentic intonation and rhythm, and to understand native speakers of the language, the cassette is indispensable. If it is intelligently used, in conjunction with the pronunciation guide, the familiar problems of speaking and understanding a new language should be solved.

The authors of the language books in the Master series are all resourceful and successful teachers of individuality and experience. They have tried to ensure that those who use these books thoughtfully may experience the pleasure and satisfaction of successful language-study without the direct intervention of a teacher. All concerned with the project hope that the books will establish for the learner a continuing involvement with the infinite variety and endless fascination of languages.

BETTY PARR
Editorial Consultant

INTRODUCTION: HOW TO USE THIS BOOK

GENERAL PLAN

This book is intended for complete beginners in Italian but it also provides a most useful refresher-course for those with some knowledge of the language. Each chapter is built around dialogues on which are based a series of exercises that help to recreate the process of learning a language in the country where it is spoken. The pronunciation guide (pp. xv–xvii) is an important element and should be studied in conjunction with the accompanying cassette, on which all the dialogues and all the examples in the pronunciation guide are recorded.

DIALOGUES

Each chapter has four dialogues. The main characters in two of these are teenagers, while the other two dialogues are concerned principally with business people and their friends and relations. In this way you become familiar with an informal and a more formal type of language. Furthermore, the two sets of dialogues present similar topics, so that the basic vocabulary and grammatical points are repeated, thus facilitating the learning process. The dialogues of the first five chapters are translated into English in the reference material section (pp. 261–8). They are not literal translations. They give the phrases that English people would use in the circumstances described in the dialogues (e.g. 'tutto bene in viaggio?' is translated 'did you have a good journey?'. The literal meaning is 'all well on the journey?').

VOCABULARY LISTS

The vocabulary lists which follow the dialogues in each chapter give the meaning of all new words in order of their appearance and provide useful grammatical information. In addition, they indicate in **bold type** the stressed vowel in any word which does not follow the rule of accenting the penultimate syllable (e.g. **bene** is regular, but **essere** is not, so the list shows **essere**, to help you to pronounce it correctly).

The supplementary vocabulary lists in the grammar reference section give you further words relating to the topics of each chapter. You may wish to compile your own vocabulary book, listing the words alphabetically as you meet them.

EXPLANATIONS

Each section provides background notes with information about Italy and practical suggestions useful during a visit to the country. In addition, this section takes you step by step through the dialogues, pointing out the basic phrases relating to the theme of the chapter and explaining essential points about the grammar, their peculiarities and any important differences from English. There are plenty of examples, with a translation next to them, most of which are taken from the dialogues. In this way you are able to check your comprehension of the dialogues and learn the language in context. If you wish to consolidate your knowledge further, you could use the translations of the examples and translate them back into Italian for extra practice.

If you wish to explore in greater depth the grammar of the language, there is a grammar reference number relating to each topic to guide you through the grammar reference section. This section has three functions: first, to group together all the aspects of a grammar topic which have been presented over various chapters; second, to provide a summary of the grammatical contents of the book, to help you to revise or check quickly; third, to give you the opportunity of acquiring a sounder grammatical knowledge of the language.

EXERCISES

These are graded at two levels. Those marked **A** are for students seeking mainly to understand and speak the language in circumstances similar to those presented in the dialogues, while the **B** section is offered to those who wish to pursue the details of the grammatical points raised and reach a stage of competence that will enable them to use the language more creatively. The dialogues include expressions which the students will need to learn in order to be able to use them in conversation, as well as expressions which they will recognise and understand, though not necessarily expect to use themselves. The exercises are planned to help students to practise speaking, while the cassettes are aimed more at helping them with aural comprehension.

SOME ADVICE

Learning a language is an individual matter, and people learn languages in different ways. However, here are a few suggestions which you may find useful, some of which should help you to have fun in the learning process. Persuade a friend to learn Italian with you. Comparing progress is a challenge which helps you to overcome moments of frustration and prompts you to find spare time in your day. Either on your own or with someone else, play out the various roles, as if you were one of the characters. Think yourself into a situation where you would have to ask somebody for something—a drink, a piece of information—and work out what you would actually have to say. Try working through the exercises and seeing how long it takes you to do them correctly. The next time you do them, try to better your own record. To help your memory and your spelling, type out the dialogues and the exercises. Concentrating on a keyboard does wonders.

It is very important to use the cassettes consistently. Listen to the examples from the pronunciation guide or to a sentence of a dialogue, use the pause button, repeat the words.

The inclusion of revision sections every five chapters is intended to help you to check on your progress. And now, buon lavoro! Enjoy your work!

GUIDE TO PRONUNCIATION

It is fairly easy to pronounce Italian more or less correctly. Most sounds have approximate equivalents in English and the few new ones are not difficult to imitate, if you listen very carefully to the cassette, which contains recordings of all the examples in this guide, as well as all the dialogues in the book. Particular attention must be paid to the intonation and rhythm of the language, which are different from English.

1. Each vowel is always pronounced as described below, whatever its position in a word.
2. To speak Italian with its well-known musical rhythm, pronounce each vowel clearly and separately, even if it is within a group. *Example*: aiuto = a + i + u + to (help!)

It must be emphasised that the English sounds given are only approximate and not identical. Listen to the cassette to get the right effect.

Approximate English sounds		*Examples*
a	*ca*r	m*a*drig*a*le (madrigal)
*e	b*e*d	ser*e*nata (serenade)
i	*ea*t	vio*li*no (violin)
*o	h*o*t	*o*pera (opera)
u	r*oo*m	m*u*sica (music)

**e* and *o* are pronounced more 'open' or more 'closed' according to regional variations.

THE CONSONANTS

The following consonants or groups of consonants are always pronounced as indicated below, whatever their position in a word. The presence of an 'h' after 'c' or 'g' makes the sound hard.

ce	as *ch* in chest	con*ce*rto (concert)
ci	as *ch* in chin	Giacomo Puc*ci*ni
che	as *k* in Kent	or*che*stra (orchestra)
chi	as *k* in kilo	*chi*tarra (guitar)

ge	as *j* in jet	Michelan*ge*lo
gi	as *j* in jolly	*Gi*otto
ghe	as *ge*t	spa*ghe*tti
ghi	as *g*immick	In*ghi*lterra (England)
gli	approximately as *ll* in million but more marked	Modi*gli*ani
gn	approximately as *ni* in onion but more marked	Pietro Masca*gni*
h	is silent	no difference between *a* (at) and *ha* (has)
qu	as in s*qua*t	*qua*rtetto (quartet)
r	is trilled by vibrating the tongue against the hard palate	o*r*gano (organ)
sce	as in *she*pherd	*sce*riffo (sheriff)
sci	as in *shi*ft	fa*sci*smo (fascism)
t	is pronounced with the tip of the tongue on the back of the top teeth	*T*osca
z	as *ts* in bets	*Z*effirelli

DOUBLE CONSONANTS

These are stressed more in Italian than in English and are pronounced almost twice without a pause between the two letters:

Federico Fe*ll*ini (as a*ll l*ength)
Paolo Ro*ss*i (as mi*ss*pent)
la pe*nn*a (as p*en-kn*ife)

STRESSES

The majority of Italian words are stressed on the last vowel but one, and there is no accent to indicate it:

buongiorno, signorina

Accents are written only when the stress falls on the last vowel of a word. In this case the stressed vowel has a sharp sound:

sì (yes)
è (it is)
città (city)

When a word does not follow these two rules, the stressed vowel is printed in the vocabulary lists of this book in **bold** type:

> **ca**mera (room)
> tel**e**fono (telephone)

THE ITALIAN ALPHABET

As you have seen, in Italian the same sound always corresponds to the same spelling and the same spelling is always pronounced in the same way. This is why there is no equivalent to the expression 'how do you spell it?'. To ask for the spelling of a foreign name, Italians will ask you; come si scrive? (lit: *How do you write it?*).

Here is the Italian name for each letter of the alphabet (in brackets):

> a (a); bi (b); ci (c); di (d); e (e); effe (f); gi (g); acca (h); i (i); i lungo (j); cappa (k); elle (l); emme (m); enne (n); o (o); pi (p); qu (q); erre (r); esse (s); ti (t); u (u); vi (v); vi doppio (w); ics (x); i greco (y); zeta (z).

THE APOSTROPHE

The apostrophe indicates the omission of a vowel and does not affect the pronunciation.

I TEACHING UNITS

del bel paese là dove 'l sì sona
(in the fair country where the *sì* doth sound)

Dante, *Divine Comedy*, 33, 80, *c.* 1300

INTRODUCTIONS: BREAKING THE ICE; GOODBYES

1.1 DIALOGUES

Dialogue 1

Maria Pardi, an Italian businesswoman, has gone to meet Julian McKenzie, a Scottish businessman, at the airport.

Pardi: Scusi, è il signor McKenzie?
McKenzie: Sì. Sono Julian McKenzie. È la signora Pardi?
Pardi: Sì. Buongiorno. Piacere.
McKenzie: Piacere. (They shake hands).
Pardi: Ben arrivato. Tutto bene in viaggio?
McKenzie: Sì. Grazie. Tutto bene.

(On the way home, McKenzie points to a monument and asks what it is.)

McKenzie: Scusi, signora, che cos'è?
Pardi: È il Castello Sforzesco.
McKenzie: È molto bello!

Dialogue 2

At her office, Maria Pardi introduces Mr McKenzie to other people.

Pardi: Signorina Dani, buongiorno. Le presento il signor McKenzie . . . signor McKenzie, la signorina Dani . . .
Dani: Piacere.
McKenzie: Piacere. (They shake hands.)
Pardi: (to McKenzie) Le presento il regista Luigi Bianchi.

Bianchi: Molto lieto.
McKenzie: Molto lieto.

(And now the usual questions to break the ice.)

Dani: È qui in Italia per lavoro o in vacanza?
McKenzie: Eh, no! Non sono qui in vacanza. Sono qui per lavoro, purtroppo.
Bianchi: È qui con la famiglia o è solo?
McKenzie: Sono qui solo.
Pardi: Signor McKenzie, le presento il dottor Rossi . . .
McKenzie: Molto lieto.
Rossi: Piacere.
Pardi: Il dottor Rossi non è italiano, è svizzero.
Rossi: (to McKenzie) È inglese?
McKenzie: No! No! Non sono inglese. Sono scozzese. La ditta è inglese. È a Londra.

(Later, Miss Dani is the first to leave.)

Dani: Buonasera a tutti. A domani.
McKenzie: Buonasera, signorina. A domani.

Dialogue 3

Tim Yeats, an English student, is going to spend some time in Italy as a guest of an Italian student, Lucio Pardi. Lucio meets Tim at the station in Milan.

Lucio: Scusa, sei Tim Yeats?
Tim: Sì.
Lucio: Sono Lucio Pardi.
Tim: Ciao!
Lucio: Ciao! Ben arrivato! (They shake hands.) Tutto bene in viaggio?
Tim: Sì. Grazie. Tutto bene.

(On the way home, Tim points to a monument.)

Tim: Scusa, Lucio, che cos'è?
Lucio: È la chiesa di San Babila.
Tim: È molto bella!

Dialogue 4

At Lucio's home Tim is introduced to Lucio's sister, Carla, and a few friends.

Lucio: Carla . . . Tim . . . Tim . . . Roberto, il ragazzo di Carla . . .
Carla e Roberto: Ciao! Ben arrivato!
Tim: Ciao! (They shake hands.)
Roberto: Sei qui a Milano per studio o in vacanza?
Tim: Sono qui per studio, purtroppo!
Lucio: Julie è qui?
Roberto: No, non è qui. (To Tim) Julie è l'amica francese di Carla.
Julie: (Arriving) Sono qui, sono qui. Ciao a tutti.
Lucio: Ciao. Sei sola o con Maria?
Julie: Sono sola.
Roberto: Julie, ti presento Tim, lo studente inglese, ospite di Lucio.
Tim: Ciao.
Julie: Ciao. (Later, Roberto leaves.)
Roberto: Ciao, Tim. A domani.
Tim: Ciao, Roberto. Arrivederci

1.2 VOCABULARY

As explained in section 1.3, Italian nouns are either feminine (f) or masculine (m); this is indicated in the vocabulary lists because the gender ought to be learnt together with each word. Irregular plurals (m and f) are listed next to their singular forms. Adjectives are given in the sing. masc. and fem. (e.g. famoso-a). Irregular verbs are indicated as irreg. For verbs with an * see 4.3 (k). Words are normally accented on the penultimate vowel (see 'Stresses' in the guide to pronunciation). If a word does not follow these rules, the accented vowel is printed in **bold** type.

Dialogue 1

scusi	excuse me (formal)
è (**e**ssere irreg.)	he, she, it is; you are (formal)
il (m sing.)	the
il signore (abbr. signor) (m)	Mr, sir, gentleman
sì	yes
sono (essere)	I am

la (f sing.)	the
la signora (f)	Mrs; Madam; lady
buongiorno	good morning; good afternoon
piacere	how do you do? (lit. pleasure)
ben arrivato-a	welcome (lit. well arrived)
tutto; -bene	everything; everything is fine
bene	fine; all right
il viaggio (m); in-	journey; during the journey
grazie	thank you
che cosa? che cos'è?	what? what is it?
il castello (m) -Sforzesco	castle; -of the Sforzas
molto	very
bello-a	beautiful, pretty, nice

Dialogue 2

la signorina (f)	Miss; young lady
le presento	may I introduce you? (formal) (lit. I introduce to you)
il regista (m) la regista (f)	film director
lieto-a; molto-	pleased; pleased to meet you
qui	here
in	in
l'Italia (f)	Italy
per	for
il lavoro (m); per-	work, job; on business
o	or
la vacanza (f); in-	holiday; on holiday
no	no
non	not
purtroppo	unfortunately
con	with
la famiglia (f)	family
solo-a	on one's own; alone
il dottore (abbr. dottor) (m)	Dr; doctor
italiano-a	Italian
svizzero-a	Swiss
inglese-e	English
scozzese-e	Scottish; Scot
la ditta (f)	firm
a	at; in; to
Londra (f)	London
buonasera	good evening
tutti -e (pl.)	everybody
domani; a-	tomorrow; see you tomorrow

Dialogue 3

scusa	excuse me; pardon (familiar)
sei (essere)	you are (familiar)
ciao	hallo; hi; cheerio
la chiesa (f)	church
di	of

Dialogue 4

il ragazzo (m)	boy; boyfriend
la ragazza (f)	girl; girlfriend
e	and
Milano (f)	Milan
lo studio (m); per-	study; to study
l' (m and f sing.)	the
l'amico (m) (pl. -ci)	friend (m)
l'amica (f) (pl. -che)	friend (f)
francese -e	French
ti presento (familiar)	I introduce (to) you
lo (m sing.)	the
lo studente (m)	student (m)
la studentessa (f)	student (f)
l'ospite (m and f)	guest
arrivederci	goodbye

(For supplementary vocabulary lists see p. 314.)

1.3 EXPLANATIONS

(The grammar references indicated from (d) begin on p. 322.)

(a) Greetings

Italians shake hands when they are introduced, when they have not seen each other for some time, when they depart after being introduced and when they are going away for a time.

Ciao! (hello and goodbye) is used with people that one would usually call by their first name:

Ciao, Carla, tutto bene?	Hello, Carla, everything all right?
Ciao, Roberto, a domani.	Cheerio Roberto, see you tomorrow.

Buongiorno (lit. *good day*) is used in the morning and in the afternoon, meeting people or taking leave of them:

Buongiorno, signora Bianchi.	Good morning, Mrs Bianchi.
Buongiorno, signor Rossi.	Good afternoon, Mr Rossi.

Buonasera (good evening) is used until late in the evening.

Buonanotte (good night) is used when retiring for the night.

Arrivederci is used to say goodbye formally and informally.

(b) Forms of address
While in English everybody is addressed as 'you', in Italian a person may be addressed in a familiar or in a more formal way. The familiar form is used with friends, relatives, children, teenagers, colleagues, i.e. people called by their first name. The formal form is used with everybody else. The following sections (c–e) will give you your first examples.

(c) Attracting people's attention
To attract people's attention, the familiar form is scusa:

Scusa, Carla ...	Excuse me, Carla ...

The formal form is scusi:

Scusi, signor Bianchi ...	Excuse me, Mr Bianchi ...

You may also attract people's attention by calling them:

Signore ...	Sir ...
Signora ...	Madam ...
Signorina ...	Miss. It is common practice and quite polite to call an unmarried woman, signorina.

(d) Introductions – *grammar ref. 49*
To introduce people in the familiar form, you simply say their names. Or you use the formula ti presento ...

Ti presento Carla.	This is Carla.

To introduce people formally, either you simply say:

. . . la signorina Dani.	. . . Miss Dani.

Or, more elaborately, you use the formula le presento:

Le presento il dottor Rossi.	Let me introduce to you Dr Rossi.
Le presento il regista Bianchi.	Let me introduce to you the film director Bianchi.

As you see, unlike English, Italians put the article il, la (the) in front of signore, signora, signorina or any professional title in introductions.

A familiar reply to an introduction may be ciao! or, more colloquially, salve!

A formal reply is either piacere! (how do you do) or molto lieto (pleased to meet you) if you are a man, molto lieta if you are a woman.

(e) Essere (to be) – *grammar ref. 58*
In Italian there are two words for 'you'. There is the familiar form tu and the formal form lei. Voi (2nd person pl.) is used when referring to more than one person (*8.3(g)*). The verb with tu is different from the verb with lei, as you can see in the following examples.

To ask people about their identity, the familiar form is sei:

(tu) Sei Tim Yeats?	Are you Tim Yeats?

The formal form is è:

(lei) È il signor McKenzie?	Are you Mr McKenzie?
(lei) È il dottor McKenzie?	Are you Dr McKenzie?

To reply and say who you are, you say: sono . . .

Sì, (io) sono il dottor Rossi.	Yes, I am Dr Rossi.
Sì, (io) sono Tim.	Yes, I am Tim.
Sì, sono l'amica di Carla.	Yes, I am Carla's friend.

To describe someone else's identity, you say: è . . .

(Lui) È Tim Yeats.	He is Tim Yeats.
(Lei) È l'amica di Carla.	She is Carla's friend.

To sum up, the pattern of the verb essere in the singular is this:

io sono	I am
tu sei	you are (familiar)
lei è	you are (formal)
lui, lei è	he, she, it is

Io, tu, lei etc. (the subject pronouns) are usually left out in Italian. Tu and its verb form are used to address people familiarly, lei to address people formally.

Notice: in Italian the verb ending of the formal form lei has the same ending as the 3rd person sing. (he is). This characteristic applies to *all* verbs.

(f) How to ask a question – *grammar ref. 75*
Questions are usually formed by simply raising the tone of the voice at the end of the sentence, or, like English, by using words such as che cos'è? What is it?

Signor McKenzie è scozzese?	Are you Scottish Mr McKenzie?
Sei francese?	Are you French?
È la chiesa di San Babila?	Is it Saint Babila's church?

(g) How to affirm and to deny – *grammar ref. 77*
The simplest form of affirmation is sì. The simplest form of negative is no. These forms are equivalent to the English: 'Yes, I am'; 'yes, he does'; 'no, I am not'; 'no he doesn't' etc.

Sei scozzese? Sì.	Are you a Scot? Yes, I am.

Alternatively, for a negative, the word non is placed in front of the verb:

Non sono scozzese.	I am not Scottish.
Non sono in vacanza.	I'm not on holiday.

(h) The possessive form with ''s' – *grammar ref. 16*
The form *'s* does not exist in Italian. It is expressed by the word di:

È l'amica di Carla.	She is Carla's friend.
È la chiesa di San Babila.	It is Saint Babila's church.

(i) Nouns and definite articles (the) – *grammar ref. 1; 13*
All Italian nouns are either masculine or feminine. Their gender ought

to be learned by heart together with the word, because there is no infallible way of guessing it. Articles vary according to the gender of the noun they define:

	masculine singular	feminine singular
before a consonant	*Il* castello	*la* chiesa
before a vowel	*l'* ospite	*l'* amica
before *s* +a consonant and z	*lo* studente	

(j) Adjectives: singular forms – *grammar ref. 37*
To state your nationality, you say:

Sono italiano (if you are a man)	I am Italian.
Sono italiana (if you are a woman)	I am Italian.
Sono inglese (man or woman)	I am English.

Similarly, to describe something, you say:

Il Castello Sforzesco è bell*o*.	(the word castello is masculine)
La chiesa è bell*a*.	(the word chiesa is feminine)
È una chiesa frances*e*.	It's a French church.
È un castello frances*e*.	It's a French castle.

To sum up: in the singular, some adjectives end in -e, for masculine and feminine forms. Others end in -o and change into -a when qualifying a feminine noun. Adjectives are usually placed *after* the noun(s) they refer to.

To reinforce an adjective, the word molto is placed in front of it:

È molto bello, il ragazzo di Carla.	Carla's boyfriend is very handsome.
Carla è molto bella.	Carla is really pretty.

Proverbio: Il buon giorno si vede dal mattino.
A happy day starts the way.

1.4 EXERCISES

(The key to these exercises begins on p. 269.)

A (for students who wish to acquire a basic knowledge of Italian)

Exercise 1

Play the following roles. Speak up. Remember that the more you practise, the more you learn, as with a musical instrument.

(i) You are Mr McKenzie visiting a firm. What would you reply?

— Le presento il signor McKenzie. . . . Piacere.

— . . .

— Tutto bene in viaggio?

— . . .

— (When you leave) Buonasera, signor McKenzie.

— . . .

(ii) You are Mr McKenzie and are introduced to other staff of the firm.

— La signorina Dani, il signor McKenzie.

— . . .

— Molto lieta. È qui in vacanza o per lavoro?

— . . .

— È qui solo o con la famiglia?

— . . .

(iii) You are Tim. You have missed Lucio at the station. So you go to his home and introduce yourself to his mother.

— . . . (Ask her whether she is Mrs Bruni.)

— . . . (Say who you are.)

— . . . (Reply that you're happy to meet her.)

— . . . (Ask whether Lucio is there.)

— . . . (Say hello and shake hands with Lucio.)

Exercise 2

Which is the right answer to each question?

1. Tutto bene? (a) Sì, grazie. (b) Piacere. (c) Molto lieto.
2. Sei scozzese? (a) Sì, sono in vacanza. (b) No, non sono francese. (c) Sì. Sono scozzese.
3. Scusi, è solo? (e) No, sono qui per lavoro. (b) Sì, sono qui a Milano. (c) No, sono con la famiglia.

Exercise 3

At Lucio's home, his friends want to make Tim feel at home. Imagine you're Tim, and answer their questions.

— Sei qui solo a Milano?

— Sei qui in Italia per studio?

— Sei Tim Yeats?

— Sei inglese?

B (for students who wish to progress beyond a basic knowledge)

Exercise 4

You are overwhelmed with enquiries. Answer according to the situations in the dialogues.

1. La chiesa di San Babila è bella?
2. Il signor McKenzie è a Milano per lavoro o per studio?
3. La famiglia McKenzie è a Milano?
4. Julie è l'amica di Tim?
5. Julie è svizzera?
6. Il regista Bianchi è francese?
7. Sei italiano?

Exercise 5

Julian McKenzie has missed Mrs Pardi at the airport. Translate the message he leaves for her with her secretary:

I am Julian McKenzie, the Scottish friend of Maria Pardi. Everything is fine in London. I'll see you tomorrow.

Exercise 6

Tim rings up Italian friends in Florence. Translate their telephone call.

— Is it Mr Gardi? — Yes, I am Mr Gardi. — I am Tim Yeats. Good morning. I'm in Milan with Lucio Bruni's family. — Are you on your own? — Yes. I'm on my own. The family is in London. — Are you here on holiday? — No. I'm not here on holiday. I'm here to study. — Did you have a good journey? — Yes, thank you. — Goodbye, Tim. — Goodbye, Mr Gardi.

Exercise 7

Write down all the words you have learnt which require il in front of them. Do the same exercise with l'.

BOOKING ACCOMMODATION; ASKING THE WAY IN TOWN

2.1 DIALOGUES

Dialogue 1 All'Ente Turismo

Tim is looking for accommodation for a friend who is coming to Milan. He goes to the Tourist Office.

Impiegato: Ciao.
Tim: Buongiorno. C'è un ostello della gioventù qui a Milano?
Impiegato: Sì. C'è un ostello molto grande.
Tim: C'è un posto per una settimana?
Impiegato: No. È tutto esaurito.
Tim: Allora . . . una pensione non molto cara. È per uno studente straniero.
Impiegato: Allora . . . (looking in the register) C'è una pensione non molto cara in via Verdi 3. È la pensione Firenze.
Tim: C'è una camera singola da lunedì prossimo?
Impiegato: Sì. Una camera singola . . . Sì . . . c'è. Seimila per notte.
Tim: La colazione è inclusa?
Impiegato: No. Non è inclusa. Che nome?
Tim: Che nome? Ah! Steve Lloyd (spelling it) Esse, ti, e, vi, e. Elle, elle, o, i greco, di: Steve Lloyd.

Dialogue 2 Per strada

Tim stops a teenager to check his way. He addresses him informally.

Tim: Scusa, per piacere . . . per via Verdi?
Ragazzo: Scusa, che via?
Tim: Per via Verdi.

Ragazzo: È in centro. Verso l'università.
Tim: È lontano?
Ragazzo: No. Sempre dritto fino a piazza Garibaldi.
Tim: Grazie. Ciao. (After a while he stops another teenager.) Scusa, per piacere ... dov'è via Verdi?
Ragazzo: È subito qui a destra dove c'è una banca. Poi sempre dritto e a sinistra.
Tim: (he misunderstands) Allora, subito qui a sinistra ...
Ragazzo: No! No! Subito a destra. Poi sempre dritto ...
Tim: Ah! Sì. Grazie.
Ragazzo: Prego. Ciao!
Tim: (to himself) A destra, sempre dritto, a sinistra.

Dialogue 3 Per strada

Mr McKenzie is looking for accommodation for himself and his wife, who is coming to Milan. He meets Miss Dani.

McKenzie: Buongiorno, signorina Dani.
Dani: Buongiorno, signor McKenzie. Tutto bene?
McKenzie: Sì, grazie. Tutto bene. Scusi, signorina Dani, dove c'è un albergo qui vicino, per piacere?
Dani: Di prima o di seconda categoria?
McKenzie: Di prima categoria. E non molto rumoroso.
Dani: C'è un albergo di prima categoria in via Torino.
McKenzie: Dov'è via Torino?
Dani: La prima a destra. Poi sempre dritto e, in fondo, la seconda a sinistra.
McKenzie: Molte grazie. Arrivederci.

(He checks with a policeman.)

McKenzie: Scusi, dov'è l'albergo Trieste?
Vigile: Sempre dritto, dopo la stazione.
McKenzie: Grazie. Molte grazie.
Vigile: Buongiorno.

Dialogue 4 All'albergo

Portiere: Signore, buongiorno. Prego?
McKenzie: Buongiorno. C'è una camera matrimoniale con bagno?
Portiere: Per quanto tempo? Per una notte?
McKenzie: No. Per una settimana. Da sabato prossimo.
Portiere: Sì. C'è una camera libera da sabato prossimo.
McKenzie: Quant'è per una notte?

Portiere: Centomila lire per notte.
McKenzie: E c'è l'aria condizionata?
Portiere: Sì, c'è l'aria condizionata, la televisione . . .
McKenzie: Bene, bene. La colazione è esclusa o inclusa?
Portiere: È esclusa. Che nome, prego?
McKenzie: Sally e Julian McKenzie.
Portiere: Grazie. Buongiorno.
McKenzie: Buongiorno.

'C'è un albergo qui vicino, per piacere?'

2.2 VOCABULARY

Dialogue 1

l'ente turismo (m)	tourist office
l'impiegato (m) l'impiegata (f)	clerk
c'è	there is
un (m)	a
l'ostello (m) della gioventù	youth hostel
grande-e	large; big
il posto (m)	place; seat

una (f)	a; an
la settimana (f)	week
tutto-a esaurito-a	fully booked
allora	then; well; so
la pensione (f)	boarding house
caro-a	expensive; dear
uno (m)	a; an
straniero-a	foreign; foreigner
la via (f)	road
Firenze (f)	Florence
la camera singola (f)	single bedroom
da	from
il lunedì (m) (pl. invar.)	Monday
prossimo-a	next
sei	six
mila (f pl.)	thousands
la notte (f); per-	night; a night
la colazione (f)	breakfast
incluso-a	included
che . . . ?	what . . . ? which . . .
il nome (m)	name

Dialogue 2

la strada (f)	road,street
per piacere	please
per . . .	the way to
il centro (m); in-	the centre; in the-
verso	in the direction of; near
l'università (f) (pl. invar.)	university
lontano-a	far; far away
sempre	always
dritto-a; sempre dritto	straight; straight on
fino a	as far as
la piazza (f)	square
dove; dov'è?	where; where is it?
subito	immediately
la destra (f); a destra	right; on the right
la banca (f) (pl. -che)	bank
poi	then
la sinistra (f); a sinistra	left; on the left
prego; prego?	don't mention it; can I help you?

Dialogue 3

l'albergo (m) (pl. -ghi)	hotel
vicino-a; qui-	near; nearby
primo-a	first
la categoria (f); di prima-	class; category; first class
secondo-a	second
rumoroso-a	noisy
il fondo (m); in-	end; at the end
molte grazie	many thanks
il vigile (m)	traffic warden; policeman
dopo	after
la stazione (f)	station

Dialogue 4

il portiere (m)	receptionist
la camera matrimoniale (f)	double bedroom
il bagno (m)	bathroom
il tempo (m); per quanto – ?	time; for how long?
il sabato (m)	Saturday
libero-a	free; vacant
quanto-a; quant'è?	how much; how much is it?
cento	hundred; one hundred
lire (f pl.)	liras
l'aria condizionata (f)	air-conditioning
la televisione (f)	television

2.3 EXPLANATIONS

(a) Background information

Ente Turismo: every small town in Italy has a tourist office. They are often inside the railway station or in the city centre. Sometimes they are called Azienda di Soggiorno. They provide information about accommodation, sightseeing and outings.

Accommodation: hotels in Italy are classified as di lusso (luxury), di prima categoria . . . first, second, third, fourth class. A pensione corresponds to bed and breakfast or to a boarding house; pensione completa means full board, mezza pensione means half board.

Breakfast: traditionally it is not included, although a continental breakfast is more and more frequently offered with package tours. VAT is added to the hotel bill. The Italian word for it is IVA (Imposta sul Valore Aggiunto).

(b) Asking whether people or things are available: c'è? (is there?)
If looking for someone or something, the most frequent expression is c'è . . .?

C'è un albergo qui vicino?	Is there a hotel nearby?
C'è un posto libero?	Is there a vacant place?
C'è il dottor Bianchi?	Is Dr Bianchi there?

The reply may be:

Sì, c'è.	Yes, there is.
or	
No, non c'è.	No, there isn't.

As you will notice, no change in word order is required to form a question; the intonation conveys it, as explained in chapter 1.

(c) The indefinite article (a, an) – *grammar ref. 7*
Like the definite articles, the indefinite articles vary according to the gender of the noun they define. There are two masculine articles: uno is used before words starting with *s* + a consonant or *z*; un before all other words:

C'è un albergo non lontano?	Is there a hotel not far away?
C'è un ragazzo inglese qui?	Is there an English student here?
Sei uno studente straniero?	Are you a foreign student?

There are also two feminine articles: un' is used in front of words starting with a vowel; una in front of all other words:

C'è un'università a Milano?	Is there a university in Milan?
È una camera grande?	Is it a large room?

(d) Indicating for how long: per (for) – *grammar ref. 61*
If asked per quanto tempo? (for how long?) the easiest reply is: per . . .

Per quanto tempo sei qui?	How long are you here for?
Per una settimana.	For a week.
Per un giorno.	For a day.

(e) Starting from . . . : da – *grammar ref. 16*
To indicate the day when you wish to start, you say da . . .

da lunedì from Monday; da lunedì prossimo from next Monday; da lunedì notte from Monday night.

(f) These are the weekdays
lunedì, martedì, mercoledì, giovedì, venerdì, sabato e domenica. They are all masculine nouns, except domenica (Sunday) and they do not start with a capital letter.

(g) Asking prices: quant'è?
Information about fees, prices, costs can be obtained with the following question: quant'è?

Quant'è una camera matrimoniale?	How much is a double bedroom?
Quant'è per una notte?	How much is it for one night?
Quant'è la colazione?	How much is breakfast?

(h) Numbers (*for cardinal and ordinal numbers, see grammar ref. 11*)
The word mila attached to any number from two onwards means 'thousand'; seimila – six thousand. But *one* thousand is mille. One hundred or a hundred is cento. Notice that 'a' or 'one' is dropped.

Prices: from 1100 to 1900, prices are expressed in the following way: 1100 = millecento; 1200 = milleduecento; 1300 = milletrecento. Notice the following difference:

Una camera per una notte.	A room for one night.
Mille lire per notte.	One thousand liras a night.

(j) Asking the way: dov'è?
Finding your way you need just two words: scusi, per . . . ? This is the simplest and most common way of asking for directions (Can you direct me to . . . ? Excuse me, what is the way to . . . ?)

A more specific question is dov'è (where is?) or more forcefully dove c'è un . . . ? (where is a . . . ?)

Dov'è la stazione?	Where is the station?
Dov'è un ostello?	Where is a youth hostel?
Dov'è Tim?	Where is Tim?
Dove c'è un ostello?	Where is there a hostel?

Understanding directions: most directions are idiomatic expressions (a destra, on the right; in fondo, at the end, etc.) and ought to be learned by heart. La prima and la seconda (a sinistra *or* a destra), the first and the second (on the left or on the right), are feminine because the word la strada (f) is implied.

(k) Being asked your identity: che . . . ? (what? which?) – *grammar ref. 76(b)*

Che nome, prego? 'Your name, please?' (lit. what name?) is usually the question asked in hotels and offices to find out people's identity.

Che + a noun is also used to put very simple questions. It may be used both with masculine and feminine words, for people and things. For instance, you may use it to ask people to repeat something:

Che via?	What, which road? (did you say?)	Ah! via Verdi!
Che albergo?	What, which hotel? (did you say?)	Ah! l'albergo Londra!

Or, you may use it for more specific information:

Che studente inglese? Which English student? (are you looking for?)

(l) Addresses

Addresses are expressed and written in the following order:

Signor Franco Pardi
via Verdi 9
25015 Sirmione (Brescia)

The name of the province goes on the right in brackets, the postal code goes on the left.

(m) How to thank people

The shortest way of expressing thanks formally or informally is grazie (thank you or thanks). To thank someone more warmly, you may say molte grazie, 'thank you very much', or mille grazie (lit. one thousand thanks). When people thank you, you are expected to reply, always, prego or prego, di niente, 'it's all right', 'don't mention it', 'it's a pleasure'. If it's a reciprocal favour, you say grazie a lei (formal) or grazie a te (informal) (lit. thanks to you).

Prego has a variety of meanings which are all very common. For instance: 'Can I help you?' 'What can I do for you?' (see dialogue 4) 'After you!' 'Go ahead!' 'Help yourself!'

Proverbio: Chi cerca trova.
Nothing venture, nothing win. (He who seeks will find.)

2.4 EXERCISES

A

Exercise 1

Tim goes home and is asked endless questions by Lucio's mother about accommodation for his friend. Play Tim's role.

Mamma: Ciao, Tim. Allora, c'è un ostello qui a Milano?
Tim: ...
Mamma: C'è un posto da lunedì prossimo?
Tim: ...
Mamma: E allora, c'è una pensione non molto cara?
Tim: ...
Mamma: È libera per una settimana?
Tim: ...
Mamma: E la colazione è inclusa?
Tim: ...

Exercise 2

Lucio's mother is not happy and sends Tim to enquire at another boarding house for a single room with a bath for his friend.

Portiere: Buongiorno.
Tim: ...:
Portiere: Prego?
Tim: ...:
Portiere: Con bagno?
Tim: ...:
Portiere: Per quanto tempo?
Tim: ...:
Portiere: Che nome, prego?
Tim: ...:
Portiere: Grazie.
Tim: ...:

Exercise 3

After leaving the hotel, Mr McKenzie can't find his way back to the office. He asks a policeman for via Garibaldi. With the help of the indications in brackets, reproduce what Mr McKenzie says.

McKenzie: . . . (he attracts his attention)

Vigile: Prego?

McKenzie: . . . (he asks where via Garibaldi is)

Vigile: È verso via Mazzini.

McKenzie: . . . (he checks if it is on the right or on the left)

Vigile: No. È sempre dritto.

McKenzie: . . . (he checks if it is after a bank and a large hotel)

Vigile: Sì.

McKenzie: . . . (he thanks him and says goodbye)

Exercise 4

Your friend does not know any Italian at all. She asks you to enquire the way to various places.

Friend: Ask about the station. *You*: Scusi, per la stazione?

Ask for the university; for Garibaldi square; San Siro stadium; the hotel in Trieste road; the tourist office.

B

Exercise 5

Tim is doing his first homework in Italian. He has an old-fashioned grammar and he has to put the correct indefinite article un, uno, una, un' in front of each word:

stazione; università; piazza; pensione; bagno; settimana; via; nome; strada; amica.

Exercise 6

Tim is only half listening and occasionally he has to ask again. Play Tim's part, filling in the missing words, as in the example.

Lucio: C'è . . . strada . . . *Tim*: Dove c'è una strada qui vicino?

Lucio: C'è . . . ostello della gioventù; c'è . . . camera singola; c'è . . . pensione; c'è . . . chiesa.

Exercise 7

Tim explains to a newly acquired Italian friend, Luca, how to reach Lucio's house by car. Looking at the map on p. 24, give Tim's directions.

Tim: Pronto, Luca? Ciao. Sono Tim. L'indirizzo di Lucio è via Roma 8.

Luca: È qui vicino?

Tim: . . .

Luca: Verso l'Ente Turismo?

Tim: . . .
Luca: In via Venezia?
Tim: . . .
Luca: A sinistra, c'è l'albergo Italia?
Tim: . . .
Luca: E poi?
Tim: . . .
Luca: È via Roma?
Tim: . . .
Luca: Scusa, che numero?
Tim: . . .
Luca: Grazie. Ciao. Arrivederci.
Tim: . . .

Exercise 8

Tim tries to advise an Italian friend about a cheap boarding house in London. Can you join in and say this in Italian?

Here is Victoria Station. Immediately on the right, there is a hotel. It is the hotel Victoria and there is a bank. After the first street on the right, there is a bank and a tourist office. On the left, there is a cheap (not very expensive) boarding house. It is six pounds (sterline) a night [illegible] a single room. There isn't (a) bath, there isn't a (la) TV, there isn't [illegible]ir conditioning. English breakfast is included!

ASKING ABOUT TRANSPORT IN TOWN; COURTESIES

3.1 DIALOGUES

Dialogue 1 Alla stazione della metro
At the tube station.

McKenzie: Buongiorno, scusi . . .
Vigile: Prego?
McKenzie: Per andare a San Giuliano c'è la metropolitana?
Vigile: No. Non c'è fino a San Giuliano. La metro va solo fino a piazzale Bologna.
McKenzie: E poi? Che cosa devo prendere?
Vigile: A piazzale Bologna deve cambiare e prendere il sette.
McKenzie: E il sette va fino a San Giuliano?
Vigile: No. Poi deve prendere il pullman, il numero otto.
McKenzie: Il pullman, ogni quanto c'è?
Vigile: C'è ogni mezz'ora.
McKenzie: La metropolitana, l'autobus, e un pullman ogni mezz'ora! Un taxi, un taxi, per piacere! È più veloce!
Vigile: D'accordo. Il tempo è denaro.

Dialogue 2 Al posteggio dei taxi
At the taxi rank.

McKenzie: Buongiorno. È libero?
Tassista: Sì. Buongiorno. Dove va?
McKenzie: A San Giuliano, per piacere. Sa dov'è?
Tassista: Sì. So dov'è. Prego.
Tassista: (Approaching San Giuliano) Che indirizzo?
McKenzie: L'indirizzo è via Verona 3. È la ditta Pradella.
Tassista: Ah, sì. Lo so. (As they approach) È questo palazzo qui a sinistra, dopo il semaforo.

McKenzie: (Taking out his wallet) Quant'è?
Tassista: Diecimila.
McKenzie: Ecco a lei. (He hands him the money) Grazie. Buongiorno.

(McKenzie entering the building meets an old acquaintance)

Uomo d'affari: Buongiorno, signor McKenzie. Come va?
McKenzie: Bene, grazie. E lei?
Uomo d'affari: Non c'è male. Grazie. Tutto bene a casa?
McKenzie: Sì. Sì. Grazie.

Dialogue 3 Alla fermata dell'autobus

Tim decides to get a taxi to go to his school for foreign students. The taxi driver addresses him informally.

Tim: Buongiorno.
Tassista: Dove vai?
Tim: Devo andare alla Scuola Internazionale. Scusi, quant'è, per piacere?
Tassista: Eh . . . duemila, tremila, circa.
Tim: Come, scusi?
Tassista: Duemila, tremila, circa . . .

(Tim thinks it's too expensive and looks for a bus)

Tim: Grazie . . . Scusi . . . dove c'è un autobus per corso Venezia?
Tassista: C'è il dodici.
Tim: Dov'è la fermata per il dodici, per piacere?
Tassista: È qui dietro l'angolo. Di fronte c'è l'albergo Bologna.
Tim: E per il biglietto?
Tassista: Devi andare all'edicola.
Tim: Che cos'è?
Tassista: È un giornalaio. Sai che cos'è?
Tim: Sì. Lo so. Buongiorno. Molte grazie.
Tassista: Ciao.

Dialogue 4 Alla fermata del tram

Tim: Scusi, signorina, ogni quanto c'è il dodici?
Signorina: Ogni quarto d'ora.

(The number 12 arrives and Tim gets on. After a while he checks.)

Tim: Scusi, signora, ma il dodici non va in corso Venezia?
Signora: No. Il dodici non va in corso Venezia.
Tim: Dove devo scendere, allora? Alla prossima fermata?
Signora: No. Devi scendere qui. A questa fermata. A questo semaforo.

(Tim gets off at the stop and asks a young girl.)

Tim: Scusa, che autobus va in corso Venezia?
Ragazza: Il quindici va fino a via Parigi, vicino allo stadio.
Tim: La fermata, dov'è?
Ragazza: La fermata è proprio qui. Ma la metro è più comoda.
Tim: E se vado a piedi?
Ragazza: (she laughs) Allora, sempre dritto! In fondo a corso Genova a sinistra . . . subito a destra, poi a sinistra . . .
Tim: Ciao. Grazie.
Ragazza: Prego. Ciao.

(Tim takes out his pocket dictionary and looks up the expression *never mind*. He reads *pazienza*. But at the school he is cheered up by Julie.)

Julie: Ciao, Tim. Come va?
Tim: Bene. Grazie. E tu? Tutto bene?
Julie: Sì. Grazie. Non c'è male.

'Dov'è la fermata del tram?'

'Per Corso Vittorio Emanuele, per favore'

3.2 VOCABULARY

Dialogue 1

andare	to go
la metropolitana *or* la metro (f)	tube
va (andare, irreg.)	he, she, it goes; you go (formal)
solo	only
il piazzale (m)	large square
devo (dovere, irreg.)	I must
prendere	to take
deve (dovere)	he, she, it must; you must (formal)
cambiare	to change
il pullman (m) (pl. invar.)	coach
il numero (m)	number
ogni; -quanto	each; every; how often (lit. how much)
mezzo-a	half
l'ora (f); mezz'ora (f)	hour; half an hour
l'autobus (m) (pl. invar.)	bus
…xi *or* tassì (m) (pl. invar.)	taxi

più	more
veloce-e	fast
d'accordo	quite right
il denaro (m)	money

Dialogue 2

il tassista (m)	taxi-driver
sa (sapere, irreg.)	he, she, it knows; you know (formal)
so;lo so (sapere)	I know; I know (it)
l'indirizzo (m)	address
questo-a	this
il palazzo (m)	building
dopo	after
il semaforo (m)	traffic lights
ecco; -a lei	here it is; here you are (formal)
come? come va?	how? how are you? (lit. how goes it?)
l'uomo (m) (pl. uomini)	man, men
gli affari (m pl.) uomo d'-	business; businessman
male; non c'è -;	bad; not bad
la casa (f)	house; home

Dialogue 3

vai (andare)	you go (familiar)
la scuola (f)	school
internazionale-e	international
circa	approximately
come?	I beg your pardon? (lit. how?)
il corso (m)	avenue
Venezia (f)	Venice
dietro	behind
di fronte	opposite
l'angolo (m)	corner
il biglietto (m)	ticket
devi (dovere)	you must (familiar)
l'edicola (f)	news-kiosk
il giornalaio (m)	newsagent
sai (sapere)	you know (familiar)

Dialogue 4

il tram (m) (pl. invar.)	tram car, street car
un quarto (m); -d'ora	a quarter; a quarter of an hour

ma	but
scendere	to get off
Parigi (f)	Paris
lo stadio (m)	football ground
proprio	precisely
comodo-a	convenient
se	if
vado (andare)	I go
il piede (m); a piedi	foot; on foot

3.3 EXPLANATIONS

(a) Background information

Bus tickets: must often be purchased before getting on the vehicle. They are on sale at newsagents, tobacconists, coffee bars and at the underground stations. It is worth buying a booklet of tickets since inside towns the fare is often the same irrespective of distances. Some buses have automatic ticket machines on the bus, and these need short change—hard to come by often.

Tramcars: some Italian towns such as Milan and Turin still have tram cars as a major means of public transport.

Maps of the underground stations are displayed inside train compartments and in the stations.

(b) Finding out how to go to a place: andare a – *grammar ref. 64*

To go to a place (building or town) you say: per andare a . . . ?

Scusi, per andare a S. Siro?	Excuse me, to go to San Siro?
Lucio! Per andare a casa?	Lucio! To go home?

But to go to a specific address, you say: per andare in . . . ?

Scusi, per andare in via Verdi?	. . . to go to Verdi road?
Scusi, per andare in piazza Roma?	. . . to go to Rome square?

To ask about a means of transport, you say: che cosa va a/in . . . ?

Per piacere, che cosa va in via Firenze?	. . . what do I take to . . . ? (lit. what goes to . . . ?)
Per piacere, che cosa va a San Giuliano?	. . . what do I take to . . . ?

The answer may be:

La metro va fino a . . .	The tube goes as far as . . .
La metro va vicino a . . .	The tube goes near to . . .

Or, more specifically, you may ask:

Che autobus va a San Giuliano?	What bus do I take to . . . ?
Che tram va vicino a piazza Roma?	What tramcar goes near Rome square?

To indicate the number of a bus or a tramcar, people say: il numero sette or il sette, l'otto, il dieci etc.

To know where people are going, you say:

Scusa, Lucio, dove vai?	Lucio, where are you going? (familiar)
Signor Gardi, dove va?	Mr Gardi, where are you going? (formal)

Notice: like the verb essere (1.3(e)), the verb andare uses the 3rd person sing. for formal address.

(c) Present and Present Continuous – *grammar ref. 61*

As you will have noticed above, Italian uses the same forms to express a regular action and a continuous action, as the following shows:

(io) vado	I go; I'm going
(tu) vai	you go; you're going (familiar)
(lei) va	you go; you're going (formal)
(lui, lei) va	he, she, it goes; is going

(d) Asking how frequently: ogni quanto?

The word order for this kind of question is flexible:

Il pullman, ogni quanto c'è?	How often is the bus?
Ogni quanto c'è il pullman?	

(e) Asking what you have to do: dovere (must) – *grammar ref. 64*

Che autobus devo prendere?	What bus do I take? What bus do I have to take?
Che cosa devo prendere?	What (bus, etc.) do I take?

Dove devo scendere?	Where do I get off? Where do I have to get off?
Dove devo cambiare?	Where do I change (bus)?

As indicated in the above translations, the verb **dovere** is also used when English does not need it. It is also used where English would have 'must', 'have to . . .,' to indicate an obligation:

(io) devo	I must; I have to
(tu) devi	you must; you have to (familiar)
(lei) deve	you must; you have to (formal)
(lui, lei) deve	he, she, it must; has to

(f) a + articles; di + articles – *grammar ref. 16*

The word a always combines with the article in this way:

a + il = *al* Vado al telefono.	I go to the telephone.
a + l' = *all'* Vado all'ente turismo.	I to go the tourist office.
a + lo = *allo* Vado allo stadio.	I go to the stadium.
a + l' = *all'* Vado all'università.	I'm going to the university.
a + la = *alla* Vado alla scuola.	I'm going to the school.

So far you've seen the following words requiring *a* before the noun that follows: *vicino* allo stadio (near the stadium); *di fronte* all'albergo (opposite the hotel); *in fondo* alla strada (at the end of the road).

Notice: a must always be used in front of towns, cities, villages:

Sono a Londra.	I am in London.

The word di combines with the article in the following ways:

di + il = *del* il numero del telefono	the telephone number
di + l' = *dell'* la camera dell'albergo	the hotel room
di + lo = *dello* la via dello stadio	the road by the sports-ground
di + l' = *dell'* la via dell'università	the road by the University.
di + la = *della* la stazione della metro	the tube station

(g) Asking people whether they know: sapere (to know) – *grammar ref 64*

To put a question informally, you say: sai . . . ?; formally, you say: sa . . . ?

Scusi, sa dov'è il tram?	. . . do you know where the tram is?
Scusa, sai che cos'è?	. . . do you know what it is?
Scusi, sa ogni quanto c'è?	. . . do you know how frequent it is?

To say 'yes, I do', or 'yes, I know', you have to say: sì, lo so (lit. yes, I know it). Similarly, to say 'no, I don't', or 'I don't know', you have to say: no, non lo so. Here is the pattern of sapere:

(io) so	I know
(tu) sai	you know (familiar)
(lei) sa	you know (formal)
(lui, lei) sa	he, she, it knows

(h) Being specific: questo-a (this) – *grammar ref. 17*

Questo-a may be used in front of nouns, or on its own:

Questo biglietto è caro, purtroppo.	This ticket is dear, unfortunately.
Questa è la fermata dell'8 (otto)?	Is this the bus stop for the number 8 (bus)?

Questo-a becomes quest' in front of words starting with a vowel: quest'ostello.

(i) Comparing: più (more) – *grammar ref. 46*

To make a comparison, the word più is placed in front of the adjective. In a question, the most frequent word order is the following:

È più veloce un taxi o la metro?	Is a taxi or the tube faster?
È più caro quest'albergo qui?	Is this hotel more expensive?

In a statement or in a reply, the word order is flexible:

È più veloce la metro. La metro è più veloce.	The tube is faster.

A more complete reply would be: è più veloce la metro *del* taxi—the tube is faster *than* the taxi. Notice that, in this case, too, as an element of comparison, di combines with the article (see above (*f*)).

(j) Courtesies: e tu?; e lei? (and you?) – *grammar ref. 48*
Come va? 'How are you?' (lit. how does it go?) is a very frequent familiar and formal form. The replies may be: bene, grazie, or va bene, grazie; non c'è male; così, così (so, so).
And an automatic question in reply: e lei? (formal) or e tu? (familiar).

(k) How to indicate you haven't understood: scusi?
The simplest form is scusi? (formal) I beg your pardon? or Scusa? (familiar) Can you say it again? Che cosa? (What?) is rather abrupt.

Proverbio: Chi va adagio va sano e va lontano.
Better to be safe than sorry. (He who goes slowly goes safely and travels far.)

3.4 EXERCISES

A

Exercise 1
Several people are stopped by acquaintances on the road. Exchange a few courtesies as in the following example:
Q. Buongiorno, signorina. Come va? *A*. Bene, grazie. E lei?
Q. Tutto bene in viaggio? *A*. Sì, grazie. Non c'è male.

1. Buongiorno, signor McKenzie. Come va? *A*. . . .
   Tutto bene all'albergo? *A*. . . .
2. Ciao, Lucio. Come va? *A*. . . .
   Tutto bene all'università? *A*. . . .
3. Buongiorno, signora. Come va? *A*. . . .
   Tutto bene a casa? *A*. . . .
4. Ciao, Carla. Come va? *A*. . . .
   Tutto bene in ditta? *A*. . . .

Exercise 2
You've just arrived. You've booked at the hotel Trieste. Ask for the information you need:

1. Stop a passer-by.
2. First of all, ask where the Trieste hotel is.

3. Then ask whether there is an underground.
4. Since the answer is no, find out how you get there.
5. Check whether you have to change (buses).
6. Ask whether bus number 7 goes as far as Venice Avenue.
7. The answer is negative, so ask where you have to get off.
8. And, at long last, ask where the bus stop is!

Exercise 3

Mr McKenzie comes back to his office from S. Giuliano. He must go to Milan. The address is Garibaldi Road 11. Play his part, basing the replies on dialogue 2.

Tassista: Buongiorno.
McKenzie: ...
Tassista: Che indirizzo?
McKenzie: ...
Tassista: Che numero?
McKenzie: ...
Tassista: Diecimila.
McKenzie: ...

Exercise 4

Tim has extended his Italian. Before, he could only say, Scusi, per via Torino? Now, he can say: Che autobus va in via Torino? Can you do the same? Have you improved as he has?

— Scusi, per via Garibaldi?
— Scusi, per via Verona?
— Scusi, per corso Venezia?
— Scusi, per piazzale Firenze?

Exercise 5

Tim decides to go and see the Italian World Champion Football Team. He asks for the famous stadium of San Siro. Being guided by the gentleman's answers, can you provide his questions?

Tim: ...
Signore: Prego?
Tim: ...
Signore: No. Non c'è la metropolitana per San Siro.
Tim: ...
Signore: Sì, c'è un autobus.
Tim: ...
Signore: No. Non va dritto fino a San Siro.
Tim: ...
Signore: La fermata è proprio qui di fronte.

B

Exercise 6

What about a bit of fun? Here is a list of questions, but the answers do not correspond. Can you match the questions to the right answers?

1. Ogni quanto c'è?	(a) Per un giorno.
2. Che indirizzo?	(b) Va verso piazza Roma.
3. C'è un ostello?	(c) Sì, a sinistra.
4. Quant'è?	(d) Tremila lire.
5. Per quanto?	(e) Via Garibaldi 3.
6. A sinistra?	(f) No, non c'è un ostello.
7. Dove va?	(g) C'è ogni quarto d'ora.

Exercise 7

Mr McKenzie has left a few questions for Miss Dani. Can you guess her replies? They are all negative. For instance:

McKenzie: Ma non è il numero dodici?
Dani: No. Non è il numero 12.

1. Ma non c'è un autobus?
2. Ma non c'è un taxi?
3. Ma il sette non va in via Torino?
4. Ma non c'è ogni ora?
5. Ma l'indirizzo non è via Trento 10?
6. Ma non c'è il bagno?

Exercise 8

McKenzie is welcomed back by Mrs Pardi. Can you reproduce their conversation in Italian?

Pardi: Good morning, Mr McKenzie. How are you?
McKenzie: Very well. Thank you.
Pardi: Everything's fine in San Giuliano?
McKenzie: Yes. Thank you. Everything is fine. (He looks up a map.)
Pardi: Where do you have to go?
McKenzie: I have to go to Cavour Street.
Pardi: Don't you know where it is?
McKenzie: No. I don't. Is it nearby?
Pardi: Yes. It's the first on the left.
McKenzie: Then, I'll walk.

Exercise 9

Can you reproduce Tim and Roberto's dialogue in Italian?

Roberto: Tim, hallo! Where are you going?
Tim: I'm going to the stadium.
Roberto: On foot? But do you know where it is?
Tim: Yes, I know. It's far away.
Roberto: There is the metro and there is the number five tram. It goes straight to the stadium.
Tim: Fine. Thank you. Bye.
Roberto: Cheerio.

GETTING TO KNOW OTHER PEOPLE; TALKING ABOUT YOURSELF

4.1 DIALOGUES

Dialogue 1 In classe

In class Tim is taught how to get to know his school friends. The teacher addresses the students with the familiar form.

Professore: (to a student) Come ti chiami?
Studente: Mi chiamo Ivan.
Professore: E la tua compagna, come si chiama?
Ivan: La mia compagna si chiama Dolores Suarez.
Professore: (to Ivan) Ivan, di dove sei?
Ivan: Sono russo. Sono di Mosca.
Professore: E la tua compagna, di dov'è?
Ivan: È spagnola.
Professore: (to Dolores) Dolores, sei di Madrid?
Dolores: No. Sono di un piccolo paese vicino a Madrid.
Professore: (to Julie) Julie, parli bene l'italiano?
Julie: No. Non parlo bene l'italiano.
Professore: Sai bene il francese?
Julie: Sì. Lo so bene.
Professore: Perchè sei in Italia?
Julie: Perchè desidero imparare bene l'italiano.

Dialogue 2 Dopo l'intervallo

Tim is now taught to talk about his favourite things and people.

Professore: Hans, qual è il tuo sport preferito?
Hans: Il mio sport preferito è il nuoto.
Professore: Juan, qual è la tua attrice preferita?
Juan: La mia attrice preferita è Ornella Muti. È italiana.

Professore: (to another student) E la tua?
Studente: Io preferisco Jane Fonda.
Professore: Sai bene l'italiano?
Studente: No. Non lo so bene. Ma capisco un poco.
Professore: Quanto resti in Italia?
Studente: Scusi? Non capisco. (The teacher explains.)
Studente: Ah! Resto un mese qui a Milano. Poi vado a Firenze.
Professore: (to Ivan) E tu, quando riparti per il tuo paese?
Ivan: Riparto tra un mese.
Professore: A Mosca, studi o lavori?
Ivan: Lavoro. Sono professore di russo.
Professore: (to another student) E tu, dove lavori?
Studente: Sono impiegata in una ditta italiana a Parigi.

Dialogue 3 In un ufficio

McKenzie checks with the receptionist about his appointment with the assistant-director of the Pradella company.

McKenzie: (to the receptionist) Buongiorno. Devo incontrare il vice-direttore.
Portiere: Come si chiama?
McKenzie: Julian McKenzie. Sono dell' Avonex di Londra.
Portiere: Prego. Si accomodi. (He rings up) Secondo piano.
Vice-direttore: (he welcomes him at the door) Ben arrivato! Conosce il mio collega, Franco Marconi?
Marconi: (shaking hands) Molto lieto. Vado spesso in Inghilterra.
McKenzie: Piacere.
Vice-direttore: Signor McKenzie, desidera cominciare con questo catalogo? Io aspetto Luca Briato.
McKenzie: Sì. Preferisco ordinare subito.

(after a while and after other transactions)

McKenzie: . . . Va bene. Chiedo la conferma a Londra.
Vice-direttore: (pointing to a pen on the table) Signor McKenzie, questa penna è sua?
McKenzie: Uh! Sì! Grazie. È la mia.

Dialogue 4 Una colazione di lavoro

Mr McKenzie is sitting next to a businessman he has never met before, but a conversation starts off easily in Italy.

Rotondi: (to McKenzie, pointing to a folder on his chair) È sua questa cartella?
McKenzie: No. Non è mia. (Pointing to his neighbour) Forse è la sua.
Rotondi: (offering a cigarette) Fuma?
McKenzie: Sì. Grazie. È la mia marca preferita.
Rotondi: Per che ditta lavora?
McKenzie: Lavoro per l'Avonex di Londra. Lei, per che ditta lavora?
Rotondi: Per la Sampiro Internazionale.
McKenzie: È una società per azioni?
Rotondi: Sì. È una società per azioni.
McKenzie: Dov'è la sede principale?
Rotondi: È a Parigi, con una filiale a New York. Quanto resta in Italia?
McKenzie: Resto qui un mese. Ma ritorno presto. Lei è di Milano?
Rotondi: Sì. Sono di Milano. Ma abito a Parigi.
McKenzie: Quando riparte?
Rotondi: Riparto questa sera . . . o resto fino a domani.

4.2 VOCABULARY

Dialogue 1

la classe (f)	class; classroom
il professore (m)	teacher, lecturer
la professoressa (f)	teacher, lecturer
come?	how?
chiamarsi	to be called
il tuo (m) la tua (f)	your, yours (familiar)
la compagna (f) il compagno (m)	friend, companion
il mio (m) la mia (f)	my, mine
di dove?	where . . . from? from where . . . ?
russo-a	Russian
Mosca (f)	Moscow
spagnolo-a	Spanish
piccolo-a	small
il paese (m)	village; country; nation
parlare	to speak
perchè	why; because
desiderare	to wish
imparare	to learn

Dialogue 2

l'intervallo (m)	interval; break
quale? (m and f)	which? which one?
lo sport (m) (pl. invar.)	sport
preferito-a	favourite
il nuoto (m)	swimming
l'attore (m)	actor
l'attrice (f)	actress
*preferire	to prefer
*capire	to understand
un poco; un po' (abbr.)	a little
quanto	how long (lit. how much)
restare	to stay; to remain
il mese (m)	month
quando	when
ripartire	to leave; to go back
tra, fra	in (referring to time)
studiare	to study
lavorare	to work

Dialogue 3

l'ufficio (m)	office
incontrare	to meet
il vice-direttore (m)	assistant director
s'accomodi	go in; take a seat (formal)
il piano (m)	floor
conoscere	to know
il/la collega (m and f) (pl. -ghi, -ghe)	colleague
spesso	often
l'Inghilterra (f)	England
cominciare	to start, to begin
il catalogo (m) (pl. -ghi)	catalogue
aspettare	to wait
ordinare	to order
va bene	that's fine; okay; it's all right
chiedere	to ask
la conferma (f)	approval; confirmation
la penna (f)	pen
il suo (m) la sua (f)	your, yours (formal)

Dialogue 4

la colazione (f) -di lavoro	lunch; breakfast; business lunch
la cartella (f)	folder; brief-case

suo (m) sua (f)	his, her, its
fumare	to smoke
la marca (f) (pl. -che)	brand
la società (f) (pl. invar.)	company
l'azione (f) per azione	share; limited (Ltd); Plc
la sede (f)	headquarters
principale-e	main
la filiale (f)	branch
ritornare	to return
presto	soon
abitare	to live
fino a	until

4.3 EXPLANATIONS

(a) Telling people where you come from: sono di . . .
Asking familiarly, one says: di dove sei? (where do you come from?)
Asking formally, one says: di dov'è? (lit. of where are you?)

The answer may be formed by essere + an adjective of nationality, or essere + di + the name of a town, or village. But *not* by the name of a nation.

Sono inglese.	I come from England; I'm English.
Sono di Londra.	I am from London.

Asking where a third person comes from, you say:

Il direttore, di dov'è? / Di dov'è, il direttore?	Where does the director come from? (lit. where is the director from?)

The answer is:

Il direttore è di Londra.	The director comes from London.

(b) Saying you know a language: sapere
The verb to use is sapere (irreg.) which you have already met (*3.3(g)*).
To ask, you say:

Tim, sai l'italiano? (familiarly) Signora, sa l'italiano? (formally)	Do you know Italian?

To reply, you may say:

Sì, so l'italiano.	Yes, I know Italian.
Sì, lo so.	Yes, I know it.
No, non lo so.	No, I don't know it.

About a third person, you ask or reply:

Il direttore sa l'inglese? Sa l'inglese, il direttore?	Does the director know English?
Sì, il direttore sa l'inglese.	Yes, the director knows English.

The names of languages may be used with or without the article:

Impara l'inglese? Impara inglese?	Does he learn English?

And the names of languages are all masculine. So you say:

L'italiano è bello e facile!	Italian is nice and easy!

(c) Saying you speak a language: parlare

The question may be:

Tim, parli inglese?	Tim, do you speak English? (familiar)
Signora, parla inglese?	Signora, do you speak English? (formal)

The reply may be:

Sì, parlo inglese!	Yes, I speak English!
No, non parlo inglese.	No, I don't speak English.
Sì, lo parlo un poco; bene; molto bene.	Yes, I speak it a little; well; very well.

As you may have guessed, there is no Italian equivalent to the English replies, 'Yes, I do'; 'No, I don't'. You may say: sì or no.

To ask about someone else, you say:

Parla bene l'inglese il direttore? Il direttore, parla bene l'inglese?	Does the director speak English well?

(the word order is optional)

The answers may be:

Sì, lo parla bene.	Yes, he speaks it well.
No. Non lo parla bene.	No, he doesn't speak it well.

(d) Verbs of the 1st conjugation: the present tense–*grammar ref. 58*
The endings of the verb parl-are are very important because all regular verbs ending in -are (this is the infinitive, the ending given by dictionaries) follow the same pattern as parlare.

The ending -are is removed and a new ending is added, as follows:

(io) parl + o	I speak
(tu) parl + i	you speak (familiar)
(lei) parl + a	you speak (formal)
(lui, lei) parl + a	he, she, it speaks

Remember that with all verbs the formal lei uses the same form as the 3rd person sing. (*1.3(e)*).

Verbs ending in -care and -gare add an h before the endings beginning with *i* (tu, noi) to keep the hard sound of the infinitive.

(e) Talking of your job: lavorare
You may use specific verbs (lavorare, studiare are regular verbs of the 1st conjugation) or an expression with the verb essere + un + a noun:

Lavoro in una ditta.	I work in a company.
Studio all'università.	I am at the university (lit. I study).
Sono un impiegato.	I am an office clerk.
Sono un professore.	I am a teacher.

If you are more specific, the article is dropped before the noun:

Sono professore di russo.	I am a teacher (m) of Russian.
Sono portiere in una ditta.	I am a receptionist (m) in a firm.

(f) Saying how long you're staying: present continuous and immediate future – *grammar ref. 61*

To form the question with 'how long', you may use either quanto (lit. how much) or quanto tempo (lit. how much time) and the verb restare (regular,. 1st conjugation) in the present tense (see (*d*) above).

Tim, quanto tempo resti in Italia? (familiar) Signora, quanto tempo resta in Italia? (formal)	how long are you staying in Italy?

To answer, you say:

Resto un poco; molto; fino a. . .	I'll be staying a little; a long time; until . . .

To talk about someone else, you say:

Quanto resta il direttore?	How long is the director staying?
Il direttore resta fino a domani.	The director is staying until tomorrow.

As you see from the examples above, the endings of the present tense, of the present continuous and of the immediate future are the same in Italian. The context is a sufficient indication. Here are a few other examples:

Che cosa aspetti, Tim? — What are you waiting for, Tim?
Aspetto l'autobus. — I'm waiting for the bus.
(after aspettare, *for* is dropped in Italian)
Quando ritorni? — When will you go back?
Ritorno domani. — I'll go back tomorrow.

(g) Telling people what your name is: chiamarsi – *grammar ref. 54*

Che nome? is the question usually asked in hotels and offices. In everyday conversation, people prefer:

Come ti chiami? (familiar) Come si chiama, signora? (formal)	What's your name? (lit. how do you call yourself?)

The reply is:

Mi chiamo . . .	My name is . . . (lit. I call myself.)

Asking about someone else, you say:

Come si chiama il direttore? Il direttore, come si chiama?	What's the director's name? (lit. how does he call himself?)

To be more precise, you may ask:

Come si chiama, di nome?	What's his first name?
Come si chiama di cognome?	What's his surname?

(h) Saying whether you know people: conoscere
You use this verb to say you know people or places:

Conosci Londra?	Do you know London? (familiar)
Conosce la signora?	Do you know Mrs . . . ? (formal)
Sì, conosco Londra.	Yes, I know London.
Ma non conosco Edinburgo.	But I don't know Edinburgh.

To ask whether another person knows, you say:

Il direttore conosce Londra?	Does the director know London?

The reply is:

Sì, il direttore conosce Londra.	Yes, the director knows London.

(For the pronunciation of -sci; -sce, see the guide to pronunciation.)

(i) Verbs of the 2nd conjugation: the present tense – *grammar ref. 58*
All regular verbs ending in -ere follow the same pattern as conosc-ere. The ending -ere is removed and the necessary ending is added:

(io) conosc + o	I know
(tu) conosc + i	you know (familiar)
(lei) conosc + e	you know (formal)
(lui, lei) conosc + e	he, she, it knows

(j) Saying when you go back: ripartire
Verbs of the 3rd conjugation – *grammar ref. 58*
To ask you say:

Quando riparti, Tim? (familiar) Quando riparte, signora? (formal)	When do you go back home?

The answers may be:

Riparto domani.	I'll go back tomorrow.
Non riparto fino a domani.	I'm not going back until tomorrow.

About someone else:

Quando riparte il direttore?	When is the director going back home?
Il direttore riparte domani.	The director goes back tomorrow.

All regular verbs ending in -ire (this is the infinitive, the ending given in dictionaries) follow the same pattern as ripart-ire. They are verbs of the 3rd conjugation. The ending -ire is removed and the necessary ending is added as follows:

(io) ripart + o	I go back home
(tu) ripart + i	you go back home (familiar)
(lei) ripart + e	you go back home (formal)
(lui, lei) ripart + e	he, she, it goes back home

To sum up, here is a table showing all three conjugations:

(io)	lavor*o*,	conosc*o*,	ripart*o*	I
(tu)	lavor*i*,	conosc*i*,	ripart*i*	you, (familiar)
(lei)	lavor*a*,	conosc*e*,	ripart*e*	you, (formal)
(lui) (lei)	lavor*a*,	conosc*e*,	ripart*e*	he, she, it

(k) Saying what you prefer: preferire – *grammar ref. 59*
To ask people, you say:

Preferisci l'italiano o il francese? (familiar)	Do you prefer Italian or French?
Preferisce l'italiano o il francese? (formal)	

The answer is:

Preferisco . . .	I prefer . . .

To ask about someone else:

La signora Bianchi preferisce Londra o Parigi?	Does Mrs Bianchi prefer London or Paris?
Preferisce Parigi a Londra.	She prefers Paris to London.

Other verbs have the same pattern as preferire. One of them is capire: Scusi, non capisco. (I don't understand). They are indicated with an * in the vocabulary list.

(l) Stating what belongs to you: the possessives – *grammar ref. 32*
To say my or mine, you use il mio if you refer to a masculine noun; la mia if you refer to a feminine noun:

Sì, grazie, è il mio catalogo.	Yes, thank you, it's my catalogue.
No, non è il mio (catalogo).	No, it's not mine.
Sì, è la mia penna.	Yes, it's my pen.
No, non è la mia (penna)	No, it's not mine.

Similarly, to ask people, you say il tuo or il suo if you are referring to a masculine noun la tua or la sua if you are referring to a feminine noun:

È il tuo catalogo? (familiar) È il suo catalogo? (formal)	Is it your catalogue? Is the catalogue yours?
È la tua penna? (familiar) È la sua penna? (formal)	Is the pen yours? Is it your pen?

Unlike English, the possessive does not indicate whether the person who possesses the object is a man or a woman. It indicates only the gender of the thing possessed:

È sua questa penna?	Is it his pen? *as well as* Is it her pen?
È suo questo catalogo?	Is it his catalogue *as well as* Is it her catalogue?

Notice that in expressions such as it's mine, is it yours?, etc., the definite article may be omitted: è la mia; è mia.

(m) Expressing your preference: qual è? – *grammar ref. 76(b)*
You also use the possessives to indicate your favourite thing or person:

È il mio collega preferito.	He is my favourite colleague.

To ask you say:

Qual è il tuo attore preferito?
Qual è la sua attrice preferita?

Qual(e) is used in front of masculine *and* feminine nouns.

(n) Expressing possession with di – *grammar ref. 16*

Questa penna è di Tim.	This is Tim's pen.

4.4 EXERCISES

A

Exercise 1
What would you reply to this question 'Scusi, è un professore di inglese?' if the following words described one of your jobs?

studente; vice-direttore; portiere; vigile; tassista; uomo d'affari; impiegato; impiegata; segretaria.

Exercise 2
Tim's friend, Steve Lloyd, has arrived and is checking in at the boarding house Tim has booked for him. Can you play his role?
Steve: . . . (Is there a single room for Steve Lloyd?)
Signora: Sì. Sei tu? Sei l'amico di Tim Yeats?
Steve: . . . (Yes.)
Signora: Parli italiano?
Steve: . . . (A little. Very little.)

Signora: Di dove sei?
Steve: . . . (I come from Cambridge.)
Signora: Studi all'università di Cambridge?
Steve: . . . (No. At the University of London.)
Signora: Resti a Milano per una settimana?
Steve: . . . (Yes, I'll be staying for a week.)

Exercise 3
Mr McKenzie finds a friendly neighbour at the hotel restaurant. Play McKenzie's role.
Signore: È inglese?
McKenzie: . . . (He says he is from Edinburgh.)
Signore: Ah! Sa bene l'italiano!
McKenzie: . . . (He says he knows it a little.)
Signore: È in Italia per lavoro?
McKenzie: . . . (He says he works for a firm in London.)

Exercise 4
Tim is the object of the curiosity of Lucio's friends. Reply for him.
Amico: Come ti chiami?
Tim: . . . (He says he is called Tim Yeats.)
Amico: Di dove sei?
Tim: . . . (He says he is English.)
Amico: Conosci bene l'Italia?
Tim: . . . (He says he doesn't. A little.)
Amico: Ma capisci l'italiano?
Tim: . . . (He says he understands a little. But he doesn't speak it.)
Amico: Dove abiti?
Tim: . . . (He says he lives in Cambridge.)
Amico: Preferisci Londra o Cambridge?
Tim: . . . (He says he prefers Cambridge.)

Exercise 5
Tim's Italian is not yet fluent, but he can already give his opinion. Follow his example:
Jane Fonda? È la mia attrice preferita!

L'Italia? È . . . !
Il castello di Warwick? È . . . !
Il nuoto? È . . . !
Via Veneto? È . . . !

B

Exercise 6

State that you must do what you intend doing. Use the expression as in the example:
Sì. Chiedo la conferma. Devo chiedere la conferma.

1. Sì. Riparto domani.
2. Sì. Aspetto la segretaria.
3. Sì. Scendo qui.
4. Sì. Resto fino a giovedì.

Exercise 7

To each question, reply that you do it every evening, as in the example:
Aspetti il 12? Aspetto il dodici ogni sera!

1. Scendi qui?
2. Vai alla Scuola Internazionale?
3. Riparti per San Giuliano?
4. Incontri Carla?
5. Vai a piedi?

Exercise 8

At the school, the teacher is trying to find out what belongs to whom. Can you help him, as in this example:
È tuo questo biglietto? No, non è mio. Il mio è più caro.

È tua questa penna?	(Say it's not yours. Yours is nicer.)
È tuo questo catalogo?	(Say it's not yours. Yours is smaller.)
È tua questa cartella?	(Say it's not yours. Yours is larger.)
È tuo questo denaro?	(Say it's not yours. Yours is English.)

Exercise 9

The conversation at the hotel restaurant carries on. It's now McKenzie's turn to put questions. Play his role, helped by the replies.
McKenzie: ...
Signore: Lavoro a Roma.
McKenzie: ...

Signore: Ritorno a casa ogni settimana.
McKenzie: . . .
Signore: Preferisco Milano.
McKenzie: . . .
Signore: È più rumorosa Roma.
McKenzie: . . .
Signore: Arrivederci. A domani.

Exercise 10

Today McKenzie talks about Sally, his wife.
Signore: Conosce l'Italia?
McKenzie: (Yes. She knows Italy. She prefers Rome.)
Signore: Come si chiama?
McKenzie: (Her name is Sally.)
Signore: Lavora a Londra?
McKenzie: (Yes. She works in London.)
Signore: È scozzese?
McKenzie: (Yes. She is Scottish.)

CHANGING MONEY; MAKING TELEPHONE CALLS

5.1 DIALOGUES

Dialogue 1 All'ufficio cambi

Tim: Devo cambiare . . . come si dice in italiano? . . . un 'traveller's cheque' . . .
Lucio: Si dice 'traveller's cheque' o 'assegno da viaggio'.
Tim: Sai quando chiude l'ufficio cambi?
Lucio: Sì. Chiude a mezzogiorno. Ma non so quando apre.

(After a while at the exchange office)

Tim: Buongiorno.
Impiegata: Prego?
Tim: Devo cambiare un assegno da viaggio, per piacere.
Impiegata: Ecco il modulo. Hai il passaporto?
Tim: Sì . . . (he can't find it). Mi dispiace, ma non ce l'ho.
Impiegata: Non hai il passaporto?
Tim: No. Non ce l'ho proprio . . . Un momento . . . No, no. Ma non posso cambiare un assegno da viaggio senza il passaporto?
Impiegata: No, mi dispiace.
Tim: Ah! Ho la patente. Va bene?
Impiegata: No. Mi dispiace. Non posso. Devi ritornare.

Dialogue 2 Al telefono al bar

Tim goes to a coffee bar where there is a public telephone.

Tim: Buongiorno. Un gettone, per piacere.
Barista: Ecco il gettone. Devi telefonare qui in città?
Tim: Sì. Quant'è? Cento lire? (He hands him a large banknote)

Barista: Sì. Non hai moneta? Non hai un pezzo da mille lire?
Tim: No. Mi dispiace.

(Tim inserts the phone token, and dials)

Lucio: Pronto?
Tim: Lucio? Ciao. Sono Tim. Hai un momento di tempo?
Lucio: Sì. Certo!
Tim: Non ho il passaporto! E non posso cambiare l'assegno da viaggio.
Lucio: Eh, no, certo. E dove hai il tuo passaporto?
Tim: In camera. Puoi venire qui?
Lucio: Dove sei?
Tim: Sono al Bar Italia in via Bologna.
Lucio: Sono lì tra poco.
Tim: Va bene. Grazie. Sei un amico!

'Posso cambiare £10 sterline?'

Dialogue 3 In banca

McKenzie: Buongiorno. Ho bisogno di cambiare un assegno da viaggio.

Banchiere: Bene. Ha il passaporto?
McKenzie: Sì. Eccolo.

(The British passport sparks off a conversation)

Banchiere: Io ho un figlio in Inghilterra.
McKenzie: Lavora o studia?
Banchiere: Studia inglese presso una scuola per stranieri. Ha bisogno di imparare la lingua per lavoro.

(The necessary paper is filled in for McKenzie to sign)

Banchiere: Ecco il modulo. Deve firmare qui, per piacere.
McKenzie: Quant'è la sterlina oggi?
Banchiere: È duemila lire. Eh! la lira scende!
McKenzie: Posso parlare con il direttore della banca?
Banchiere: Ha un appuntamento?
McKenzie: Mi dispiace, non ce l'ho.
Banchiere: Eh, allora oggi non può. Domani va bene?
McKenzie: Va bene. Domani.

Dialogue 4 Alla SIP
At the Public Telephone Office

McKenzie: Buongiorno. Ho bisogno di un gettone, per piacere.
Telefonista: Deve telefonare in città o fare un'interurbana?
McKenzie: Devo telefonare in città, ma non so il numero.
Telefonista: La guida del telefono è lì dietro.
McKenzie: Quant'è? Cento lire?
Telefonista: Sì. (He pays with a five thousand liras note.)
Telefonista: Non ha moneta?
McKenzie: No. Mi dispiace. Ho un pezzo da duemila.
Telefonista: Va bene. Ecco a lei, duecento, trecento . . . quattrocento, cinquecento . . . mille . . . duemila.

(There is no reply and McKenzie comes back.)

McKenzie: Non risponde. È la Camera di Commercio. Chissà quando chiude?
Telefonista: Chiude a mezzogiorno. Ha mezz'ora di tempo.
McKenzie: Grazie. Buongiorno.
Telefonista: Buongiorno.

5.2 VOCABULARY

Dialogue 1

dice (dire, irreg.); come si -?	to say; how do you say?
l'assegno (m); - da viaggio	cheque; traveller's cheque
chiudere; chiuso-a	to close; closed
l'ufficio cambi (m)	currency exchange office
mezzogiorno (m)	midday
aprire; aperto-a	to open; opened
il modulo (m)	form
hai (avere, irreg.)	you have (familiar)
il passaporto (m)	passport
mi dispiace	I'm sorry
ho (avere); ce l'ho	I have; I have got it
proprio	really
un momento (m); -di tempo	one moment; a spare moment
posso (potere, irreg.)	I can; I may
senza	without
la patente (f)	driving licence

Dialogue 2

il telefono (m)	telephone
il gettone (m)	telephone token
il/la barista (m and f)	barman; barmaid
telefonare	to ring up
la città (f) (pl. invar.)	town; city
la moneta (f)	change (small coins)
un pezzo da mille (m)	a one thousand liras note
pronto?	hallo? (on the phone)
certo	certainly; surely
puoi (potere)	you can (familiar)
in camera	in the bedroom
il bar (m) (pl. invar.)	bar; coffee-bar
lì	there; over there
tra poco	in a while (lit. within little)

Dialogue 3

avere bisogno di	to need
il banchiere (m)	banker, bank clerk
ha (avere)	he, she, it has; you have (formal)
eccolo (m); eccola (f)	here it is

presso	at; at somebody's home
la lingua (f)	language
firmare	to sign
la sterlina (f)	pound (currency)
oggi	today
scendere	to go down
il direttore (m) la direttrice (f)	director
la banca (f) (pl. -che)	bank
l'appuntamento (m)	appointment; date
può (potere)	he, she, it can; you can (formal)

Dialogue 4

il/la telefonista (m and f)	telephone operator
fare	to make
l'interurbana (f)	trunk call
la guida (f)	telephone book
rispondere	to answer
la Camera di Commercio (f)	Chamber of Commerce
chissà	I wonder (lit. who knows)

5.3 EXPLANATIONS

(a) Background information

Ufficio cambi and banks: a currency exchange office is often available at tourist offices, in railway stations and at airports. Banks are not open in the afternoon and are closed all day on Saturday and Sunday. The Italian currency is the lira, which is divided according to the decimal system.

Telephones: telephones are found in public boxes, in bars and wherever this sign (SIP) is visible. You would not find telephones in post offices. In large towns and small places there is a public telephone office (Telefono Pubblico or SIP) where you may find telephone directories and get help with trunk and international calls. To make telephone calls you need special tokens which are sold in bars, at newsagents and are available from slot machines in the telephone boxes. Dial 10 for the operator and 12 to enquire about a number. 113 for emergency calls.

Proverbio: Paese che vai, usanza che trovi
Many countries, many customs.

(b) Asking how a word is expressed in Italian: si dice – *grammar ref. 64*
To ask, you say: Come si dice 'a bank' in italiano? (how do you say ... in Italian?) The reply is: Si dice ... (lit. one says) both for singular and plural words. Dice is the irregular 3rd person singular of dire (to say).

(c) Asking when a place opens or closes
You may say:

Questa banca è aperta?	Is this bank open?
Questa banca è chiusa?	Is this bank closed?

or you may ask:

Quando apre questa banca?	When does this bank open?
Quando chiude questa banca?	When does this bank close?

The word order with quando is flexible, so you could say: la banca, quando apre?

The replies could be:

tra poco; tra mezz'ora; tra un quarto d'ora; tra un momento; subito; lunedì; etc.

(d) Handing out something: ecco (here is, here are)
This very frequent word is used to accompany the gesture of handing over something: money, a document, coffee etc. Or to point to someone or something:

Ecco il passaporto.	Here is your passport.
C'è Tim? Sì. Eccolo. (m)	Is Tim there? Yes, here he is.
C'è Carla? Sì. Eccola. (f)	Is Carla there? Yes, here she is.

The second form is used if you do not repeat the noun.

(f) Saying whether you have something or not: avere (to have) – *grammar ref. 58*
The question is:

Scusa, hai il passaporto?	Have you got your passport? (familiar)

Scusi, ha il passaporto?	Have you got your passport? (formal)

If the answer is *affirmative*, you say:

Sì, ho il passaporto.	Yes, I have the passport.
Sì, ce l'ho.	Yes, I have got it.

If the answer is *negative*, you say:

Mi dispiace, no, non ho il passaporto.	I'm sorry, I haven't the passport.
Mi dispiace, non ce l'ho.	I'm sorry, I haven't got it.
No, sono senza.	No, I am without it.

Non ce l'ho may be used with masculine *and* feminine nouns.

If the question has an indefinite article, the reply may include the word ne: – *grammar ref. 27*

Hai un gettone? Sì, ne ho uno.	Have you got a token? Yes, I have got one.

The singular form of the present tense of **avere** is as follows:

(io) ho	I have, I have got
(tu) hai	you have, you've got (familiar)
(lei) ha	you have, you have got (formal)
(lui, lei) ha	he, she, it has

(g) Expressing a need: ho bisogno di . . . (I need)

Ha bisogno di un gettone?	Do you need a telephone token?
Hai bisogno del passaporto?	Do you need the passport?
Sì, ho bisogno del passaporto.	Yes, I need the passport.

If you don't repeat the noun, the word **ne** must be inserted:

Ne ho bisogno.	I need it. (lit. I have need of it.)

The word di is used also when avere bisogno is followed by a verb:

Ho bisogno di andare in banca.	I need to go to a bank.

(h) Asking whether you can or may do something: posso *– grammar ref. 64*

To ask whether it's *possible* for you to do something, you say:

Posso cambiare questo assegno?	Can I change this cheque?

To ask whether you *may* do something, you say:

Posso parlare con il direttore?	May I speak to the director (manager)?

To ask other people, you say:

Puoi venire qui?	Can you come here? (familiar)
Può cambiare questo assegno?	Can you change this cheque? (formal)

About someone else:

Scusi, il mio amico può telefonare?	Can my friend ring up?
Certo può telefonare se desidera.	Yes, he can if he wishes.

The full pattern of the verb potere is:

(io) posso	I can
(tu) puoi	you can (familiar)
(lei) può	you can (formal)
(lui, lei) può	he, she, it can

(i) Dealing with money: un pezzo da *– grammar ref. 16*

You may be asked:

Scusi, ha moneta?	Excuse me, have you got change? (formal)

The answer may be:

Ho un pezzo da mille, duemila etc.	I have a one thousand liras note.

(j) Your identity over the phone

When you pick up the receiver you say Pronto? or Pronto? Chi parla? You don't say your telephone number. Then you add: Sono (Tim) (it's Tim); to say 'Speaking' you say Sono io.

5.4 EXERCISES

A

Exercise 1

Here is a list of words in English. Ask how you say them in Italian and provide the reply, as in the example:
(the passport) Come si dice 'the passport' in italiano, per piacere? Si dice il passaporto.

the driving licence; a telephone token; the signature; the church; to walk; a quarter of an hour; the traffic lights; I am sorry.

Exercise 2

Ask when the following places open and close.
Example: (banca) – Quando apre e quando chiude questa banca?

ufficio cambi; ditta; scuola; edicola; ostello; banca; albergo.

Exercise 3

Tim is often absent-minded and forgets things. Lucio tries to help him. Can you play Tim's role?

Lucio: Tim, hai il passaporto?
Tim: (Say you haven't got it.)
Lucio: Ma non devi cambiare un assegno?
Tim: (Say you've got the driving licence.)
Lucio: Puoi cambiare un assegno senza il passaporto?
Tim: (Say you don't know. But say you don't know where the passport is.)
Lucio: Non lo sai?
Tim: (Say that maybe it's in the bedroom.)
Lucio: Hai moneta?
Tim: (Say you've a one thousand liras note.)
Lucio: Ma non devi fare un'interurbana?
Tim: (Say yes, you have to make a trunk call.)
Lucio: Allora, hai bisogno di moneta!

Exercise 4

Match the words on the left with the words on the right to form meaningful questions:

Può chiedere . . . ?	in banca
Può andare . . . ?	una camera
Può cambiare . . . ?	a Londra
Può firmare . . . ?	lunedì
Può parlare . . . ?	fino a domani
Può telefonare . . . ?	un assegno
Può restare . . . ?	questo numero
Può ripartire . . . ?	un modulo
Può verificare . . . ?	con la mia segretaria

Exercise 5

Match the sentences on the left with the sentences on the right to form meaningful statements:

Ho bisogno di un albergo.	Devo andare al posteggio.
Ho bisogno di un taxi.	Devo andare a Venezia.
Ho bisogno di un pullman.	Devo andare in un albergo.
Ho bisogno di una camera.	Devo restare qui un mese.

B

Exercise 6

Answer these questions in relation to dialogues 1 and 2.

Che cosa deve cambiare Tim?
Quando chiude l'ufficio cambi?
Tim ha il passaporto?
Tim deve ritornare all'ufficio cambi?
Dove ha il passaporto Tim?
Dov'è Tim quando telefona?
Quant'è un gettone?

Exercise 7

Lucio arrives with the passport and Tim now goes to the bank. Play his part.

Banchiere: (recognizes him) Ah! Hai il passaporto?
Tim: . . .
Banchiere: Hai bisogno di cambiare l'assegno da viaggio?
Tim: . . .

Banchiere: Allora, il passaporto, prego.
Tim: . . . (handing it over)
Banchiere: (he hands out the money) mille, duemila, tremila, quattromila, cinquemila, seimila, settemila, ottomila . . .
Tim: . . . (he checks them again)
Banchiere: Va bene?
Tim: . . .
Banchiere: Arrivederci.

Exercise 8
McKenzie has left some scattered notes on his table for Miss Dani. Can you arrange them in a meaningful sequence?

E non posso telefonare a Franco perchè non ha il telefono. Si chiama Franco Lugli. Aspetto un'interurbana da Londra. Oggi ho un appuntamento con un amico. Abita vicino all'albergo Flora. Ma non posso andare. Devo prendere un taxi subito.

REVISION AND SELF-ASSESSMENT TEST FOR CHAPTERS 1-5

Exercise 1 (Revise ch. 1)

Suggest a question to fit each of the following answers:

— Sì, tutto bene in viaggio.
— Sì. Sono la signora Pardi.
— Sì. Sono Lucio.
— No, sono Julie.
— Sì. È la chiesa di San Babila.

(For each correct answer, you earn one point)

Exercise 2 (Revise ch. 2)

1. To ask where someone is from, do you say?:
scusi, di dov'è? or scusi, dov'è? or scusi, c'è?

2. To ask whether there is accommodation available, do you say?:
c'è una camera libera? c'è un tavolo libero? c'è un'edicola?

3. To ask where something is, do you say?:
ogni quanto c'è? ecco? dov'è?

4. To ask whether something is far away, do you say?:
è vicino? è lontano? è sempre dritto?

(For each correct answer you earn one point)

Exercise 3
According to the numbers, ask where that street number is as in the example: Dov'è via Verdi 3?

4 1 5 8 7 6 10

(For each correct answer you earn one point)

Exercise 4 (two points for each correct answer)
Play Tim's role at the bus stop.
Tim: (how frequent is bus number 12?)
Signore: Il dodici è ogni quarto d'ora.
Tim: (Does the underground go as far as San Siro?)
Signore: No. La metro non va fino a San Siro.
Tim: (Ask where the bus stop is.)
Signore: La fermata è proprio qui.
Tim: (Ask if it is near the traffic-lights.)
Signore: Sì. È vicino al semaforo.
Tim: (Say thank you very much.)
Signore: Prego.

Exercise 5 (one point for each correct answer)
Imagine you always underestimate the cost by one thousand liras, as McKenzie does in the example:
McKenzie: Quant'è? Duemila lire? *Tassista*: No. Tremila.

Tassista: No, ottomila. No, seimila. No, tremila. No, quattromila. No, duemila. No, settemila.

Exercise 6 (two points for each correct answer)
Ask a question, joining each pair of words as in the example:
(bello) chiesa di San Paolo, chiesa di San Pietro – È più bella la chiesa di San Paolo o la chiesa di San Pietro?

1. (comodo) la pensione Firenze, la pensione Venezia.
2. (grande) l'università di Milano, l'università di Torino.
3. (lontano) la filiale di via Roma, di via Venezia.
4. (piccolo) Venezia, Verona.
5. (vicino) piazzale Garibaldi, piazzale Mazzini.

Exercise 7 (two points for each correct answer)
Ask a question with each of the following words according to this model:

Dov'è il mio gettone? Non lo so dov'è il tuo. Il mio è qui.
assegno da viaggio; biglietto; cartella; pezzo da diecimila; penna.

Exercise 8 (two points for each correct answer)
You work in London, but you don't live there. You are in Italy on business and will stay for a week. You understand Italian but you

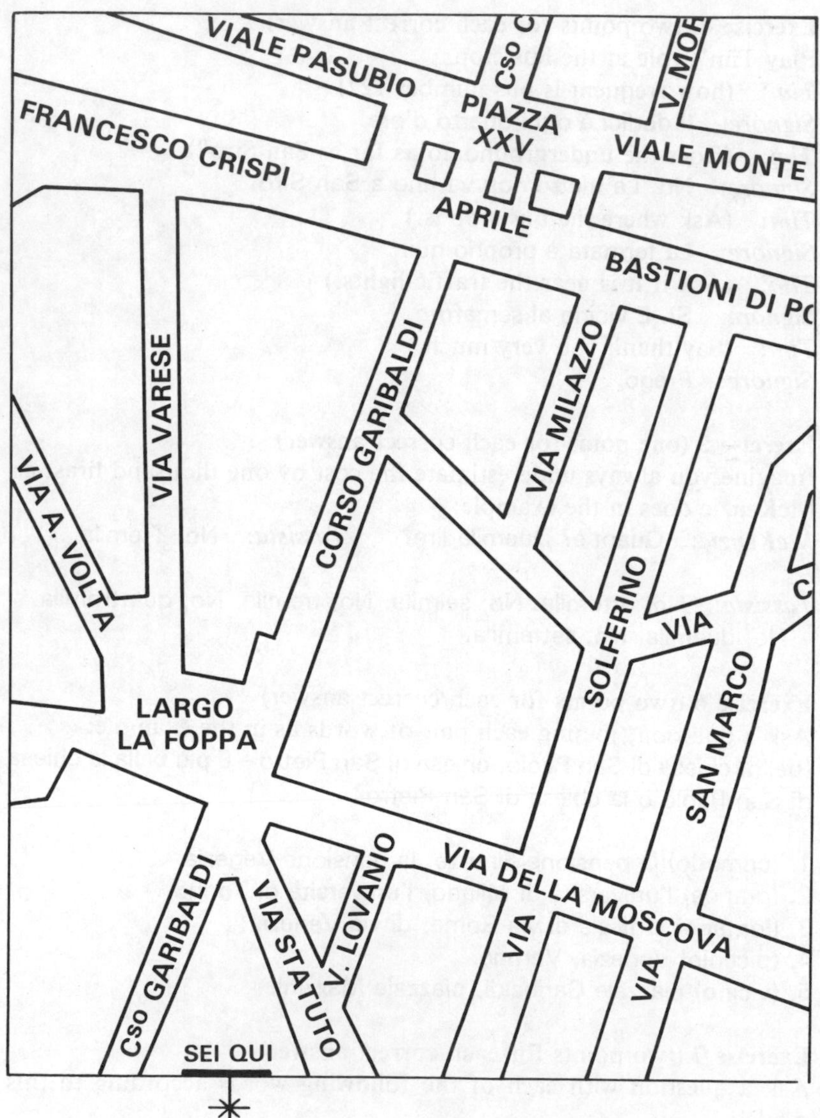

don't speak Italian very well. Say all this to people asking about you. (They address you formally.)

— Dove lavora, signore/a?
— Abita a Londra?
— Perchè è in Italia?
— Quanto resta in Italia?
— Capisce l'italiano?

Exercise 9 (three points for each correct question)
Suggest the right question to each answer formally.

1. La signora si chiama Giovanna.
2. Mi chiamo Giovanna.
3. In italiano si dice un albergo di prima categoria.
4. Mi dispiace, non so dov'è piazza Roma.
5. Purtroppo non posso arrivare tra un quarto d'ora.
6. Sono di Madrid.

Exercise 10 (three points for each correct answer)
Look at the map of the centre of Milan and answer the following questions:

1. Via Pasubio è vicino a via Crispi?
2. Via Lovanio è a destra o a sinistra di corso Garibaldi?
3. Via Della Moscova è in fondo a corso Garibaldi?
4. Via Della Moscova è dopo via Statuto?
5. C'è Largo La Foppa in fondo a corso Garibaldi?

More than 80 points: bravissimo! bravissima! Excellent.
Between 50 and 80: il lavoro va bene. Good.
Below 50: così, così. So, so.

ORDERING DRINKS; ASKING FOR ADVICE IN SHOPS

6.1 DIALOGUES

Dialogue 1 **In gelateria**

Tim and Julie go to an ice-cream parlour near the school.

Tim: Ci sono posti liberi, per favore?
Cameriere: Sì. C'è un tavolo a destra, vicino alla terrazza.

(The students sit down.)

Cameriere: Prego?
Julie: Io prendo un gelato al cioccolato. E tu, Tim?
Tim: Un gelato alla frutta.
Cameriere: Va bene. Allora due gelati.

(They are joined by other foreign students and staff.)

Professore: Cameriere! Scusi, ci sono altri tavoli liberi?
Cameriere: Sì. C'è un altro tavolo fuori in terrazza.

(They all go out and start deciding what they want.)

Gustav: Io vorrei un bicchiere di latte, e tu, Martha?
Martha: Io vorrei un succo di frutta. E lei, professore?
Professore: Prendo un frullato. Questi frullati sono famosi in tutta la città.
Lise: Che cosa sono i frullati?
Professore: Il frullato è un succo fatto di frutta e latte.
Cameriere: Allora, frullati per tutti?

'Preferisci il gelato alla crema o alla frutta?'

Dialogue 2 In pasticceria

After a few days, Mr McKenzie decides to present Mrs Pardi with a small gift. He goes to a sweet shop.

Proprietaria: Buongiorno. Prego?

McKenzie: Devo fare un regalino, ma non so che cosa. Sono indeciso. Vorrei un consiglio.

Proprietaria: È per un uomo o per una donna?

McKenzie: Una donna.

Proprietaria: Una scatola di cioccolatini? O una scatola di biscotti? Di Amaretti di Saronno?

McKenzie: Che cosa sono gli Amaretti di Saronno?

Proprietaria: Sono questi biscotti qui un poco amari, fatti a Saronno, una cittadina qui vicino.

McKenzie: Va bene. Mi dia una scatola di cioccolatini e una scatola di Amaretti.

Proprietaria: Un pacchetto solo o due pacchetti?

McKenzie: Due pacchetti, per favore. Quant'è in tutto?

Proprietaria: Dodicimila.

McKenzie: Ecco a lei. Grazie e arrivederci.

'Qui ci sono autori italiani?'

Dialogue 3 In libreria

Mr McKenzie decides to buy something to read to improve his Italian.

Libraio: Buonasera. Prego?
McKenzie: Vorrei un vocabolario italiano-inglese.
Libraio: Un'edizione economica o un vocabolario più grande?
McKenzie: Ma . . . non so. Vorrei vedere una buona edizione, ma non molto cara.
Libraio: I vocabolari sono tutti qui, su questo scaffale.

(McKenzie picks up one or two dictionaries and asks for the price.)

McKenzie: Quant'è questo vocabolario?
Libraio: I prezzi sono tutti dietro la copertina.
McKenzie: Va bene. Mi dia questo. (He would also like some works of Italian literature.) Vorrei anche vedere alcuni libri in italiano, ma facili.
Libraio: Romanzi brevi o racconti?
McKenzie: Ma, non so . . . Forse un'antologia di racconti.

'Una scatola di cioccolatini o una scatola di biscotti?'

Libraio: In questi scaffali ci sono gli autori stranieri tradotti. Qui ci sono altri autori italiani contemporanei, Buzzati, Moravia, Vittorini, Pasolini, Silone . . .
McKenzie: Va bene, grazie . . .

Dialogue 4 In un negozio di dischi

Tim wants to find out something about Italian music.

Commesso: Ciao.
Tim: Vorrei regalare un disco di musica italiana.
Commesso: Preferisci musica classica o musica leggera?
Tim: Musica leggera, musica folcloristica. Vorrei un consiglio. Vorrei alcuni nomi di cantanti italiani.
Commesso: Che cantanti? I complessi? I cantautori?
Tim: Scusi, non capisco. Che cosa sono i cantautori?
Commesso: Sono cantanti e anche autori, come Bob Dylan.
Tim: Quali sono gli italiani più famosi?
Commesso: Lucio Battisti, Fabrizio De André, Domenico Modugno . . .
Tim: Ci sono album con i testi dietro la copertina?
Commesso: Sì. Sono questi album qui.
Tim: (He picks out one.) Vorrei ascoltare quest'album di Guccini. (He likes it) Va bene. Prendo questo. Quant'è?
Commesso: Ottomila. Devi fare lo scontrino. Ciao.

6.2 VOCABULARY

Dialogue 1

la gelateria (f)	ice-cream parlour
ci sono	there are
per favore	please
il cameriere (m)	waiter
la cameriera (f)	waitress
il/la tavolo-a (m and f)	table
la terrazza (f); in –	terrace, balcony; on the –
il gelato (m)	ice-cream
il cioccolato (m); al –	chocolate; chocolate-flavoured
la frutta (f); alla –	fruit; fruit-flavoured
altro; altra; un altro (m) un'altra (f)	other; another
fuori	outside
vorrei (volere, irreg.)	I would like
il bicchiere (m)	glass

il latte (m)	milk
il succo (m) (-chi); -di frutta	juice; fruit juice
il frullato (m)	fruit shake
questi-e	these
sono (essere)	they are
famoso-a	famous; well-known
tutto il, tutta la	the whole; all the
fatto-a (fare, irreg.)	made

Dialogue 2

la pasticceria (f)	confectioner's
il proprietario (m) la proprietaria (f)	owner
il regalo (m); il regalino (m)	gift, present; small gift
indeciso-a	uncertain
il consiglio (m)	advice
la donna (f)	woman
la scatola (f)	box
il cioccolatino (m)	small chocolate
il biscotto (m)	biscuit
amaro-a	bitter
un poco	slightly
la cittadina (f)	small town
mi dia (dare, irreg.)	give me (formal)
il pacchetto (m); fare un –	packet; to wrap up
in tutto	in all

Dialogue 3

la libreria (f)	bookshop
il vocabolario (m)	dictionary
l'edizione economica (f) (pl. -che)	paperback edition
vedere	to see
buono-a	good
tutti-e; tutti i; tutte le	all
lo scaffale (m)	shelf
il prezzo (m)	price
la copertina (f); dietro la –	cover; on the back cover
questo-a	this one
anche	also, too
alcuni-e	some
il libro (m)	book
facile-e	easy

il romanzo (m)	novel
breve-e	short
il racconto (m)	short story
l'antologia (f)	anthology
l'autore (m) l'autrice (f)	author
contemporaneo	contemporary

Dialogue 4

il commesso (m) la commessa (f)	shop assistant
il disco (m) (pl. -chi)	record
regalare	to give a present
la musica (f)	music
classico-a (pl. -ci, -che)	classic
leggero-a	light
folcloristico-a (-ci, -che)	folk
il/la cantante (m and f)	singer
il complesso (m)	pop group
il cantautore (m)	singer and song writer
come	such as, like
quali? (m and f pl.)	which? which ones?
il testo (m)	text
ascoltare	to listen
l'album (m) (pl. invar.)	album; LP
lo scontrino (m); fare lo –	cash slip; to get the –

6.3 EXPLANATIONS

(a) Background information

The gelateria has the same social function as a café. It does not serve alcoholic drinks. A large variety of ice-creams and fruit drinks are sold on the premises or to take away, especially in summer. In winter, the most popular items are hot chocolate drinks, cones of whipped cream (un cono di panna montata), and cakes (paste).

Small and medium sized shops are still predominant in Italy. They are usually run on a family basis and foreign tourists receive a great deal of personal attention, even if they don't speak Italian.

Regional variations in food are a striking feature of Italian culture. Every region—very often every single town—has its own food specialities (cakes, biscuits, liqueurs). Try them by asking: vorrei una specialità del posto (I'd like a local speciality).

Proverbio: Tutti i gusti sono gusti.
Every man to his taste.

(b) Fillers

Every language has a group of words which are used to 'oil' conversations. Some of the most frequent English expressions are: 'well', 'so', 'then', 'fine'. Similarly, Italian people frequently use allora, va bene, ecco, dunque. Look out for other 'fillers' in the next chapters.

(c) About more than one: plural forms

(i) The articles (masculine) – *grammar ref. 13* There are two forms of plural masculine articles:

i in front of most words
gli in front of words starting with a vowel, *s* + consonant and *z*

Ecco i libri italiani.	Here are the Italian books.
Ecco gli altri libri.	Here are the other books.
Ecco gli studenti inglesi.	Here are the English students.

(ii) Plural nouns and adjectives (masculine) – *grammar ref. 3; 37*

To form the plural of masculine nouns and adjectives, you change their last vowel into -i.

È un regista famoso? Sì, sono tutti registi famosi.
È un autore inglese? Sì, sono tutti autori inglesi.
È un romanzo facile? Sì, sono tutti romanzi facili.

Ending in -io – grammar ref. 5

If a noun or an adjective ends in -io, simply drop the o for the plural:

Vorrei un consiglio.	I would like advice.
Vorrei alcuni consigli.	I would like a few words of advice.

Exceptions to this rule are indicated in the vocabulary lists.

Ending in -co, -ca, -go, -ga – grammar ref. 6

Nouns and adjectives ending in -co or -ca in the singular form end in -chi in the plural. Similarly those ending in -go or -ga, change it into -ghi in the plural. This is in order to keep the hard 'c' and 'g' sound—(see the pronunciation guide).

Hai un disco di Modugno?	Ho due dischi di Modugno!
Hai un collega inglese?	Ho due colleghi inglesi!
Hai un succo di frutta?	Ho due succhi di frutta!

Nouns ending with a consonant – grammar ref. 4
These, most of them of foreign origin, do not change in the plural:

Vorrei un album di Guccini.	I would like one LP by/of Guccini
Ecco a lei due album di Guccini.	Here are two LPs by/of Guccini

These and other irregular plural forms are indicated in the vocabulary lists.

(d) Ordering something: vorrei (I'd like)
The simplest form is:

Un gelato, per favore.	An ice-cream, please.

or, more gracefully:

Vorrei un gelato, per favore.	I'd like an ice-cream, please.
Mi dia un gelato, per favore.	I'll have ... (lit. give me).

To say 'please', there is no difference between per piacere and per favore.

(e) Offering something to other people
You say this, addressing the person:

E tu?	And you? (familiar)
E tu, che cosa prendi?	And what do you take? (familiar)
E lei?	And what about you? (formal)
E lei, che cosa prende?	And what do you take? (formal)

You may sum up with:

per tutti ...	for everybody ...

(f) Expressing what you wish to do
According to what you wish, you say:

Vorrei ascoltare un disco.	I'd like to listen to a record.
Vorrei anche vedere questo album.	I'd also like to see this album.

The word anche is placed *after* the main verb.

(g) . . . sono . . . (are) – *grammar ref. 58*
Most of the expressions based on è (is) which have been met and used in the previous chapters can be used in the plural with sono (are):

Ci sono (gelati alla frutta)?	Are there (ice-creams with a fruit flavour)?
Che cosa sono?	What are they?
Quali sono?	Which are they?
Dove sono?	Where are they?
Che (libri) sono?	What (books) are they?
Di dove sono?	Where do they come from?

To reply to all these questions, you use sono (they are).

The pronoun loro (they) is usually omitted; a question is formed by raising the tone of the voice at the end of the sentence. To reply in the negative the word non is inserted before the verb:

Ci sono tavoli liberi?	Are there vacant tables?
No, non ci sono tavoli liberi.	No, there aren't vacant tables.

If you do not repeat the noun, the expression ce ne must be inserted instead of the noun: – *grammar ref. 27*

Non ci sono tavoli liberi. Non ce ne sono.	There aren't vacant tables.
Ci sono tavoli liberi. Ce ne sono.	There are vacant tables.

(h) Saying something is not available (there are no . . .)
The expression non ci sono corresponds to two expressions in English:

Non ci sono dischi di musica classica.	There are no records of classical music. There aren't any records of classical music.

(i) Saying what you want to buy (some, other, these)
You start with:

Vorrei prendere . . .	I would like to take . . .
Vorrei comprare . . .	I would like to buy . . .
Prendo . . .	I take, I'll take . . .
Compro . . . (comprare)	I buy, I'll buy . . .

Io, tu, lei, which are usually left out, are put before the verb only if the speaker wants to emphasize who chooses what.

If you wish to specify a quantity, you may say:

Vorrei prendere questi gelati.	I'd like to take these ice-creams.
Vorrei prendere alcuni gelati.	I'd like to take (some) ice-creams.
Vorrei prendere altri romanzi.	I'd like to take other novels.
Io compro anche una penna.	I'll also buy a pen.
Mi dia un altro biscotto.	May I have another biscuit? (lit. give me)
Mi dia un'altra scatola.	May I have another box?
Desidero un solo vocabolario.	I wish to have only one dictionary.
Desidero una sola camera.	I require only one room.

(j) Indicating flavours: al – *grammar ref. 16*
a + the definite article is used with words relating to food to indicate flavours or ways of cooking:

Un gelato al cioccolato.	A chocolate-flavoured ice-cream.
Un gelato alla frutta.	A fruit-flavoured ice-cream.
Un cioccolatino al liquore.	A chocolate filled with liqueur.

(k) Talking of music, arts: adjectives in -a – *grammar ref. 37*
Adjectives ending in -a are useful when talking of arts and social arts subjects. They too form their plural in -i:

È un autore realista.	Sono autori realisti.
È un autore marxista.	Sono autori marxisti.
È un romanzo surrealista.	Sono romanzi surrealisti.

6.4 EXERCISES

A

Exercise 1
Order the following drinks or sweets, as in the example:
(ice-cream) Vorrei un gelato, per favore.

a fruit-flavoured ice cream; two glasses of milk; three fruit juices; a box of biscuits.

Exercise 2

You've enjoyed your drink or ice-cream and would like to order a second one:
(ice-cream). Scusi, mi dia un altro gelato, per favore.

a fruit-flavoured ice-cream; a fruit juice; a chocolate-flavoured ice-cream; a glass of milk.

Exercise 3

You would like to choose from a selection. What would you say?

Ecco un disco di Modugno. Scusi, ci sono altri dischi di Modugno?

Ecco un album di Battisti.
Ecco un vocabolario italiano.
Ecco a lei un romanzo inglese.
Ecco a lei un racconto americano.
Ecco un gettone.

Exercise 4

Here is a series of answers. Can you supply the questions?
A. Sono assegni da viaggio. *Q*. Che cosa sono?

1. I taxi sono lì fuori.
2. Questi sono amaretti di Saronno.
3. Questi studenti sono di Parigi.
4. Sì, ci sono negozi aperti.
5. Sono racconti contemporanei.
6. Sì, ci sono tavoli liberi.

Exercise 5

Match each noun with its appropriate adjective. The endings will help you.

Nouns: romanzo; albergo; pensione; autori; cantanti; musica; strada; gelato.
Adjectives: folcloristica; rumorosa; americano; completa; caro; contemporanei; folcloristici; buono.

B

Exercise 6

An Italian friend rings up Tim to see how his day went. Reproduce Tim's replies in Italian.

Hallo! Not too bad, thank you, and you? An ice-cream parlour, near the school. No, not on my own, with other foreign students. They are not all English. Oh, yes! Also foreign businessmen, French, American . . . No, a fruit juice. The others – ice-creams, glasses of milk, fruit shakes. No, not at home, in a record shop. Not near the station. It is the shop after the university. Yes, bus number 13 as far as Piazza Garibaldi and then on foot. No, not (of) classical music, folk music. Yes, two albums of well-known Italian singers. They are very good (belli). They are Battisti and De André. No! Not twenty thousand liras! Sixteen thousand! They are not very expensive. Yes, there are the texts on the back of the sleeve (cover). Okay. See you tomorrow.

Exercise 7

Can you write this essay in Italian? The title is: *Montenapoleone Road.* It is a very famous Italian street. It goes from Manzoni road to San Babila square. Opposite there is the Scala. Not far away, on the right, there is the Duomo, (which is) Milan's very beautiful church. On the right or on the left of this road—I'm not sure—there is the British Council. The address is Manzoni Road 18. One building in Montenapoleone road is the house of a famous author, a poet (un poeta) Nobel Prize winner (il Premio Nobel) Eugenio Montale. There are shops, first class hotels, but there are no buses. The tube is nearby. There is a tube station in San Babila Square and there are two buses in via Manzoni.

DOING THINGS WITH OTHER PEOPLE; INSISTING ON PAYING

7.1 DIALOGUES

Dialogue 1 Al bar

Tim has cashed his cheque and wants to offer Lucio a drink.

Tim: Lucio, non hai voglia di prendere qualcosa?
Lucio: Sì. Prendiamo un caffè?
Tim: Grazie. Non bevo mai caffè. Perchè non beviamo qualcosa di fresco? Un'aranciata o una birra?
Lucio: (he asks the waiter) Ha birra inglese?
Cameriere: Mi dispiace. Ci sono solo queste marche, tedesche e danesi.
Tim: Va bene. Bevo una birra. (He starts ordering . . .).
Cameriere: Devi fare lo scontrino.
Tim: Come? Scusi, non parlo italiano molto bene.

(Lucio is quicker than Tim to go to the cash desk.)

Tim: Lucio, pago io!
Lucio: No. Offro io.
Tim: Offro io! Dai!
Lucio: Paghi tu un'altra volta.
Tim: Grazie, allora. (Back to the counter)
Lucio: Un caffè e una birra. Mi dia anche un bicchiere d'acqua.
Cameriere: Scusa, la birra alla spina o in bottiglia?
Tim: In bottiglia, grazie (Raising his glass) cin . . . cin . . .

Dialogue2 La colazione a casa
Breakfast at home

Lucio: Mamma, oggi prepariamo una colazione inglese.
Tim: Signora, ci sono uova fresche?
Mamma: Sì. In frigo ci sono sei uova tutte fresche.
Lucio: Tim, mangiamo anche salsicce?
Tim: Sì. Ho bisogno di alcune fette di pancetta, di alcune salsicce, di alcuni pomodori e alcune fette di pane tostato.
Lucio: C'è latte, per favore?
Mamma: Sì, certo. Eccolo. È freddo, va bene?
Lucio: Sì, grazie.
Mamma: E da bere? Tè o caffè, questa mattina?
Lucio: Tè con latte, oggi. Proprio una colazione inglese!
Mamma: Tim, il caffè con lo zucchero o senza?
Tim: Con lo zucchero, grazie (Serving the eggs and the toast) Ecco la colazione!
Lucio: Buona!

'Prendiamo un caffé?'

Dialogue 3 L'aperitivo
Mrs Pardi, Mr McKenzie and other colleagues go to the bar before lunch.

Rossi: (to the ladies) Signore, un caffè? Un aperitivo?
Pardi: Io e la signorina Dani prendiamo una minerale. Analcolica!
Rossi: E lei signor McKenzie?
McKenzie: Vorrei un Martini.
Rossi: Rosso o bianco?
McKenzie: Rosso con una fetta di limone.
Rossi: . . . Io ho voglia di . . . un amaro con acqua. Ho sete.
Rossi: (at the cash desk) Un Martini, un amaro e due minerali.
Cassiera: Duemilacinque, prego.
McKenzie: Per favore, pago io!
Rossi: No, no. Offro io.
McKenzie: Permetta . . . Offro io questa volta.
Rossi: No, no. Un'altra volta.
McKenzie: Grazie.
Cameriere: Scusi, signore, l'amaro liscio o con ghiaccio?
Rossi: Con ghiaccio e con alcune olive e queste patatine . . . Cin . . . cin . . .

Dialogue 4 La colazione in albergo

Mr McKenzie and an English businessman have breakfast together.

Cameriere: Buongiorno, signori. Tè o caffè?
McKenzie: Questa mattina cominciamo con un tè.
Cameriere: Con latte o con limone?
McKenzie: Con latte, grazie.
Cameriere: Ecco lo zucchero.
McKenzie: No, no, grazie, non prendo mai lo zucchero con il tè. Desideriamo anche uno yogurth, due uova sode e alcune fette di pane tostato.
Cameriere: Con miele e marmellata?
McKenzie: C'è marmellata di arancia?
Cameriere: No, mi dispiace. Ci sono solo marmellate alla frutta.
McKenzie: C'è burro salato?
Cameriere: No, mi dispiace. Non è facile fare una colazione inglese in Italia!
McKenzie: Non importa. Non si preoccupi.
Cameriere: Buona giornata!

7.2 VOCABULARY

Dialogue 1

aver voglia di qualcosa	to feel like (to have a desire for) something

il caffè (m) (pl. invar.)	coffee
bevo (bere, irreg.)	I drink
mai	never
fresco-a (pl. -chi; -che)	fresh, cool
l'aranciata (f)	orange squash
la birra (f)	beer, lager
tedesco-a (pl. -chi, -che)	German
danese-e	Danish
pagare	to pay
offrire	to offer
dai!	come on!
una volta	once (lit. one time)
l'acqua (f)	water
alla spina	draught (beer)
la bottiglia (f)	bottle
cin . . . cin . . .	cheers!

Dialogue 2

la mamma (f)	mother, mummy
preparare	to prepare
la colazione (f); fare –	breakfast; to have –
l'uovo (m) (pl. le uova (f))	egg
il frigorifero, il frigo (m)	fridge
mangiare	to eat
la salsiccia (f) (pl. -ce)	sausage
la fetta (f)	slice
la pancetta (f)	bacon
il pomodoro (m)	tomato
il pane (m)	bread
tostato-a	toasted
freddo-a	cold
bere	to drink
il tè (m) (pl. invar.)	tea
il limone (m)	lemon
lo zucchero (m)	sugar

Dialogue 3

l'aperitivo (m)	aperitif, drink before a meal
la minerale (f)	mineral water
l'analcolico (m) (pl. -ci)	non alcoholic drink
rosso-a	red
bianco-a (pl. -chi, -che)	white
l'amaro (m)	aperitif with a bitter taste

l'acqua (f)	water
il cassiere (m) la cassiera (f)	cashier
aver sete	to be thirsty (lit. to have thirst)
permetta . . . (permettere)	allow me (formal)
liscio-a	straight
il ghiaccio (m)	ice
l'oliva (f)	olive
la patatina (f)	crisp
la patata (f)	potato

Dialogue 4

lo yogurth (m) (pl. invar.)	yoghurt
sodo-a; uovo –	hard; hard-boiled egg
il miele (m)	honey
la marmellata (f)	jam, marmalade
l'arancia (f) (pl. -ce)	orange
il burro (m)	butter
salato-a	salted
non importa	it doesn't matter
non si preoccupi (preoccuparsi)	don't worry (formal)
la giornata (f); buona-	day, daytime; have a good day

7.3 EXPLANATIONS

(a) Background information

Bars: Bars and cafés in Italy play the same role as pubs and cafés in England. Outsidc cafés, there are often tables where people sit, drink and talk. Bars are open uninterruptedly from 7 o'clock in the morning until midnight. Alcoholic drinks are served at all times. Items cost more if they are served at a table rather than if you stand at the bar, and there are often two price scales on display.

Drinks: The favourite drink is the caffè espresso (a small cup of strong black coffee). The cappuccino (black coffee with milk froth) is a favourite drink with foreigners. Beer is usually drunk in the summer as a refreshing drink. As a social drink, it is substituted by aperitifs, of which there is a large choice.

Breakfast: English breakfast is usually not available in Italy. Some supermarkets sell foreign products (cereals etc.). Italian breakfast is only a cup of espresso coffee taken at the bar (the first social activity of the day). Another popular type of breakfast at the bar is the cappuccino with a cake (brioche, pronounced briosh).

(b) A drink for two: noi (we . . .) – *grammar ref. 58*
All verbs (1st, 2nd, 3rd conjugations) take the ending -iamo to indicate that the subject of the verb is *we* (1st person pl.):

rest – are (1st conj.)	rest + iamo
prend – ere (2nd conj.)	prend + iamo
offr – ire (3rd conj.)	offr + iamo
*prefer – ire (3rd conj.)	prefer + iamo

This form is used: to make a suggestion, (let's) – *grammar ref. 61*

Prendiamo un caffè?	Shall we take a coffee? What about a . . .?
Perchè non prendiamo un tè?	Why don't we take a cup of tea?

to announce a plan:

Oggi prepariamo una colazione inglese.	Today we'll prepare an English breakfast.

to make a statement:

Mi dispiace, non capiamo l'italiano.	Sorry, we don't understand Italian.

to make a proposal:

Beviamo alla tua salute!	Let's drink to your health!

(c) Verbs changing their spelling: – *grammar ref. 60*
See in the grammar ref. section how some verbs (pagare, cominciare) modify their spelling to keep the same sound as the infinitive. (Revise the pronunciation guide, the letters chi, ci, ghi, gi)

Pago io!	I'll pay!
No, paghiamo noi!	No, we'll pay!

(d) What you never do: non . . . mai (never) – *grammar ref. 78*
The word 'never' is expressed in Italian with two words: non . . . mai.

Non beviamo mai alcolici.	We never drink alcoholic drinks.

But, to be really emphatic you can say:

Mai prendo il caffè a colazione.	I never take coffee at breakfast.

(e) More than one: feminine plural

The article – *grammar ref. 13* Before feminine plural words the article is le:

Le uova sono fresche?	Are the eggs fresh?
Sono buone le patatine?	Are the crisps good?

Feminine plural nouns and adjectives: – *grammar ref. 3; 37*
Feminine nouns and adjectives ending in -a change it into -e
Feminine nouns and adjectives ending in -e change it into -i

Una birra inglese, per favore. Due birre inglesi, per favore.
Una minerale italiana, per favore. Due minerali italiane, per favore.

These endings apply to words which you've already learnt in the singular form:

Ci sono altre salsicce?	Are there other sausages?
Sì, ci sono alcune salsicce nel frigo.	There are some sausages in the fridge.
Hai bisogno delle fette di pane?	Do you need the slices of bread?
Ho bisogno di tutte le fette.	I need all the slices.
Queste bottiglie sono grandi.	These bottles are large.

Change of spelling, words in -ca, -ga – *grammar ref. 6*
Like the masculine words, some feminine words (ending in -ca, -ga) change in the plural form to keep the same sound as in the singular:
l'amica, le amiche; la collega, le colleghe.
The plurals are indicated in the vocabulary lists.

(f) More than one: nouns ending with an accent – *grammar ref. 4*
Nouns ending in -à, -è, -ì do not change in the plural:

Milano e Roma sono due città molto belle.	Milan and Rome are two very nice cities.
Tutti i lunedì vado a Roma.	Every Monday I go to Rome.
Bevono due tè.	They drink two teas.

(g) Saying what you fancy . . . aver voglia di
You may be vague and just say:

Ho voglia di qualcosa.	I feel like having something.

Or be more specific, adding a noun, singular or plural:

Hai voglia di un cappuccino?	Do you fancy a white coffee?

or adding a verb:

Ha voglia di mangiare un'arancia?	Do you fancy eating an orange?

A negative reply may be:

No, grazie, non ho voglia di uova.	No, thank you. I don't fancy eggs.

Or, if you wish to say you don't fancy anything:

Non ho voglia di niente.	I don't want anything (lit. I don't have a wish for nothing) *see grammar ref. 78*

(h) Insisting it's your turn: offro io
You express your determination, by placing the subject pronoun io, after the verb:

Pago io!	I should like to pay myself.
Offro io! Dai!	It's on me. Come on!

You may add:

Paghi tu un'altra volta!	You'll pay another time!
Offre lei la prossima volta!	You'll offer the next time!

To reply:

Grazie, allora. Molto gentile.	It's very kind of you.

(i) Words

(i) bere: the infinitive is irregular. The present tense is regular (*see grammar ref. 64*)

(ii) mamma (f) is used for calling her. To speak about her, you say: mia madre, or mia mamma.
(iii) l'uovo is masc. in the sing., but it is fem. in the plural.
(iv) volta (f) is used only in expressions such as these:
una volta (once); tre volte (three times); alcune volte (a few times).

Proverbio: Buon vino fa buon sangue.
Wine makes glad the heart of man.
(lit. Good wine makes good blood)

7.4 EXERCISES

A

Exercise 1
You have just arrived in Italy with a friend and would like to try everything. Say it according to the model:
un'aranciata? Sì, grazie, prendiamo due aranciate.

un caffè? un tè? un cappuccino? un bicchiere di latte? una birra alla spina? un aperitivo liscio? un amaro con ghiaccio? un succo di frutta? un cioccolatino? un'arancia?

Exercise 2
You want to offer a drink. Say it according to the model:
hai voglia di prendere qualcosa? Di un caffè?

a fruit shake; a cup of tea; an aperitif; a red Martini; a coffee with milk without sugar; a few olives; a few crisps; a glass of cold milk.

Exercise 3
Here is a list of verbs. Put them in the right slots to form meaningful sentences:
restiamo; andiamo; ascoltiamo; leggiamo; compriamo; mangiamo; parliamo.
1. purtroppo, non . . . mai un mese in Italia.
2. Mi dispiace, non . . . mai frutta a colazione.
3. Non . . . mai in ufficio a piedi.
4. Eh No! Non . . . mai libri cari.
5. Non . . . mai la televisione.
6. Non . . . mai racconti tradotti.
7. Non . . . francese a casa.

Exercise 4
You are in various shops. Order the following things in the simplest way, as in the model:
(aperitif): Due aperitivi, per favore.

biglietto; birra; camera singola; aranciata; gelato; disco; modulo; penna; scatola di cioccolatini; pacchetto di patatine; sterlina.

Exercise 5
Mr McKenzie thinks it is his turn to offer Mr Rossi a drink. Can you play his role with the help of Mr Rossi's answers?
McKenzie: ...
Rossi: Sì, grazie. Ho proprio voglia di un caffè.
McKenzie: ...
Rossi: No, grazie. Senza latte.
McKenzie: ...
Rossi: No, grazie, non prendo zucchero.
McKenzie: (he orders at the cash-desk)
Rossi: Pago io, per favore.
McKenzie: ...
Rossi: Grazie. Molto gentile.

B

Exercise 6
Can you order your breakfast in Italy?

I'll start with tea. Milk, but no sugar. Then I'll have two slices of toasted bread with butter, salted, if possible, and marmalade. I'll also have fruit-flavoured yoghurt, a fruit juice, two slices of bacon and one sausage. No, thank you. I don't take tomatoes.

Exercise 7
You want to organize a party and you need a few of each of the following items. Say it according to the model:
(salatino) Ho bisogno di alcuni salatini.

birra; aranciata; bicchiere; oliva; disco; bottiglia di acqua minerale; biscotto; gelato; Martini; analcolico.

Exercise 8
With a friend you ring up a hotel to book two rooms and you reply to the receptionist's questions:

— Ask whether there are two single bedrooms with bathroom.
— Say that you're staying for three weeks.
— Say that you are going back next Wednesday.
— Say you are waiting for two colleagues.
— Ask when the hotel closes.
— Say you will arrive in two hours.

Exercise 9
People are enquiring about your movements. Can you reply as in the following example?
Dove vai? (say you are going to listen to a record) Vado a ascoltare un disco.

to learn English; to study Italian; to work in England; to open the shop; to close the office; to take the bus; to change money; to drink a glass of water.

Exercise 10
Write the first page of your diary in Italy. It will be a souvenir when you speak Italian fluently.

Today, like every Thursday, I start with a light breakfast. A cup of tea, with milk, without sugar. My favourite breakfast consists of a boiled egg and a slice of bread. Then, with two friends (f), I walk to the SIP where I work. We don't take the bus because the office is not far away. I speak French, English and German and every hour I listen to a hundred trunk calls. I sign almost one hundred forms. At midday the office closes and we go back home. There I prepare ... (arrivederci alla prossima volta) till the next time.

ORDERING MEALS; SAYING SOMETHING IS VERY GOOD

8.1 DIALOGUES

Dialogue 1 Alla tavola calda

Mr McKenzie, Mrs Pardi and Mr Rossi go to the snack bar for lunch. They each sit on a stool.

Rossi: (to everybody) Che cosa ordiniamo?
Pardi: (pointing to the counter) Per me quell'insalata lì e quel prosciutto crudo.
McKenzie: (to the waiter) Avete dei panini?
Cameriere: Sì, abbiamo dei panini al prosciutto, al formaggio . . .
McKenzie: Mi dia un panino al prosciutto crudo.
Rossi: Nient'altro? Un'insalata anche per lei?
McKenzie: Va bene. Ma non vorrei mangiare molto.
Cameriere: E per lei, signor Rossi?
Rossi: Prendo un panino al salame e della frutta.
Cameriere: Qualcosa da bere?
Pardi: Prendo della birra alla spina.
McKenzie: Per me un bicchiere di latte freddo.
Rossi: Per me una mezza bottiglia di vino rosso.

(Before they start eating)

Rossi: Buon appetito!
Pardi: Grazie, altrettanto.

Dialogue 2 Uno spuntino all'albergo

A snack at the hotel

Rossi: Devo lavorare molto. Ordino qualcosa da mangiare per telefono anche per lei?

McKenzie: No, no. Questa volta offro io. Che cosa prende?
Rossi: Prendo un panino al formaggio, un piatto di insalata mista e una macedonia di frutta.
McKenzie: Che cosa significa macedonia di frutta?
Rossi: Significa 'fruit salad'.
McKenzie: E da bere? Che cosa ordino per lei?
Rossi: Mezza bottiglia di vino rosso.

(McKenzie picks up the phone)

McKenzie: Vorrei ordinare qualcosa da mangiare in camera.
Portiere: Prego. Che cosa desidera?
McKenzie: Due panini al prosciutto cotto, due insalate e . . . avete della macedonia di frutta fresca?
Portiere: Freschissima! E da bere? Del vino bianco leggero?
McKenzie: Mezza bottiglia di vino bianco e una di vino rosso. Un momento . . . Per me l'insalata non condita. Senza olio. Mi scusi. Sono un inglese stravagante!

Dialogue 3 In pizzeria

Lucio and Tim decide to have an evening out with Laura and another friend.

Lucio: Buonasera. C'è il menù, per piacere?
Cameriera: Eccolo. Che cosa porto da bere?
Lucio: Avete della birra ghiacciata?

DA FRANCO PIZZERIA

Pizza Margherita	L2.300
Pizza Napoletana	L2.500
Pizza Quattro Stagioni	L2.500
Pizza Capricciosa	L2.500
Pizza Farcita con funghi	L2.800
Pizza Al Gorgonzola	L2.800

Tim: Una birra ghiacciata!? (he shakes his head in horror). In inglese si dice 'no comment'.

Lucio: Prendiamo due pizze alla napoletana?

Tim: (reading the menu) Che cosa significa alla napoletana? Com'è?

Lucio: La pizza napoletana è la pizza originale. C'è sopra del sugo di pomodoro, della mozzarella, delle acciughe e del basilico.

Tim: Che cos'è la mozzarella? È tenera?

Lucio: Sì. È tenerissima. È quel formaggio bianco lì. Allora una pizza napoletana anche per te, Tim?

Tim: Sì. Per me una pizza napoletana. Non grande. E da bere un bicchiere di vino bianco. Con ghiaccio, per favore.

Lucio: Vino con ghiaccio??!! In italiano si dice 'tutti i gusti sono gusti'. Ma anche in Italia si dice 'no comment'.

Tim: Buon appetito! e cin . . . cin!

Dialogue 4

The two girls arrive.

Lucio: Salve, Laura! Come va?

Laura: Così, così.

Cameriera: Buonasera. Prego?

Laura: Come sono quelle pizze là alla napoletana?

Tim: Sono buonissime, leggerissime.

Laura: Avete delle pizze ai funghi? Ho fame!

Cameriera: Sì. Abbiamo delle pizze ai funghi saporitissime.

Silvia: Va bene. Per noi una pizza ai funghi e basta.

Cameriera: E qualcosa da bere per voi?

Silvia: Per me nient'altro. Grazie. Non ho sete e sono a dieta. E per te, Laura?

Laura: Scusi, dopo la pizza . . . ho voglia di quel dolce alla crema. Mi dia anche un succo di pomodoro. Tim, ci sono le pizze in Inghilterra?

Tim: Sì. Ma non sono buonissime. Perchè è difficile trovare la mozzarella e l' origano.

Lucio: Eh! Ma sono più facili da digerire con della birra inglese!

Tim: Cameriere, scusi . . . dov'è un gabinetto?

8.2 VOCABULARY

Dialogue 1

me	me
quello-a; quelli-e	that; those

l'insalata (f)	salad
il prosciutto (m); al prosciutto	ham; with ham
crudo-a	raw; uncooked
avete (avere) (pl.)	you have
del	some
il panino (m)	roll; sandwich
abbiamo (avere)	we have
il formaggio (m)	cheese
nient'altro	nothing else
molto	a lot
il salame (m)	salami
il vino (m)	wine
l'appetito (m); buon-	appetite; enjoy your meal
altrettanto	the same to you

Dialogue 2

al telefono (m); per –	on the phone; by phone
il piatto (m)	plate, dish
misto-a	mixed
la macedonia (f)	fruit salad
significare; che cosa significa?	to mean; what does it mean?
cotto-a	cooked
condito-a	dressed (with oil)
l'olio (m)	oil
un inglese (m)	an Englishman;
un'inglese (f)	an Englishwoman
stravagante-e	extravagant, eccentric

Dialogue 3

la pizzeria (f)	pizza parlour
il menù (m) (pl. invar.)	menu, list
portare	to bring; to carry; to take
ghiacciato-a	iced
la pizza (f)	pizza
napoletano-a; alla napoletana	Neopolitan; Neapolitan style
originale-e	original
sopra	on; above; on top of
il sugo (m) (pl. -ghi)	sauce
la mozzarella (f)	name of a cheese
l'acciuga (f) (pl. -ghe)	anchovy
l' origano	oregano, marjoram
tenero-a	soft
te	you (familiar)
il gusto (m)	taste

Dialogue 4

salve	hi!
così	so
là	there
il fungo (m) (pl. -ghi)	mushroom
la fame (f); avere fame	hunger; to be hungry
saporito-a	tasty
noi	us
basta	that's all; enough
la sete (f) avere sete	thirst; to be thirsty
la dieta (f); essere a –	diet; to be on a –
il dolce (m)	cake
la crema (f) dolce alla –	custard; cake with custard
trovare	to find
*digerire	to digest
il gabinetto (m)	toilet

8.3 EXPLANATIONS

(a) Background information

Quick lunches are not an Italian institution as they are in the Anglo-Saxon world. The midday lunch (il pranzo) is still the most important meal of the day and the family generally gathers at home. However, the increasing number of commuters and tourists has led to the opening of plenty of snack-bars and pizzerie in the largest cities and in tourist centres.

Beers. The word birra in Italian usually means lager and is normally served cold or iced. To have an English beer you have to ask for a specific brew. Danish and German beers are more easily available than British beers.

Proverbio: Tutti i gusti sono gusti
Every man to his taste.

(b) Before starting a meal

Before a drink people say: cin . . . cin – cheers.
Before a meal, at home or in public places, it is a sign of politeness to wish people: buon appetito—enjoy your meal (lit. good appetite). The reply is: grazie, altrettanto (lit. thank you, the same to you).

(c) Saying what you want for yourself: per me (for me) – *grammar ref. 47*

After the preposition per, these are the pronouns used:

Per me, una pizza.	A pizza, for me.
E per te?	And for you, Carla? (familiar)
Signora, per lei?	And for you, madam? (formal)
Per noi, due pizze.	For us, two pizzas.
Laura e Silvia, per voi? (pl.)	Laura and Silvia, for you?
Anche per noi . . .	For us, too . . .

Referring to someone else, you say:

Per lui, una birra.	For him, a beer.
Per lei, un gelato.	For her, an ice-cream.
Per loro . . .	For them . . .

These are the personal pronouns used after all prepositions.

(d) Indicating quantities: del, dello, etc. (some, any) – *grammar ref. 28*

To say some, as you know, alcuni-e, is to be used in front of plural nouns (6.3(i)). Another word often used is del, dello (di + def. art.) which takes different endings according to the word following it:

(il vino) C'è del vino?	Is there any wine?
(lo zucchero) Ho bisogno dello zucchero	I need sugar.
(la crema) Ha della crema?	Have you any cream?
(l'acqua) Vorrei dell'acqua.	I would like some water.
(i gelati) Mi dà dei gelati?	Can I have some ice-cream cones?
(gli studenti) Ci sono degli studenti.	There are some students.
(le camere) Ci sono delle camere?	Are there some rooms?

These forms are used also in negative sentences. They are equivalent to the English forms: 'not' . . . any . . . and 'no'.

Non c'è della birra.	There is no beer.
Non ci sono dei panini.	There are no rolls.

In Italian, as in English, it's not compulsory to use del or alcuni. It is equally correct to say: Hai birra? They are almost always omitted in negative sentences: Non ho panini. (I have no sandwiches).

(e) Asking for some more: dell'altro + noun

For sing. masc. nouns, you say:

Mi dà dell'altro pane, per favore?	Can you give me some more bread, please?
Mi dà dell'altro aceto?	Can you give me some more vinegar?

For sing. fem. nouns:

Vorrei dell'altra acqua minerale.	I would like some more mineral water.
Vorrei dell'altra birra.	I would like some more beer.

For pl. nouns:

Prendo degli altri panini.	I'll take some more sandwiches.
Prendo delle altre arance.	I'll take some more oranges.

(f) Referring to people and things in the distance: quello (that) – *grammar ref. 18*

While questo (this) follows a regular pattern (questo, questa, questi, queste), quel (quello) has the same pattern as del (dello) modelled on the definite articles:

(il libro) quel libro	that book
(lo scaffale) quello scaffale	that shelf
(la bottiglia) quella bottiglia	that bottle
(l'edicola) quell'edicola	that newsagents
(i dolci) quei dolci	those cakes
(gli yogurt) quegli yogurt	those yoghurts
(le patatine) quelle patatine	those crisps

(g) Asking people if they have something: avete (you, pl.) – *grammar ref. 58*

Here are the plural forms of the verb avere. Avete is frequently used to address shopkeepers, to find out if goods are available.

Avete delle pizze?	Have you got pizzas?
Sì, abbiamo pizze ai funghi . . .	Yes, we have pizzas with mushrooms.

Referring to other shops, you say: hanno (they have)

In quella tavola calda hanno buone pizze.	In that snack bar they have good pizzas.

(h) Qualcosa da . . . (something to)
Notice the following expressions:

Qualcosa da bere?	Something to drink?
Nient'altro da bere, per me.	Nothing else to drink, for me.
Sono a dieta.	I am on a diet.

Qualcosa and nient'altro (nothing else), if followed by a verb, require da before the verb. *See also 10.3(i).*

(i) Replying to an offer: sì, grazie.
Unlike English, when offered something, in Italian you may say grazie both if you accept and if you refuse:

Caffè? Sì, grazie.	Coffee? Yes, please.
Caffè? No, grazie.	Coffee? No, thank you.

(j) Being emphatic: -issimo (very . . .) – *grammar ref. 43*
To ask what something is like, you may say:

Com'è quell'aperitivo?	What is that aperitif like?
Come sono quei funghi?	Those mushrooms, what are they like?

To reply, you may say:

Sono buoni	They are good
Sono così, così	They are so, so
Sono molto buoni	They are very good.

Or you may build up a new word. You cut out the last vowel of the adjective and add a new ending: -issimo. This forms the feminine in -a and the plural in -i and -e.

Quei funghi sono buonissimi.	Those mushrooms are very good.
Quelle pizze sono freschissime.	Those pizzas are really fresh.

Notice that adjectives ending in -co, -go add h before -issimo to preserve the hard sound of the letter c or g: bianco – bianchissimo.

(k) Asking the meaning of words
The most formal expression is:

Che cosa significa 'mozzarella'?	What does 'mozzarella' mean?
Che cosa significano 'i funghi'?	What does 'i funghi' mean?

(l) Words
Notice that **facile** (easy: ch. 6) requires **da** if followed by a verb:

Facile da digerire.	Easy to digest.
È un libro facile da leggere.	It's a book easy to read.

8.4 EXERCISES

A

Exercise 1
It's your turn to pay. Can you order in the same way as in the model?
Un panino per me. E per voi? Anche per noi. Due panini, per favore.

1. Un caffè per me. E per voi?
2. Un tè per me. E per voi?
3. Un analcolico, per me. E per voi?
4. Una birra per me. E per voi?
5. Una pizza al prosciutto per me. E per voi?

Exercise 2
At the grocer's, find out whether things are available, according to this example:
Buongiorno, avete del prosciutto?

Here is your shopping list:
insalata; formaggio; latte; burro; marmellata; salsicce; uova; aranciate.

Come back later. Ask if they have some more of the same goods:
Scusi, avete dell'altro prosciutto?

Exercise 3
You want to make sure of prices and qualities before you buy:
Commesso: Buongiorno, signorina, desidera?
— (Ask: How much is that salami?)
Commesso: Mille lire il pacchetto.
— (Say you will take two packets.)

Commesso: Poi? Del prosciutto? Del formaggio?
— (Ask: What is that cheese like?)
Commesso: È buonissimo.
— (Ask if he will give you a slice of that cheese.)
Commesso: Ecco una fetta. È buona?
— (Say it's very good.)

Exercise 4
You are in a food shop. Make the following requests, inserting the right form of dello:

Mi dà . . . marmellata. Poi prendiamo . . . miele e . . . acqua minerale. Vorrei anche . . . frutta e . . . pomodori.

Do the same in a bookshop:

Vorrei fare un regalo. Ma sono indeciso. Avete . . . libri inglesi tradotti? Posso vedere . . . vocabolari italiani? Scusi, ci sono . . . edizioni tascabili?

Do the same with a traffic warden:

Scusi, ci sono . . . pensioni qui vicino? E . . . telefoni? Sa se ci sono . . . negozi aperti?

Exercise 5
Make sure that what you're buying is really good. Use this model:
Scusi, come sono questi panini? Sono buonissimi o buoni?

arancia; acciuga; biscotto; cioccolatini; dolce; formaggio; fungo; gelato; limone; marmellata; salsiccia.

B

Exercise 6
Mr McKenzie wants to make sure he understands correctly what his colleagues are referring to. Can you supply his questions according to the following model:
(ditta) Quale? Quella ditta lì?

direttore; filiale; banca; catalogo; firma; albergo; banchiere; camera di commercio.

Exercise 7

Mr McKenzie wants to please his colleagues. Supply his remarks.

Signora Pardi: Com'è questa birra? È buona?
McKenzie: (It's very, very good.)
Rossi: Va bene questo formaggio?
McKenzie: (This cheese is all right. It's very, very soft.)
Pardi: Va tutto bene, allora?
McKenzie: (Everything is absolutely fine.)

Exercise 8

Answer the following questions in relation to dialogue no. 1.

1. Che cosa ordina la signora Pardi?
2. Il signor McKenzie prende un piatto di prosciutto cotto?
3. Che cosa prende il signor McKenzie?
4. Il signor McKenzie mangia l'insalata senza olio?
5. Che cosa prende il signor Rossi?

Exercise 9

Here are extracts from a bar conversation. Complete it, choosing the right word from the right-hand column. Pay attention to the endings.

Questa pizza non è . . . . È senza acciughe.
Questo latte è . . . . Desideriamo un bicchiere di latte . . . .
Sì, abbiamo il Martini . . . e il Martini . . .
Alcuni formaggi italiani sono . . . ma questo non è . . . .
Questa città è . . . . Ma questo albergo è molto . . . .
Mi dispiace, questi tavoli non sono . . . .

molli
rosso
buona
ghiacciato
bianco
liberi
rumoroso
splendida
molle
non ghiacciato

Exercise 10

Carry on with your diary, writing it in Italian:

At home I never eat a lot. I am on my own at midday. If I am with a colleague (f) we prepare some sandwiches, with cooked ham or with cheese. Or we eat a plate of salad with some slices of cheese and some slices of tomatoes. We then take a fruit-flavoured yoghurt or a fruit salad or some biscuits. I never eat bread, I never drink wine or beer because I am on a diet. Sometimes I drink a tomato juice or a fruit juice. If I am with a colleague (f), we listen to some records of classical music: English, Italian or German composers (autori). We then drink a coffee and after an hour, I go back with my colleague to the SIP. If I don't go home, I go to an ice-cream parlour or to a snack bar. There is a well-known snack bar near my office.

ASKING PERMISSION; EXPRESSING YOUR WISHES

9.1 DIALOGUES

Dialogue 1 Dal tabaccaio

Tim and Steve discover that tobacco products can be bought only at the tobacconist's.

Tim: (first going to a grocer's) Un pacchetto di sigarette . . .
Droghiere: Non abbiamo sigarette. Questa è una drogheria.
Tim: Scusi, dove possiamo comprare delle sigarette?
Droghiere: Solo dal tabaccaio. Eccolo là. Ce n'è uno a cento metri.

(Tim and Steve go there.)

Tabaccaio: Prego?
Tim: Vorrei un pacchetto di sigarette italiane.
Tabaccaio: Che marca? Con filtro o senza?
Tim: Con filtro e non molto forti. Non fumiamo spesso.
Tabaccaio: Allora potete provare queste. Sono le Nazionali Esportazioni. Volete il pacchetto da dieci o il pacchetto da venti?
Tim: Quanto costa quello da venti?
Tabaccaio: Un pacchetto da venti costa settecentocinquanta lire. Da dieci costa quattrocentocinquanta ma non Nazionale, Esportazione.
Tim: Ci dia un pacchetto da dieci, allora. E ci dia anche un accendino. Vuole della moneta?
Tabaccaio: No, ne ho, grazie. In tutto, sono duemila-settecentocinquanta.

Dialogue 2 All'edicola

Tim has to prepare an essay from an Italian magazine for his class.

Tim: Vorrei dei giornali italiani con delle illustrazioni.
Giornalaio: Vuoi dei rotocalchi o dei fumetti?
Tim: Scusi. Non capisco. Che cosa significa rotocalchi?
Giornalaio: Sono riviste illustrate di politica o di moda.
Tim: Posso guardare queste con illustrazioni a colori?
Giornalaio: Sì. Vuoi guardare anche quelle lì fuori?
Tim: Quanto costa questo settimanale?
Giornalaio: Millecinquecento. Questi, invece, mille.
Tim: Ha dei giornali stranieri?
Giornalaio: Sì. Che giornali vuoi? Francesi, tedeschi?
Tim: Inglesi.
Giornalaio: No. Quelli inglesi sono tutti esauriti. Forse ne hanno alla stazione o ne trovi dai giornalai in centro.
Tim: Grazie. Arrivederci.

(At school, he offers the cigarettes he bought with Steve.)

Tim: (to Julie) Julie, vuoi una sigaretta?
Julie: Grazie, non fumo.

'Dove possiamo trovare dei giornali stranieri?'

Dialogue 3 Dal tabaccaio

McKenzie has finished his English tobacco. He needs a new packet.

McKenzie: Ha del tabacco . . . buono . . . ?
Tabaccaio: Ne abbiamo per sigarette, per sigari. O ne desidera per la pipa?
McKenzie: Per la pipa. Voglio provare del tabacco italiano.
Tabaccaio: Vuole questo? Non è molto forte. C'è questo, più leggero . . . eccolo.
McKenzie: (pointing at the shelf behind) E quella scatola là?
Tabaccaio: È ancora più forte. Quello è il tabacco migliore.
McKenzie: Quanto costa?
Tabaccaio: Duemilasettecentocinquanta.
McKenzie: Benissimo. Ne prendo due scatole di questo e una scatola di quello. Mi dia anche dei sigari e dei fiammiferi.
Tabaccaio: Vuole provare i toscani? Sono tipicamente italiani.
McKenzie: Va bene. Due buste, per favore. Ha anche delle pellicole per fotografie?
Tabaccaio: Mi dispiace. Sono senza. Vuole provare dal fotografo a dieci minuti da qui?
McKenzie: Molte grazie.

Dialogue 4 Dal giornalaio

McKenzie and his English colleague are longing for *The Times*.

McKenzie: Buongiorno. Avete il '*Times*' di oggi?
Giornalaio: No, se volete c'è il '*Times*' di ieri e di alcuni giorni fa.
McKenzie: Sa dove possiamo trovare dei giornali stranieri?
Giornalaio: Ne possono avere alla stazione o all'air terminal . . .
McKenzie: Ci dia un quotidiano italiano, intanto.
Giornalaio: Il '*Giornale Nuovo*'? '*Repubblica*'? '*Il Corriere della Sera*'?
McKenzie: Che differenza c'è?
Giornalaio: Beh, il primo è liberale-democratico, il secondo è di sinistra . . .
McKenzie: Va bene. Prendiamo questi due. Quant'è in tutto?
Giornalaio: Cinquecento l'uno. Ha della moneta, per favore?
McKenzie: No, mi dispiace. Non importa. Ci dia alcuni gettoni.

They then get into a taxi and start lighting one of the cigars but a glance from the taxi driver makes McKenzie ask:

McKenzie: Scusi, posso fumare?

The taxi driver points to a notice saying: VIETATO FUMARE

9.2 VOCABULARY

Dialogue 1

un pacchetto da dieci	a packet of ten cigarettes
la sigaretta (f)	cigarette
il droghiere (m)	grocer
questo-a	this one
la drogheria (f)	grocer's shop
possiamo (potere)	we can; we may
comprare	to buy
ne; ce n'è uno	of it, of them; there is one
il metro (m)	metre
il filtro (m)	filter
forte-e	strong
potete (pl.) (potere)	you can
provare	to try
volete (pl.) (volere)	you want
costare	to cost
ci	us; to us
l'accendino (m)	lighter
vuole (volere)	he, she, it wants; you want

Dialogue 2

il giornale (m)	newspaper
l'illustrazione (f)	illustration
vuoi (volere)	you want (familiar)
il rotocalco (m) (pl. -chi)	tabloid
il fumetto (m)	comic
la rivista (f)	magazine
illustrato-a	illustrated
la politica	politics
la moda	fashion
guardare	to look at; to watch
il colore (m); a colori	colour; in colour
il settimanale (m)	weekly
invece	on the contrary, instead

Dialogue 3

il tabacco (m) (pl. -chi)	tobacco
il sigaro (m)	cigar
la pipa (f)	pipe
voglio (volere)	I want
ancora	even; still
il migliore, la migliore	the best
il fiammifero (m)	match
il toscano (m)	Tuscan cigar
tipicamente	typically
la busta (f)	envelope
la pellicola (f)	film
la fotografia (f)	photograph
il fotografo (m)	photographer
il minuto (m)	minute

Dialogue 4

ieri	yesterday
il giorno (m)	day
fa	ago
possono (potere)	they can
l'air terminal (m)	air terminal
il quotidiano (m)	daily newspaper
intanto	meanwhile; for the time being
la repubblica (f)	republic
la differenza (f)	difference
liberale-e	liberal
democratico-a (pl. -ci; -che)	democratic
di sinistra	on the left (in politics)
l'uno-a	each
vietato-a; -fumare	forbidden; no smoking

9.3 EXPLANATIONS

(a) Background information

In Italy, newsagents and stationers are usually in one shop. Newspapers and magazines are also sold at news-stands. They have the same opening hours as the other shops and are closed on Sunday afternoons, except in large stations and airport-lounges. Only very rarely are newspapers sold at street-corners.

Tobacco products are a state monopoly. They are sold only in authorized shops displaying this sign outside. [T]
Nationally manufactured cigarettes are the Nazionali, the Nazionali Esportazioni, the MS, the Macedonia. Foreign brands are referred to by their names.

Stamps and telephone tokens are officially accepted as a substitute for small change.

The word fumetto (comic strip) comes from the word fumo. It refers to the balloons (similar to clouds of smoke) in which words are inserted in comic strips.

Proverbio: Bacco, tabacco e Venere riducono l'uomo in cenere! (lit. Bacchus (wine), tobacco and Venus (love) reduce man to ashes).

(b) Asking where you may find something: potere (plural forms) *– grammar ref. 64*

In chapter 5.3(h), you have seen the verb potere used to ask and give permission; the same verb can be used to ask where you may find something:

Dove possiamo trovare sigarette inglesi?	Where can we find English cigarettes?
Dove posso comprare sigarette?	Where can I buy cigarettes?

People may suggest:

Potete provare dal tabaccaio qui vicino.	You may try at the tobacconist's nearby.
Ne (some) possono avere in questo bar.	They may have some at this bar.

(c) Talking of shops: da (at 's) *– grammar ref. 16*

To say you are in a shop or you are going to a shop or to somebody's house, you use da with names of people or names of trades. If you use the name of the premises, you use the preposition in or a.

Vado all'albergo.	I'm going to the hotel.
Sono in pasticceria.	I am in a sweet-shop.
Vado all'edicola.	I'm going to the news-kiosk.

But:

Sono da Carla.	I am at Carla's.
Vado dal droghiere.	I'm going to the grocer's.
Può provare dai tabaccai.	You may try at the tobacconists'.

Notice that da combines with the definite article forming other words (dal, dallo etc.)

(d) Another use of da

Da is also used to indicate quantities, or the value of an object:

Un pacchetto da dieci, per favore.	A packet of ten, please
Ho solo una banconota da mille.	I only have a one thousand liras note.
Vorrei un francobollo da cento.	I would like a one hundred liras stamp.

(e) Indicating distances

To ask how far a place is, as you know, you may say:

È lontano?	Is it far away?
È vicino?	Is it nearby?

To be more specific, you ask:

Quanto dista da qui piazza Garibaldi?	How far is Garibaldi Square from here?

You may be told the distance:

È a cento metri da qui.	It's one hundred metres from here.

Or the time it takes:

Sono a cinque minuti da ...	They are five minutes from ...

(f) Questo qui ... quello là (this one ... that one) – *grammar ref. 19–22*

Questo-a, quello-a are often used as pronouns, that is, with no noun after them. In this case they translate two English expressions: this one; that one; the . . . one:

Quel vino lì? Sì, quello lì.	That wine there? Yes, that one there.
Questa casa? Sì, questa casa qui.	This house? Yes, this one here.
Questo francese costa mille lire, quello inglese costa duemila lire.	This French one costs 1.000 liras, that English one costs 2.000 liras.
Quelle fuori? O queste dentro?	The ones outside or the ones inside?
Quello da venti costa cento lire.	The one with twenty (cigarettes) costs 100 liras.

Notice that quello follows a regular pattern if it is not followed by a noun (8.3(f)).

(g) Asking people to give you something: ci dia – *grammar ref. 49, 65*
In public places or in private, if you are on your own you say:

Per favore, mi dia.	Please, can you give me . . .

If you are with someone else:

Per piacere, ci dia.	Please, give us, (we shall have) . . .

These forms are used only with people you address formally. With friends, you say dammi (give me) and dacci (give us).

(h) Expressing your wishes: volere (to want) – *grammar ref. 64*
Vorrei is a polite form of request (6.3(d)) equivalent to the English 'I would like'. To be more emphatic – and perhaps too abrupt – you say voglio:

Voglio un bicchiere di latte.	I want a glass of milk.
Voglio bere un bicchiere di latte.	I want to drink a glass of milk.

But it's perfectly polite and formal to ask other people what they want by using this verb:

Vuoi una sigaretta, Carla?	Do you want a cigarette? (familiar)
Vuole un pacchetto da dieci?	Do you want a packet of ten? (formal)
	Would you like a packet . . .
Volete del tabacco italiano?	Do you want Italian tobacco? (pl.)

To enquire about other people, you say:

Sai che cosa vuole Carla?	Do you know what Carla wants?
Sai che cosa vogliono (Carla e Tim)?	Do you know what they want?

(i) Making polite suggestions

As in English, you may use the word **perchè** (why).

Perchè non prova dal tabaccaio?	Why don't you try at the tobacconist's?

But you may also use **volere** or **potere** addressing people familiarly or formally:

Può provare dal fotografo.	You may try at the photographer's. (familiar)
Vuole provare dal fotografo?	Do you want (would you like) to try at the ... (formal)

(j) Asking what something costs: quanto costa?

Quanto costa questa rivista?	How much does this magazine cost?
Quanto costano queste riviste?	How much do these magazines cost?

As you have already seen, the word order may be inverted in questions:

Questa rivista, quanto costa?	This magazine, how much does it cost?

(k) Understanding the meaning of ce n'è and ne: – *grammar ref. 28(a)*

There is no specific equivalent in English of the words ce n'è (ce ne è) and ne. It is very important that you don't mistake these words for a negative as they are never used for this. On the contrary, they are used to avoid repeating a word already mentioned, and they replace the word omitted. Asking: C'è un giornalaio qui? (Is there a newsagent here?) you may be told in reply:

Sì, c'è un giornalaio qui.	Yes, there is a newsagent here.

or:

Sì, ce n'è uno qui.	Yes, there is one (lit. of them) here.
Sì, ce ne sono due qui.	Yes, there are two here.

In a negative sentence, non is placed as usual before the verb:

No, non ce n'è qui.	No, there isn't one here.

(l) Words

(i) Ancora has several meanings. One of them is to reinforce a comparison:
È ancora più forte. It's even stronger.

(ii) Guardare
Guardo un quotidiano.
I look at a daily.
Notice that the verb guardare is not followed by *a* (at) in Italian.

(iii) Tipicamente. The ending -mente (invariable) usually corresponds to the English -ly (typically).
Facile, facilmente: easy, easily.

9.4 EXERCISES

A

Exercise 1

Laura wants to buy a packet of cigarettes for Tim. Complete the following conversation, guided by the answers:

Laura: . . .
Tabaccaio: Buongiorno, prego?
Laura: . . .
Tabaccaio: No, mi dispiace. Non ho delle sigarette inglesi.
Laura: . . .
Tabaccaio: Ecco delle sigarette italiane.
Laura: . . .
Tabaccaio: Sì. È un pacchetto con filtro.
Laura: . . .
Tabaccaio: Va bene. Un pacchetto da dieci.
Laura: . . .
Tabaccaio: Arrivederci e grazie.

Exercise 2

Lucio's mother thinks that Tim might like to read some foreign magazines. Can you reproduce her conversation, guided by the answers?

Mamma: . . .
Giornalaio: No, non ho delle riviste straniere, mi dispiace.
Mamma: . . .
Giornalaio: Sì, ho dei quotidiani stranieri.
Mamma: . . .
Giornalaio: Il *Times* costa millecinquecento lire.
Mamma: . . .
Giornalaio: Il *Guardian* costa duemila lire.
Mamma: . . .
Giornalaio: Ecco a lei questi due.
Mamma: . . .
Giornalaio: In tutto è tremilacinquecento lire.

Exercise 3

Tim wants to make sure that he does not annoy Lucio's mother. Can you check with him according to this model?
Signora, posso telefonare?

May I smoke?
May I listen to some records?
May I watch the television?
May I have some milk?
May I take your book?
May I take Lucio's newspaper?

Exercise 4
Tim asks Lucio whether he wants something from the local shops. Do the same according to this model:
Vuoi un panino? Vuoi della frutta?

some beer; some English magazines; some matches; an orange squash; a coloured tabloid; two films; a chocolate cake; a collection of short stories.

Exercise 5
Miss Pardi is anxious to please Mr McKenzie. She checks what he wants. Do the same according to this model:
Vuole prendere un taxi?

ordinare un frullato e un panino?
andare alla stazione?
aspettare qui in ufficio?
ritornare questa sera?
trovare quell'indirizzo?
provare quel numero di telefono?

B

Exercise 6
Answer the following questions according to the model:
Q. In Italia dove posso comprare le sigarette?
A. Può provare dal tabaccaio.

In Italia dove posso comprare dei libri?
Dove posso comprare dei giornali?
Dove posso comprare dei sigari?
Dove posso trovare dei dischi?
Dove posso mangiare un gelato?
Dove posso fare una telefonata interurbana?

Exercise 7
You are looking for something and ask where you can find it, according to this model:
dove possiamo trovare un taxi?

a coffee bar; an open bank; foreign newspapers; a bus stop; some new tickets; a Neapolitan-style pizza; a left wing newspaper; some strong tobacco.

Exercise 8

Play the students' roles in this conversation with the teacher during a break:

Professore: Fumi, Julie?

Julie: (Say you don't smoke.)

Professore: Fumi, Tim?

Tim: (Say you don't smoke. But you would like to try an Italian cigarette.)

Professore: (to everybody) Avete dei fiammiferi?

Yvonne: (Say you have some matches.)

Professore: Ivan, che cosa prendi? Caffè o aranciata?

Ivan: (Say you need a glass of fresh water.)

Professore: Tim, allora vai a comprare il regalo per il vice-direttore della scuola oggi?

Tim: (Say you're sorry, but you can't go today. You must look at some political magazines at the newsagent's).

Professore: Hai bisogno anche di alcuni quotidiani?

Tim: (Say yes, thank you. Ask if he can bring those dailies to school.) (Remember to use the formal form from student to teacher.)

Professore: Certo. Va bene.

Tim: (Say thank you very much.)

Exercise 9

Write another page of your diary in Italian.

In the office, smoking is not allowed. If I want to smoke I go outside. I smoke approximately ten cigarettes each day. But the cigarettes are not strong, they are very, very light. I often buy French cigarettes with filter. One packet costs about fifty pence (in Italian 'penny'). My assistant director, on the contrary, smokes a pipe. When I don't have to work a lot, I bring from home a daily paper or a fashion magazine and I look at the photographs. At home, instead, we read political books and novels of contemporary authors.

Exercise 10

Ask the hotel receptionist according to this model:

per favore, ci dia alcuni gettoni.

the address of the Tourist Office;
the telephone number of a taxi rank;
the bus number to go to Rome road;
the name of a snack bar where we can eat well;
today's newspaper.

ORGANISING THE WEEKEND; TELLING THE TIME

10.1 DIALOGUES

Dialogue 1

Miss Dani and Mrs Pardi talk about the plans that Mr McKenzie and a colleague are making for the week-end.

Dani: (talking about McKenzie and friend) Che cosa guardano?
Pardi: Vogliono fare una gita questo fine settimana.
Dani: Dove vanno? In montagna? Al mare? O preferiscono i laghi?
Pardi: Cercano un posto dove possono pescare il salmone.
Dani: È un po' difficile. In Italia non ci sono salmoni. Possono pescare le trote salmonate sul Lago di Garda!
Pardi: Hanno degli opuscoli?
Dani: Sì. Hanno degli opuscoli della Valtellina, delle Dolomiti ...
Pardi: Prendono un pullman o guidano loro?
Dani: Ma non so. Ci sono pullman che partono alla mattina e alla sera da Piazza Castello per la montagna, per i laghi ...

(McKenzie and his friend enter the room)

McKenzie: Signora, a che ora chiude l'autonoleggio qui vicino?
Pardi: Tutti gli autonoleggi chiudono alla una. Aprono alle tre. Ma l'autonoleggio alla stazione e all'air terminal è sempre aperto.
Dani: Dove andate, allora?
McKenzie: Andiamo sul Lago di Garda!

Dialogue 2 All'autonoleggio

McKenzie and his colleagues don't waste time. The receptionist at the car-hire firm addresses both of them.

McKenzie: Buongiorno. Vorremmo noleggiare un'automobile per questo fine settimana . . . Quanto costa?
Impiegata: Se noleggiate un'automobile di grossa cilindrata . . .
McKenzie: Scusi? Non capiamo . . . Può ripetere, per favore?
Impiegata: Se noleggiate un'automobile grande . . .
McKenzie: Ah! Sono inclusi i chilometri in questa tariffa?
Impiegata: Sì. Sono inclusi. Ma non è inclusa la benzina.
McKenzie: Quant'è in tutto, con l'assicurazione?
Impiegata: . . . Prenotate adesso?
McKenzie: Sì, va bene. Prenotiamo adesso.
Impiegata: A che ora partite venerdì?
McKenzie: No, partiamo sabato mattina tra le nove e le dieci.
Impiegata: Come pagate? In contanti? Con un assegno?
McKenzie: Con la carta di credito. Va bene? Eccola.
Impiegata: Va bene. Ecco tutto. Allora, sabato mattina.
McKenzie: Grazie e buongiorno.

'Volete visitare una città?'

Dialogue 3 All'agenzia di viaggi

Tim and Steve organise their week-end. The receptionist at the travel agency addresses them both.

Tim: Buonasera. Vorremmo alcune informazioni. Vorremmo andare da qualche parte questo fine settimana. Ci dia un consiglio.
Impiegata: Volete visitare una città o preferite andare al mare o in montagna?
Tim: No. Cerchiamo qualcosa di diverso, di nuovo. Di allegro.
Impiegata: Perchè non andate al Festival di musica folk?
Tim: Quand' è? Ha degli opuscoli?
Impiegata: È questo sabato. Oppure andate al Carnevale di Venezia. Le feste durano tutta la settimana. Finiscono domenica.
Tim: Fantastico! Sì, andiamo a Venezia sul Canal Grande.
Impiegata: I pullman partono alla mattina presto, alle sette e venti da piazza Castello.
Tim: Quanto costa andata e ritorno?
Impiegata: Diecimila lire.
Tim: C'è una riduzione per gli studenti?
Impiegata: No, ma non è caro, dai! Buon divertimento!

Dialogue 4 Alla stazione dei pullman

Saturday morning at the coach station, Tim and Steve are ready to leave.

Tim: Scusi, da dove partono i pullman per Venezia?
Autista: Partono dal marciapiede qui di fronte.
Tim: Vorremmo fare due biglietti andata e ritorno. Ventimila, vero?
Autista: No! Oggi è gratis!
Tim: Scusi, non capisco. Che cosa vuol dire?
Autista: Oggi non pagate il biglietto perchè è Carnevale.
Tim: Ah! Benone! A che ora parte il primo pullman?
Autista: Il prossimo è alle sette e venti e arriva a Venezia alle dieci meno dieci, circa, alle dieci meno cinque . . .

(On the coach)

Bigliettaio: Biglietto, prego!
Tim: Non ce l'ho. Oggi non è gratis perchè è Carnevale?
(Roars of laughter: grandi risate)
A passenger whispers to Tim: A Carnevale ogni scherzo vale! (No joke is forbidden if it's Carnival!)

10.2 VOCABULARY

Dialogue 1

la gita (f); fare una – trip; to take a trip

il fine (m) settimana	week-end
la settimana (f)	week
vanno (andare)	they go
la montagna (f); in –	mountain; in the mountains
il mare (m); al –	sea; at the seaside
il lago (m) (pl. -ghi)	lake
cercare	to look for
pescare	to fish
il salmone (m)	salmon
difficile	difficult
la trota (f)	trout
salmonato-a	salmon-flavoured
l'opuscolo (m)	leaflet; brochure
guidare	to drive
che	that, which, who
la mattina (f); alla –	morning; in the morning
la sera (f); alla –	evening; in the evening
a che ora?	at what time?
l'autonoleggio (m)	car-hire
aperto-a	open

Dialogue 2

vorremmo (volere)	we would like
noleggiare	to hire
l'automobile, l'auto (f)	car
grosso-a	large
la cilindrata (f)	capacity (of an engine)
ripetere	to repeat
il chilometro (m)	kilometre
la tariffa (f)	tariff
la benzina (f)	petrol
l'assicurazione (f)	insurance
prenotare	to book
adesso	now
tra	among; between
pagare	to pay
in contanti	cash
la carta (f) di credito (m)	credit card

Dialogue 3

l'informazione (f)	information
da qualche parte	somewhere
visitare	to visit
diverso-a	different
allegro-a	cheerful

la festa (f)	celebration
durare	to last
*finire	to finish
fantastico-a (pl. -ci; -che)	fantastic
presto	early; quick
l'andata (f)	one way
il ritorno (m); andata e ritorno	return; return (ticket)
la riduzione (f)	reduction
il divertimento (m) buon –	entertainment; enjoy yourself

Dialogue 4

l'autista (m)	driver
il marciapiede (m)	platform
fare il biglietto	to buy a ticket
vero?	is that right?
gratis	free (no cost)
voler dire	to mean
benone	very well
arrivare	to arrive
il bigliettaio (m)	the bus conductor
la risata (f)	laughter
fare uno scherzo	to make a joke

10.3 EXPLANATIONS

(a) Background information

Throughout the year major cities, as well as small places, compete with each other to organize musical, theatrical and artistic performances. To find out about them and to find out about the art treasures of the places you are visiting, go to the local Tourist Offices and ask for suggestions. Watch the advertising notices on walls where events in the province are advertised, and be adventurous! Buy the local newspapers and read the titles of the Pagina degli Spettacoli. A good network of local and long distance coaches will help you.

(b) Asking where people are going: andare (plural) – *grammar ref. 64*

If you ask people (more than one person) where they're going, you say:

Carla e Franco, dove andate adesso?	. . . where are you going now?

Carla e Franco, dove andate oggi?	. . . where are you going today?
Carla e Franco, dove andate lunedì?	. . . where will you go on Monday?

Inquiring about other people, you say:

Dove vanno i signori Franchi?	Where are the Franchis going? Where do the Franchis go?

(c) Indicating the places where you go
Italy is an extremely varied country and people frequently refer to their destinations in these ways:

Andiamo in montagna.	We are going to the mountains.
Andiamo al mare.	We are going to the coast.
Andiamo sul lago.	We are going on the lake.
Andiamo in collina.	We are going to the hills.

(d) Su (on) – *grammar ref. 16*
Su when followed by a definite article, combines with it to form a new word:

Oggi andiamo sul Canal Grande.	Today we are going on the Grand Canal.
Andate sui laghi venerdì?	Are you going on the lakes, Friday?

Su may be used also when referring to means of transport:

C'è posto sulla bicicletta?	Is there a seat on the bike?
C'è posto sull'auto?	Is there a seat in the car?

And to newspapers:

Cerco informazioni sui giornali e sulle riviste di questa città.	I look for information in the newspapers and magazines of this town.

(e) Asking two or more people what they do: voi . . . (you, pl.) – *grammar ref. 48, 58*
Remember that to address more than one person, there is only one

form (familiar and formal), the 2nd person plural: voi. You remove the usual endings of the infinitives and add the following endings:

Quando ritorn + ate (1st conj.)	When are you coming back?
Quando scend + ete? (2nd conj.)	When are you getting off?
Quando part + ite? (3rd conj.)	When are you leaving?
Che cosa *prefer + ite? (3rd conj.)	What do you prefer?

(f) To inquire about the actions of more than one person: loro (they) – *grammar ref. 58*

As above, you remove the endings of the infinitives and add the following ones. (Pay attention to the accented vowel!)

Che cosa gu**a**rd + ano? (1st conj.)	What are they looking at?
Che cosa l**e**gg + ono? (2nd conj.)	What are they reading?
Che cosa **o**ffr + ono? (3rd conj.)	What do they offer?

Preferire, capire, finire and verbs of the same type have a different ending, + iscono:

Quando finiscono?	When do they finish?

Remember that other verbs taking this ending, are listed in the vocabulary lists with an * – *grammar ref. 59*

As usual the subject pronouns voi (you), loro (they) are nearly always omitted. They are sometimes placed after the verb to emphasize who is doing the action:

Guidate voi o guidano loro?	Do you drive or do they drive?

(g) Departures and arrivals of means of transport

Quando parte questo pullman?	When does this coach leave?
Da dove partono questi pullman?	From where do these coaches leave?
Dove arriva il pullman da Venezia?	Where does the coach from Venice arrive?

(h) Asking how long events last

Quanto dura questa festa?	How long does this celebration last?
Quanto durano questi viaggi?	How long do these journeys last?
Quando finisce questa classe?	When does this lesson end?

The answers may be:

Tutto il giorno	The whole day
Per tutta la settimana	For the whole week

(i) Qualcosa di bello (something nice)

When you describe something by adding an adjective to it, the word di must be inserted between qualcosa and the adj.:

Qualcosa di allegro, voglio!	I want something cheerful

And the adjective must always be masculine and singular.

(j) The time

A che ora? At what time?

Tra le due e le tre	Between two and three

The plural feminine article le is placed before the number because the word 'hours' is implied (lit. the two hours). Therefore to say 'at two o'clock', you say: alle due, alle tre etc, and 'at one o'clock': alla una

Up to half past, minutes are added to the hour with e:

Sono le due e cinque.	It's five past two. (lit. two and five)

After half past, minutes are deducted from the following hour, with the word meno (less):

Sono le tre meno dieci.	It's ten to three. (lit. three less ten)

Official timetables are based on the 24 hour clock:

Sono le 14.35 (quattordici e trentacinque).

Che ora è? Che ore sono?	What time is it?
È la una.	It's one o'clock.
È la una e mezzo.	It's half past one.
Sono le due.	It's two o'clock.
Sono le due meno un quarto.	It's a quarter to two.

(k) What day of the week?
To indicate a specific day, you simply say the name of the day: lunedì (on Monday). To indicate each Monday, for instance, you say tutti i lunedì or ogni lunedì (on Mondays). *See also 2.3(e).*

(l) Words

(i) il fine settimana is a shortened form for il fine *della* settimana.

(ii) tra and fra are synonyms and interchangeable.

(iii) cercare (to look for) is not followed by per (for) as in English.

10.4 EXERCISE

A

Exercise 1
Insert the questions in this dialogue at a coach station.

Tim: . . .
Impiegato: Questo pullman va a Venezia.
Tim: . . .
Impiegato: Parte alle sette.
Tim: . . .
Impiegato: Arriva alle otto.
Tim: . . .
Impiegato: Ritorna a mezzanotte.
Tim: . . .
Impiegato: Il prossimo è alle nove.
Tim: . . .
Impiegato: Sono le tre.

Exercise 2
Tim and Steve go to a travel agency. Supply their questions.

Tim and Steve: (Say you would like some information.)
Impiegato: Dove volete andare?
Tim and Steve: (Say to the mountains or the seaside.)

Impiegato: Volete visitare una città o dei paesi?
Tim and Steve: (Ask for some leaflets.)
Impiegato: Ecco gli opuscoli.
Tim and Steve: (Ask where is la Valtellina.)

Exercise 3

Mr McKenzie goes to a car-hire firm with his English colleague. Fill in the missing words to form meaningful questions:

McKenzie: Vorremmo . . . un'auto, per favore.
Impiegato: Ecco gli opuscoli.
McKenzie: In queste tariffe è . . . la benzina?
Impiegato: No, non è compresa la benzina.
McKenzie: È compresa l' . . . ? E sono compresi . . . ?
Impiegato: Sì, è tutto compreso.

Exercise 4

Julie would like to join Tim and Steve at the Carnival of Venice. Can you supply her questions?

Julie: (Say you would like to book a seat on the Milan-Venice coach.)
Impiegato: Per quando?
Julie: (For next Monday.)
Impiegato: Solo andata?
Julie: (No, return for Wednesday morning.)

Exercise 5

Say you prefer to do things half an hour later than the time suggested, as in the example:

Desiderate partire alle sei? No. Preferiamo partire alle sei e mezzo.

1. Desiderate prendere la colazione a mezzogiorno?
2. Desiderate noleggiare l'automobile alle tre e mezzo?
3. Desiderate riportare l'automobile alle quattro e mezzo?
4. Desiderate visitare il castello alle undici meno venti?
5. Desiderate arrivare alle otto meno dieci?

B

Exercise 6

You tend to encourage people to postpone things one hour. Address them familiarly or formally according to the word in brackets as in the example.

(A friend): Parto alle sei. (You) Preferisci partire alle sei o vuoi partire alle sette?

(a colleague) Vado all'agenzia alle cinque e mezzo.
(the teacher) Comincio alla una.
(Miss Dani) Prendo l'autobus alle sette e mezzo.
(mother) Preparo uno spuntino alle quattro.
(waiter) Finisco il lavoro alle due meno un quarto.
(a clerk) Apro l'ufficio alle tre e venticinque.

Exercise 7

You and your friend have changed your plans and say you will go one day later:
Andate a Venezia lunedì? No, andiamo a Venezia martedì.

1. Partite domenica per il Carnevale di Venezia?
2. Finite il lavoro sabato?
3. Ritornate martedì mattina presto?
4. Volete visitare il Castello Sforzesco giovedì sera?
5. Desiderate arrivare mercoledì alle undici?

Exercise 8

Choose the right sentence according to the situation indicated in brackets:
Example: (you're on a diet) Avete voglia di qualcosa di leggero, di nuovo o di caldo?
Abbiamo voglia di qualcosa di leggero.
(you're hot) Avete voglia di qualcosa di fresco o di bianco?
(you're cold) Avete bisogno di qualcosa di buono o di caldo?
(you like strong drinks) Avete voglia di qualcosa di allegro o di liscio?
(you're a spendthrift) Avete bisogno di qualcosa di rosso o di caro?

Exercise 9

Translate into Italian one page of your diary: plans for the week-end. On Saturday Robert and Carla are going somewhere for the week-end; I don't know where. There is a festival of contemporary music at Brighton. I would like to go with some friends (m and f) who have a fast car. But petrol is expensive. If I go by coach the return ticket costs only £5. But I have to leave early in the morning, at half past six. The coaches leave for the seaside between seven and eight. And I have to stay the whole day at Brighton. The first coach leaves in the evening at twenty to nine and does not arrive here until midnight when there are no buses to go back home and so I'll have to take a taxi. I need a friend. If he/she can pay (for) the journey, I can bring some sandwiches with . . . salmon!

Exercise 10
Here is a report on what happened when Tim went back to Lucio's home, to be translated:

Lucio's mother and sister ask Tim where he is going on Saturday. They want to know how long the journey is going to last and when the Carnival of Venice ends. They ask where the coaches leave from and they want to see the brochures of the Carnival.

REVISION AND SELF-ASSESSMENT TEST FOR CHAPTERS 6-10

A competition against the clock. See the rules at the end of the exercises.

A

Exercise 1

1. In a sweet shop: say you would like to buy a box of chocolates.
2. In a book shop: say you would like to see an Italian dictionary.
3. In a record shop: say you would like to listen to some records of light music.
4. In an ice-cream parlour: say you would like another ice-cream and only one orange squash. (Use vorrei . . . or mi dia . . .).

Exercise 2

It's your turn to offer a drink. You are a mixed group and need to use the formal and the informal form:
Ask Mrs Pardi what she takes.
Then ask your friend (and you?)
Now ask your director (and you?)
Call the waiter and order for everybody . . .
Insist on paying (No, it's on me this time)
They insist and you say that they will pay next time . . . cheers!

Exercise 3

The waiter asks what he can bring for you. Say: for me . . .
You order for yourself and your wife. Say: for us . . .
Ask for some cheese. Ask for the soft one, not the white one.
Tell the waiter that the cheese is very light and everything is very, very good.
When he tells you Buon appetito, you reply . . .

Exercise 4

Match the sentences on the left with the sentences on the right to form meaningful questions: e.g. Non capisco. Può ripetere?

1. Non capisco.	(a) Può verificare?
2. Ho bisogno di un'altra camera.	(b) Può portare un panino al formaggio?
3. Ho voglia di un altro panino.	(c) Può ripetere?
4. Non ho moneta.	(d) Può ordinare un taxi?
5. Il treno parte alle sette.	(e) Può cambiare mille lire?
6. Ecco la firma.	(f) Può cercare due camere?

Exercise 5

Mr McKenzie is rather horrified at Miss Dani's questions. He replies to all of them as in the example:

Dani: In Inghilterra bevete vino a colazione?
McKenzie: No, non beviamo mai vino a colazione!

1. In Inghilterra mangiate prosciutto con lo zucchero?
2. In Inghilterra prendete l'insalata condita?
3. In Inghilterra bevete aperitivi amari?
4. In Inghilterra ordinate le pizze fredde?
5. In Inghilterra bevete birra ghiacciata?

Exercise 6

If you know what a word means, say: sì, capisco.
If you don't, say: Scusi, non capisco. Può ripetere?

l'accendino; il pane; nient'altro; intanto; alla spina; la copertina; il complesso; fatto; il frigorifero; migliore; breve; ieri; la gelateria.

Exercise 7

Tim and Lucio ask Steve whether he wants something. Then they order. Do the same according to the model:
Un panino, per te? Dei panini anche per noi e per loro, allora.

1. Un bicchiere di vino, per te?
2. Un uovo sodo, per te?
3. Una fetta di pane tostato, per te?
4. Una trota piccola, per te?
5. Un settimanale italiano, per te?

Exercise 8

To Lucio's mother reply as in the example:
Prendete il tè o cominciate con il caffè? – Io prendo il tè, loro cominciano con il caffè.

1. Cambiate gli assegni o pagate con le sterline?
2. Telefonate alla libreria o andate in discoteca?
3. Lavorate o studiate?
4. Ritornate a mezzogiorno o mangiate alla tavola calda?
5. Incontrate il professore o parlate con il dottor Segni?

Exercise 9

Are you ready to ask all these questions in Italian, if necessary?

1. Is that bus going to Venice road?
2. Is the insurance included in that price?
3. Is the petrol included in those tariffs?
4. Do those rooms have bathrooms?
5. Is that girl your Italian friend?
6. Is that red car yours?
7. Does that trip on Lake Como cost a lot?

Every exercise done correctly in 20 minutes is worth 10 points.
In 30 minutes, it is worth 5 points.
Above 70 points, is an excellent result. Bravissimo!
Between 35 and 70, is good. Bravo!
Under 35: va così, così.

TALKING ABOUT ITALY AND ENGLAND; TALKING ABOUT YOUR FAMILY

11.1 DIALOGUES

Dialogue 1 Quattro chiacchiere

Tim and Steve have joined the celebrations in Venice. A Harlequin talks to them.

Arlecchino: Di dove siete? Siete qui per il Carnevale?
Tim: Siamo inglesi. Sì, siamo qui per il Carnevale.
Arlecchino: Vi piace? O è troppo rumoroso?
Tim: No, è divertentissimo. Ci piace molto.
Arlecchino: Da quanto tempo siete in Italia?
Tim: Siamo a Milano dal 2 febbraio.
Arlecchino: (to Steve) E tu, come trovi l'Italia? Ti piace?
Tim: Mi piace moltissimo. È un paese divertente. È sempre Carnevale! Gli italiani sono fantastici.
Arlecchino: Che cosa vi piace di più?
Tim: Ci piace la vostra cucina . . . ci piacciono le italiane . . .
Arlecchino: È più cara l'Italia o l'Inghilterra?
Tim: L'Italia è cara come l'Inghilterra.
Steve: Il sole e il cielo azzurro sono più a buon prezzo . . . e il vostro vino è meno caro.
Arlecchino: Qui a Venezia è a buon prezzo l'acqua!

Dialogue 2

Other masqueraders join in: Punchinello and Colombina.

Tim: E voi? Siete tutti di Venezia?
Pulcinella: Siamo dei dintorni . . . di Padova . . . di Vicenza . . . Ma insegnamo tutti qui a Venezia.
Tim: Vivete tutti in camere in affitto?

Arlecchino: No, di giorno siamo qui a Venezia e di sera ritorniamo al nostro paese.

Tim: (incredulous) Ma vivete ancora con la vostra famiglia?

Colombina: Sì, la maggior parte dei giovani vive con i genitori.

Pulcinella: Voi no? In Inghilterra no?

Tim: No. Mio papà e mia mamma vivono a Cambridge. Anche mia sorella e mio fratello vivono a Cambridge, ma da soli.

Colombina: (really surprised) Ma sono sposati?

Tim: No. Uno è sposato, ma mia sorella no. Non importa.

Colombina: E tu sei fidanzato?

Tim: Eh! Dai! Ho diciotto anni il 22 di questo mese.

Colombina: Auguri!

Dialogue 3 Sul rapido

On an Inter-City train Mr McKenzie is going to Verona with

'Siete qui per il Carnevale?'

Mrs Pardi and his English colleague. They talk about their families.

Pardi: Che giorno arriva sua moglie?
McKenzie: Tra tre giorni, l'otto di questo mese.
Pardi: Sua figlia è sempre fidanzata con quel giovane medico indiano?
McKenzie: No! Sono sposati. Aspettano un bambino a luglio.
Pardi: Auguri! Sua moglie e suo figlio vivono ancora in campagna, vero?
McKenzie: Abbiamo un appartamento in affitto a Londra. Nostro figlio adesso insegna storia dell'arte e abita lì.
Pardi: Ma vi piace di più la campagna di Londra, vero?
McKenzie: Sì, ci piace molto la nostra campagna. È tranquilla.
Pardi: Per me e mio marito è troppo tranquilla.
McKenzie: I paesaggi italiani non sono mai tranquilli. Sono sempre drammatici . . .
Pardi: Ah, sì. Sono belli. Ma i negozi mi piacciono di più.

Dialogue 4

A passenger offers his seat near the window.

Passeggero: (to McKenzie) Le piace guardare il paesaggio? Prego. Si accomodi. Da quanto tempo siete in Italia?
McKenzie: Siamo qui da poco. Ma per me non è la prima volta.
Passeggero: (noticing his brief-case) Le piace lavorare con gli italiani?
McKenzie: Sì. Per gli inglesi è eccitante come un giallo di James Bond.
Passeggero: L'Inghilterra è meno frenetica. È più ricca di verde. È la prima volta che visitate Verona? È ricca di opere d'arte.
McKenzie: Sì. Per noi è la prima volta. Lei è di Verona?
Passeggero: Ah! Sono un veronese purosangue. Vi piace l'opera lirica?
Pardi: Sì, molto a tutti.
Passeggero: Posso invitare tutti all'Arena questa sera? C'è *Aida*.
Pardi: Grazie. Molto gentile. (They introduce one another).
Passeggero: Ecco il mio numero di telefono.
McKenzie: (softly sings) Del mio pensier tu sei regina, tu di mia vita sei lo splendor . . . [1]

[1]From *Aida*: You are the queen of my thought and the splendour of my life.

11.2 VOCABULARY

Dialogue 1

la chiacchiera (f); far quattro chiacchiere	the chat; to have a chat (lit. to make four chats)
siete (pl.) (essere)	you are
siamo (essere)	we are
vi (pl.)	to you
piacere (irreg.)	to like
troppo	too
divertente-e	amusing
ci	to us; us
da	since
febbraio (m)	February
ti	to you; you (familiar)
mi	to me; me
di più; piacere –	more; to like best
vostro-a (pl.)	your; yours
la cucina (f)	food; way of cooking
piacciono (piacere)	(to like)
il sole (m)	sun
il cielo (m)	sky
azzurro-a	light blue
a buon prezzo	cheap; at a good price
meno	less

Dialogue 2

i dintorni (m pl.)	the region around
Padova (f)	Padua
insegnare	to teach
vivere	to live
l'affitto (m); in-	rent; rented
nostro-a	our; ours
il genitore (m)	parent
la maggior parte di (f)	most of
giovane-e; i giovani	young; young people
il papà (m) (pl. invar.)	father; daddy
la sorella (f)	sister
il fratello (m)	brother
da solo-a	on one's own
sposato-a	married
fidanzato-a	engaged

l'anno (m); quanti anni hai?	year; how old are you? (lit. how many years have you?)
auguri	best wishes

Dialogue 3

la moglie (f) (pl. mogli)	wife
il medico (m) (pl. -ci)	medical doctor
indiano-a	Indian (from India)
il bambino (m) la bambina (f)	child; baby
luglio (m)	July
l'appartamento (m)	flat; apartment
la storia dell'arte (f)	history of art
tranquillo-a	quiet; peaceful
poco	not a lot
il marito (m)	husband
il paesaggio (m)	landscape
drammatico-a (pl. -ci; -che)	dramatic

Dialogue 4

il passeggero (m)	passenger
le	to you (formal)
eccitante-e	exciting
giallo-a; il giallo (m)	yellow; thriller
frenetico-a (pl. -ci; -che)	frenetic
ricco-a (pl. -chi)	rich
verde-e	green
l'opera d'arte (f)	work of art
veronese-e	from Verona
purosangue	born and bred; (lit. thoroughbred)
l'opera lirica (f)	opera
invitare	to invite
gentile-e; molto-	kind; it's very nice of you

11.3 EXPLANATIONS

(a) Expressing possession of things and people: il nostro (our, ours); il vostro (your, yours) – *grammar ref. 32*

The possessive pronouns and adjectives (4.3(1)) are used in Italian, as in English, to indicate figurative possessions of something or someone:

Mi piace la nostra campagna.	I like our countryside.

Mi piace il nostro paesaggio	I like our landscape
Il vostro vino è buono	Your wine is good
La vostra lingua è bella.	Your language is beautiful.

(b) Essere (to be): plural forms – *grammar ref. 58*
Imagine you are on a train. To find out if you are at the right station, you ask:

Scusi, (noi) siamo a Venezia?	Excuse me, are we in Venice?

Imagine you want to find out the nationality of a group of other passengers. You say:

(Voi) siete tedeschi?	Are you German?

(c) Stating for how long you have been in a place: present tense – *grammar ref. 61*
To ask 'since when?', 'for how long?' you say: da quanto tempo? (lit. since how much time?)

To say you have been in a place for a given time and are still there, you use the present tense with da:

Siamo a Firenze da un giorno.	We have been in Florence one day.

The time you give may be specific or fairly general:

Da quanto tempo siete qui?	How long have you been here?
Da molto tempo.	A long time.
Da poco tempo.	A short time.

You also use the present to indicate duration of any state or action that is still continuing.

Studiamo da tre giorni.	We have been studying for three days (and we are still studying).

(d) Dates
Unlike English, you indicate the date simply by putting the suitable masc. article (il, l') in front of the date, using the cardinal number:

Arrivo il 10 marzo.	I arrive on (the) 10th March.
Parto l'8 aprile.	I leave on (the) 8th April.

If a preposition precedes the date, the article and the preposition are joined together, as usual:

Siamo qui dal tre aprile.	We have been here since 3rd April.

To ask for today's date, you say:

Che giorno è?	What day is it?

(e) Giving your age

To ask people's age, you say: quanti anni ha? (formal) or quanti anni hai? (informal), (lit.: how many years do you have?) To tell your age you say: ho trentacinque anni (I have . . . years).

(f) A country and its people – *grammar ref. 14*

Names of nations frequently take the definite article:

L'Inghilterra mi piace.	I like England.

The name of a people is formed by putting the definite article in front of its equivalent adjective of nationality: – *grammar ref. 45.*

Gli italiani sono rumorosi.	The Italians are noisy.
La moda italiana piace alle inglesi.	(Italian fashion appeals to English women.) English women like Italian fashion.

(g) Using the verb to like: piacere – *grammar ref. 49*

To say you like something you transform the English sentence in the following way: (something) appeals to me.

L'Italia mi piace.	I like Italy. (Italy appeals to me)
L'Italia ci piace.	We like Italy. (Italy appeals to us)

Similarly, to say you like more than one thing, you use the plural verb, as follows:

Questi due ragazzi mi piacciono.	I like these two boys. (these two boys appeal to me.)
Queste tre ragazze ci piacciono.	We like these three girls. (these three girls appeal to us.)

(h) Asking people if they like something
You may use the familiar form:

Il Carnevale ti piace?	Do you like the Carnival? (the Carnival appeals to you?)

You may use the formal form:

Questa città le piace?	Do you like this town? (this town appeals to you?)

If you ask a group of people, you say:

Che cosa vi piace?	What do you like? (what appeals to you?)

(i) Talking about somebody else's likes:
If you refer to other people, you say:

I funghi piacciono a mio marito.	My husband likes mushrooms (mushrooms appeal to my husband)

The word order is flexible. You may say: A mio marito piacciono i funghi.

A Carla? Sì, i funghi le piacciono.	Carla? Yes, she likes mushrooms.
A Tim? No, i funghi non gli piacciono.	Tim? No, he doesn't like mushrooms.

(j) Saying how much you like something
The question may be:

Che cosa ti piace di più?	What do you like best?

Your answers may vary:

Venezia mi piace moltissimo; molto; poco	. . . very much; a lot; a little.

(k) Saying you like doing something: piacere + a verb
You place the verb in the infinitive after the expression mi piace, ti piace etc. which, in this case, is always singular:

Mi piace lavorare in Italia.	I like working in Italy.

(l) Making comparisons: come, meno (as, less) – *grammar ref. 46*
To say two things are alike, you use come:

L'Italia è cara come l'Inghilterra.	Italy is as dear as England.

To say one is inferior to the other, you use meno:

La campagna italiana è meno verde.	The Italian countryside is less green.

To complete the comparison, the word than is expressed with di combining with the definite article: del, della etc.

La campagna è meno divertente della città, per noi.	The countryside is less entertaining than the town, for us.

(m) Referring to members of your family: mio papà – *grammar ref. 34*
When you refer to only one member of your family, you should omit the definite article in front of the possessive adjective:

Mio figlio vive a Londra.	My son lives in London.

(n) Talking of your status
The following expressions are m and f, sing. and pl., according to the people they refer to:

Sono sposato. (m) Sono sposata. (f)	I am married.
Sono fidanzato. Sono fidanzata.	I'm engaged.
Sono nato-a a Londra nel 1950.	I was born in London in 1950.

The article *must* be put in front of the year in dates.

(p) Words
Papà: (father, dad) can be used only when calling your father directly, irrespective of his age. When you talk about him, you use mio padre or mio papà. I figli (pl.) is used to indicate sons *and* daughters.

11.4 EXERCISES

A

Exercise 1
Can you fill in the missing words?
— Tu e Carla, . . . siete qui?
— . . . qui da tre giorni.
— . . . partite?
— Partiamo . . . 29 marzo. Oggi che . . . è?
— É . . . 15 marzo.

Exercise 2
Mr McKenzie and Mr Rossi are talking about the town and the countryside. Can you complete their sentences with the correct forms of piacere?
McKenzie: . . . abitare in campagna?
Rossi: No, . . . abitare in città.
McKenzie: Perchè?
Rossi: Perchè i negozi . . . a mia moglie, le automobili . . . a mio figlio.
McKenzie: Io preferisco la campagna. Ma anche la montagna . . . e anche i laghi . . .

Exercise 3
Tim and another student talk about their school and their families. Can you play the girl's role?

Tim: Ti piace la scuola?
Studentessa: (Say you like the school a lot and you like the teachers.)
Tim: Abiti con una famiglia o in pensione?
Studentessa: (Say your father works in Milan.)
Tim: Allora sei qui con tuo papà e tua mamma?
Studentessa: (Say you live with your father and your sister. Your brother teaches at the university of Paris.)
Tim: Da quanto tempo studi italiano?
Studentessa: (Say you have been studying Italian for six months.)

Tim: Trovi l'Italia cara?
Studentessa: (Say you find Italy not too expensive.)

Exercise 4
You're involved in a discussion about two countries. Make the comparisons suggested by the graphic signs as in the example:
L'Inghilterra? È + (freddo): L'Inghilterra è più fredda.

1. La cucina italiana? È + (saporito).
2. Questo sole? È + (caldo).
3. Questo mare? È – (freddo).
4. Gli italiani? Sono–(tranquillo).
5. I prezzi? Sono = (i prezzi inglesi).
6. Le città inglesi? Sono – (frenetico).
7. Questo cielo? È + (azzurro).

Exercise 5
A special prize if you guess what this means:
GLI AZZURRI SONO I MIGLIORI!!!

Exercise 6
This is a revision of chapter 1. You have arrived on a camping site in the evening. You look for Mr Rossi, the director.
— (Say good evening.)
— Buonasera.
— (Say who you are.)
— Ben arrivato – a.
— (Ask if he is Mr Rossi.)
— Sì, sono il signor Rossi. Le presento la signora Franchi.
— (Say how do you do.)
— Piacere. Tutto bene in viaggio?
— (Say, yes, thank you. I'll see you tomorrow.)

B

Exercise 7
Tim has to write an essay for his school. Can you write it in Italian?
My mother. My mother is English. She was born in a little village in the countryside. She still likes the countryside because it's green and quiet. But now she works in a large noisy town. She has been working there for three months. Her day (giornata, f) starts at seven in the morning when she prepares breakfast for the whole family. Her breakfast is light. She only drinks a fruit juice and eats a slice of

bread. She finishes with a cup of tea without sugar. She likes her work. She works in a bookshop in the city centre. She likes everything there: the books, her colleagues. But she also likes her husband and her family. She prefers my brother because he is very entertaining and cheerful.

Exercise 8

McKenzie tells Miss Dani about their trip to Verona. Say what he told her:

Dani: Come si chiama?

McKenzie: He is called Sergio Frattini.

Dani: È giovane?

McKenzie: He isn't very young. He is fifty years old. His mother and his father too are from Verona.

Dani: E sua moglie?

McKenzie: She is younger. But she is less entertaining.

Dani: E Verona? Le piace?

McKenzie: Verona is beautiful. It's a fantastic town. It's less frenetic than Milan.

Dani: Le piace l'Arena?

McKenzie: Yes, certainly, but it has other beautiful works of art. My favourite church is San Zeno!

Exercise 9

These are the answers. Can you provide the questions?

1. Sì, la banca è ancora chiusa.
2. Purtroppo aspetto da mezz'ora.
3. Sì, sono straniera/o.
4. Sono in Italia da dieci mesi.
5. Sì, sono sposata/o con un italiano/a.
6. Sono le dieci meno venti.
7. Prego.
8. Ho tre figli.

SHOPPING; DESCRIBING GOODS; BARGAINING

12.1 DIALOGUES

Dialogue 1 **In un negozio di artigianato**

In an arts and crafts shop. Mckenzie wants to take home some souvenirs from his week-end.

McKenzie: Buongiorno, posso guardare in giro?
Negoziante: Prego. Si accomodi. Se ha bisogno, sono qui.

(McKenzie is attracted by some local rugs)

Negoziante: Questi tappeti le piacciono? Sono prodotti del nostro artigianato locale.
McKenzie: Di che cosa sono?
Negoziante: Questi sono di pura lana e quelli sono di cotone.
McKenzie: Mi mostri anche quelli di cotone. Di che colore sono?
Negoziante: Eccoli. Li tocchi. Ne ho anche alcuni rossi a strisce grigie, alcuni gialli a quadri neri.
McKenzie: Quello rosso e grigio chiaro mi piace molto. Quanto è grande?
Negoziante: Due metri per un metro e dieci centimetri.
McKenzie: E quanto costa quello di lana blu?
Negoziante: Questo di lana costa centocinquantamila lire.
McKenzie: Va bene. Lo prendo.

Dialogue 2

Mr McKenzie would like to see something else.

McKenzie: Per piacere, mi mostri anche quei portacenere.
Negoziante: Anche questi sono prodotti dell'artigianato locale.

McKenzie: Di che cosa sono questi vasi verdi?
Negoziante: Questi sono fatti di ceramica, questi di legno . . .
McKenzie: (looking at some pottery) No, questi di terracotta non mi piacciono.
McKenzie: Quanto è grande questo vaso di rame?
Negoziante: Dieci centimetri per quaranta.
McKenzie: È un po' grande. Ma lo prendo. Ha anche dei prodotti di pelle? Delle giacche? Delle borse?
Negoziante: No, non li vendiamo.
McKenzie: Allora, l'ultimo prezzo in tutto?
Negoziante: Non posso fare uno sconto grosso. Centomila.
McKenzie: È proprio l'ultimo prezzo? Niente di meno?
Negoziante: Va bene. Novantamila. Ecco il suo pacco. Grazie.
McKenzie: Grazie a lei. Arrivederla.

'Artigianato locale in piazza'

Dialogue 3 In un negozio di stampe
In a prints shop. Tim wants to buy some reproductions of Venice.

Tim: Scusi, posso guardare in giro? Cerco delle stampe.
Negoziante: Prego. È ingresso libero.
Tim: Questa stampa con Arlecchino e Pulcinella è autentica o è una riproduzione?

Negoziante: Questa è una stampa autentica. È carissima.
Tim: Mi mostri quelle riproduzioni del Carnevale in vetrina . . . (He asks for some prices) Quanto costa questa?
Negoziante: Questa con la piazza di San Marco costa diecimila.
Tim: E quella con Arlecchino in gondola?
Negoziante: Quella è una fotografia di venti anni fa. Costa cinquemila lire. La prendi?
Tim: È un po'cara. Le fotografie sono tutte in bianco e nero?
Negoziante: Queste sì. Ma ne ho anche, più recenti, a colori . . .
Tim: No, non mi piacciono. È l'ultimo prezzo per queste due?
Negoziante: Non posso fare uno sconto. Ho prezzi fissi.
Tim: Niente di meno? (With a sigh) Va bene, le prendo.

Dialogue 4 In cartoleria

Tim is in a stationery shop, looking for some posters of the Carnival of Venice.

Tim: Vorrei vedere dei (pointing at the posters) . . . come si dice?
Cartolaio: Dei manifesti. Di Venezia o di altri soggetti?
Tim: Mi mostri dei manifesti del Carnevale, di ieri e di oggi.
Cartolaio: Puoi guardare quelli vicino alla vetrina, a destra.
Tim: Non mi piacciono molto . . . sono un po' piccoli.
Negoziante: Li vuoi più grandi? Ci sono questi calendari con dodici fotografie.
Tim: (looking at one) È un po' grande.
Negoziante: (patiently) No, è trenta per quaranta. È bellissimo. Le fotografie sono di fotografi famosi.
Tim: Sì, mi piace. Lo prendo. Lo incarti e levi il prezzo, per favore.
Negoziante: Ecco e grazie, ciao!
Tim: Molte grazie, buongiorno.

12.2 VOCABULARY

Dialogue 1

il giro (m); in –	tour; around
il negoziante (m)	shopkeeper
il tappeto (m)	carpet; rug
il prodotto (m)	product
l'artigianato (m)	arts and crafts
locale-e	local
puro-a	pure
la lana (f); di pura –	wool; pure wool
il cotone (m)	cotton

mostrare	to show
li (m pl.)	them
eccoli (m pl.)	here they are
toccare	to touch
la striscia (f) (pl. -sce; a strisce)	the stripe; striped; with stripes
grigio-a (pl. -gie)	grey
il quadro (m); a quadri	check; with checks
nero-a	black
chiaro-a	light
blu (inv.)	blue
lo (m sing.)	it

Dialogue 2

il portacenere (m) (pl. inv.)	ashtray
il vaso (m)	vase
la ceramica (f) (pl. -che)	ceramic
il legno (m)	wood
la terracotta (f)	pottery
il rame (m)	copper
centimetro (m)	centimetre
la pelle (f)	leather
la giacca (f) (-che)	jacket
la borsa (f)	bag
vendere	to sell
l'ultimo-a	last; final
fare uno sconto	to offer a discount
di meno	less

Dialogue 3

la stampa (f)	print
l'ingresso (m)	entrance; hall
autentico-a (pl. -ci, -che)	authentic
la riproduzione (f)	reproduction
la vetrina (f); in –	shop window; in the shop window
la gondola (f)	gondola
la (f s.)	it
recente-e	recent
fisso-a	fixed
le (f pl.)	them

Dialogue 4

la cartoleria (f)	stationery shop
il cartolaio (m)	stationer

il manifesto (m) poster
il soggetto (m) topic
il calendario (m) calendar
incartare to wrap
levare to remove, to lift

12.3 EXPLANATIONS

(a) Conversion table

The central number can be read as either a metric or an imperial measurement, e.g., 1 metre = 3.3 feet and one foot = 0.3 metres.

inches		cm.	feet		metres
0.39	1	2.54	3.3	1	0.3
0.79	2	5.08	6.6	2	0.61
1.18	3	7.62	9.9	3	0.91
1.57	4	10.6	13.1	4	1.22
1.97	5	12.7	16.4	5	1.52
2.36	6	15.2	19.7	6	1.83
2.76	7	17.8	23	7	2.13
3.15	8	20.3	26.2	8	2.44
3.54	9	22.9	29.5	9	2.74
3.9	10	25.4	32.9	10	3.05

(b) Enquiring about materials

To say what something is made of, you may say è fatto di . . . or, simply: è di . . . (lit. it's of . . .):

Questo vaso è di rame. This vase is (of) copper.
Questi tappeti sono di lana. These carpets are (of) wool.

Therefore, to ask what something is made of, you say:

Scusi, di che cosa è? What is it (of)?
Scusi, di che cosa sono? What are they (made) of?

Equally, you say:

Prendo quello di lana. I'll take that woollen one.
Mi piace questa di pelle. I like this leather one.

(c) Colours and patterns – *grammar ref. 39*

Colours always follow the noun they describe and they usually agree with it in gender and number. Those which do not change are indicated in the vocabulary lists. To ask, you say:

Scusi, di che colore è?	What colour is it?
Di che colore sono?	What colour are they?

The reply may be:

Quella giacca è bianca.	That jacket is white.
Quelle borse sono rosse.	Those bags are red.

Or you may make up your own colour in this way:

Quella giacca è color salmone. (color(e) + any object)

To describe colours, you may use chiaro (light) or scuro (dark, deep):

I tappeti sono grigio chiaro o grigio scuro?

Notice that, in this case, these words and the colour are invariable. The following are idiomatic forms:

in bianco e nero	in black and white
a colori	coloured
a quadri	with checks, checked
a strisce	striped, with stripes

(d) Polite requests (the imperative) – *grammar ref. 65*
The endings indicating polite formal requests are as follows, for the three conjugations:

port – are (1st) port + i	bring (me), can you bring (me)
prend – ere (2nd) prend + a	take, will you take . . .
part – ire (3rd) part + a	please leave (depart)
*fin – ire (3rd) fin + isca	do finish, please

(e) Saying you buy it, you buy them: lo, la, li, le (Pronoun objects) – *grammar ref. 49*
If you use the word '*it*' referring to a m sing. object., you say lo; if it's f sing., you say la; if you use the word *them* for a masculine plural noun, you use li; for a feminine plural, you use le.
These pronouns go before the verb, as mi, ti, le, gli etc. do:

Questo tappeto? Sì, lo compro.	This carpet? Yes, I'll buy it.
Questi sigari? Sì, li compro.	These cigars? Yes, I'll buy them.
Questa birra? Sì, la bevo.	This beer? Yes, I'll drink it.

Lo (m s), la (f s), li (m pl) and le (f pl) are also used to refer to people: Sì, lo conosco—Yes, I know him; Sì, la conosco—Yes, I know her.

If you use these pronouns in a negative sentence, place non in front of them:

Mi dispiace, non le leggo. — Sorry, I don't read them.

(f) Measurements
To ask for the measurements of an item, say:

Quanto è grande? — How big is it?
Quanto è largo? — How wide is it?
Quanto è lungo? — How long is it?

Measurements are given with this formula:

1 metro per 4 metri. — 1 metre by 4 metres.

or, in a shortened form: 1 per 4 (uno per quattro); or,

È lungo quattro metri. — It's four metres long.

(g) Saying you don't like something: non mi piace

La sua famiglia non mi piace. — I don't like his family.
Queste fotografie non le piacciono? — Don't you like these photos?
Non ti piace fumare? — Don't you like smoking?

The construction remains the same as you have learnt in the previous chapter. You place non before the pronoun mi, ti etc.

(h) Un poco, un po' + an adj. ('a little' + adj.) – *grammar ref. 42*
These two words (one is an abbreviated form of the other) are frequently used as equivalent of the English expressions slightly, a bit, rather, rather too . . . . In front of an adjective they don't vary.

È un poco caro! — It's rather expensive.
Sono un po' grandi. — They are a bit too large.

(j) Bargaining for a reduction
Don't bargain in large shops or department stores or wherever you see a notice saying PREZZI FISSI (fixed prices). Italian people bargain in

shops and open markets. Make sure the tone of your voice indicates friendliness and politeness. You may start by saying:

È un po' caro.	It's a bit expensive.
È troppo caro!	It's too expensive!

Or be more straightforward and say:

È l'ultimo prezzo?	Is it your final price?
È proprio l'ultimo prezzo?	Is it really the final price?
Niente di meno . . . ?	Nothing less?

Proverbio: Chi più spende meno spende.
Cheapest is dearest.

12.4 EXERCISES

A

Exercise 1
Play the role of a fusspot (pignolo) at a restaurant.
Cameriere: Ecco la sua pizza.
Pignolo: (Say you're sorry, but it's a bit big.)
Cameriere: (the pizza is changed) Va bene questa?
Pignolo: (Say the tomato sauce is slightly salty. Ask for some crisps.)
Cameriere: Ecco. Tutto bene?
Pignolo: (Say they are slightly uncooked (raw) and the coffee is a bit cold.)
Cameriere: Ecco il conto . . . (Aside: questo è salato!)
(When something is expensive, colloquially people say it's salty.)
Pignolo: (Try to bargain: is it the final price?)
Cameriere: Mi dispiace, sono prezzi fissi.
Pignolo: (Insist: nothing less?)
Cameriere: Mi dispiace . . . no.

Exercise 2
Find out the cost of all these things: quanto costa . . . costano . . .
And how big they are: quanto è grande? quanto sono grandi . . . ?
Example: (this red rug) Quanto costa questo tappeto rosso e quant'e grande?

that red rug; this white vase; those yellow ashtrays; these photographs in black and white; those reproductions in colour.

Exercise 3
Ask whether something is made of these materials:
Example: (rame) Di che cos'è? Di rame?

lana; cotone; ceramica; terracotta; legno.

Exercise 4
You're full of enthusiasm and you say yes to every suggestion.
Example: Desideri comprare questo disco? Sì, lo compro.

1. Desideri prenotare questo viaggio?
2. Desideri ordinare una birra?
3. Desideri guardare questi opuscoli?
4. Desideri regalare questa stampa?
5. Desideri prendere queste sigarette?
6. Desideri ascoltare la televisione?

Exercise 5
You are in the wrong mood. Nothing pleases you, as in the example:
Le piace questa stampa? No, non mi piace.

1. Le piace questa fotografia?
2. Le piacciono questi regali?
3. Le piace questo vino?
4. Le piacciono queste giacche?
5. Le piacciono questi dolci?

Exercise 6 (revision ch. 2)
Ask whether there is a hotel not far away; whether there is available a double bedroom without bathroom; whether the room is noisy. Say, starting from next Monday; for a week. Ask how much it is and where the hotel is: on the right or on the left?

B

Exercise 7
Can you answer the following questions in relation to dialogues 1 and 2 using the pronouns lo, la, li, le when suitable?

1. Dov'è il signor McKenzie?
2. In quel negozio di artigianato hanno i tappeti di pura lana?
3. Hanno anche i tappeti di cotone?
4. Hanno anche alcuni tappeti rossi a strisce gialle?
5. Hanno i tappeti grigi a quadri neri?
6. Che tappeto piace al signor McKenzie?
7. Quanto è grande il tappeto rosso e grigio chiaro?
8. Compra le giacche di lana?
9. Compra le borse di pelle?

Exercise 8
Play Mr McKenzie's role at the market stall.

1. It's rather expensive. Can you show me some less expensive vases?
2. Are they local arts and crafts products?
3. What are they made of?
4. But this one is as expensive as the white one.
5. The final price?
6. Is it really your final price? Nothing less?
7. Well, I'll take it.
8. Please remove the price and wrap it.

Exercise 9
Can you reproduce in Italian Miss Dani's conversation over the phone with a friend?

1. How long have you known him for?
2. For two months?
3. Is his girlfriend pretty?
4. Do you know her?
5. Are they engaged?
6. Does she speak Italian?
7. Does she understand it a little?
8. Has he got three cars?
9. Does she drive them?
10. The blue one?

GIVING ORDERS; THE POST OFFICE SYSTEM

13.1 DIALOGUES

Dialogue 1 Dal tabaccaio

Now Tim wants some postcards of Venice.

Tim: Buongiorno. Posso guardare delle cartoline della città e dei dintorni?
Tabaccaio: Quelle della città sono da questa parte. Quelle dei dintorni sono qui a sinistra. Guarda pure, ma non mettere fuori posto.
Tim: (picks up a few postcards) Prendo queste.
Tabaccaio: Ti piacciono?
Tim: Sono le più interessanti. Sono dieci. Le conti, per favore.
Tabaccaio: Bene, mille lire, in tutto.
Tim: Mi dia anche una biro. E i francobolli, per piacere.
Tabaccaio: Per l'Italia o per l'estero?
Tim: Per l'Inghilterra. Via aerea. Vorrei anche della carta da lettere e delle buste. Le più robuste.
Tabaccaio: Mi dispiace. Siamo senza. Puoi ripassare più tardi?
Tim: Va bene. Fino a che ora siete aperti?
Tabaccaio: Siamo aperti fino alle sette. Non arrivare tardi.

Dialogue 2

Tim finds out how to send money.

Tim: Un momento . . . vendete dei biglietti di auguri?
Tabaccaio: Sì, li vendiamo. (he fetches a box) Questi sono i più grandi e anche gli ultimi.
Tim: Questo quanto costa?
Tabaccaio: Cinquecento. Vuoi anche i francobolli?

'Un pacchetto di sigarette, per favore'

Tim: Sì. È un biglietto importante. Devo includere dei soldi.
Tabaccaio: Ma non includere soldi nelle buste. È vietato.
Tim: Ah! Grazie. E come faccio?
Tabaccaio: Spedisci un vaglia. Sai compilare un vaglia?
Tim: Sì. E il biglietto? Faccio una raccomandata?
Tabaccaio: No. Le raccomandate sono sicure ma non sono veloci. Devi fare un espresso. È il più veloce.
Tim: Ho bisogno di una busta speciale?
Tabaccaio: No, metti questo francobollo e scrivi il mittente in stampatello dietro la busta.
Tim: Molte grazie. Ah, scusi! Dov'è una buca?
Tabaccaio: Sai andare in piazza? Là ce n'è una.

Dialogue 3 Alla posta
At the post office.

McKenzie: Buongiorno. Devo spedire questo tappeto in Gran Bretagna . . . Vendete della carta da pacchi e dello spago?
Impiegata: No, non li vendiamo. Li vendono in cartoleria.

(McKenzie comes back. There is no first class mail in Italy.)

McKenzie: Ecco il pacco per l'Inghilterra. Lo spedisca in prima classe.
Impiegata: Come? Può ripetere?
McKenzie: Spedisca il pacco in prima classe.
Impiegata: Non ci sono prima e seconda classe. Desidera un pacco raccomandato?
McKenzie: Sì, faccio un pacco raccomandato.
Impiegata: Con la ricevuta di ritorno?
McKenzie: Che cosa significa?
Impiegata: Quando il pacco arriva a Londra, lei riceve una ricevuta.
McKenzie: Metto il mittente in alto a destra?
Impiegata: Sì. Compili questo modulo. Scriva in stampatello.

Dialogue 4 In cartoleria

McKenzie decides to send the vase too by mail.

McKenzie: Scusi, vorrei della carta da pacchi e dello spago.
Cartolaio: Adesso è chiuso. È mezzogiorno. Ripassi più tardi.
McKenzie: Siete aperti alle tre?
Cartolaio: Sì. Siamo aperti dalle due e mezzo fino alle sette.

(later)

McKenzie: Allora mi dia della carta da pacchi e dello spago. Il più robusto. Il pacco va in Scozia. È fragile. Mi dia anche un foglio.
Cartolaio: Non metta lettere nei pacchi. È vietato.
McKenzie: Oh! Ma come faccio?
Cartolaio: Spedisca la lettera da sola.
McKenzie: Mi dia allora della carta da lettere via aerea, la più sottile, la migliore. Quant'è?
Negoziante: Tremiladuecentocinquanta. (McKenzie hands over the money.) Non ha della moneta, per cortesia?
McKenzie: Un momento . . . guardo nel portafoglio . . . No, forse nella tasca a destra . . . allora, senta: mi dia una mappa della città e un notes basso.

13.2 VOCABULARY

Dialogue 1

la cartolina (f)	postcard
la parte (f); da questa –	side; this way
pure; guarda –	also; please do look

mettere; -fuori posto	to put; to put out of place
interessante-e	interesting
contare	to count
la biro (f) (pl. inv.)	biro
il francobollo (m); – da cento	stamp; a 100 liras stamp
l'estero (m)	abroad
via aerea (f)	air mail
la carta (f) – da lettere	paper; writing paper
robusto-a	strong; robust
ripassare	to return
tardi	late

Dialogue 2

il biglietto (m); -d'auguri	card; greeting card
la lettera (f)	letter
importante-e	important
includere	include
i soldi (m pl.)	money
faccio (fare) (irreg.)	I make; I do
*spedire	to send
compilare	to fill in (a form)
il vaglia (m) (pl. inv.)	money order
la raccomandata (f)	registered letter
sicuro-a	safe
l'espresso (m)	express mail service, equivalent to 1st class mail
speciale-e	special
scrivere	to write
il mittente (m)	sender
lo stampatello	capital letters
la buca (f) (pl. -che)	letter box

Dialogue 3

il pacco (m) (pl. -chi); carta da-	parcel; wrapping paper
lo spago (m) (pl. -ghi)	string
la classe (f)	class; category
raccomandato-a	registered (mail)
la ricevuta (f)	receipt
ricevere	to receive
alto-a; in-	high, tall; on top

Dialogue 4

chiuso-a (chiudere, irreg.)	closed
la Scozia (f)	Scotland

fragile-e	fragile
il foglio (m)	sheet
sottile-e	thin
per cortesia	please (formal)
il portafoglio (m)	wallet; purse
la tasca (f) (pl. -che)	pocket
sentire	to hear
la mappa (f)	map
il notes (m) (pl. inv.)	block notes; pad
basso-a	low, small.

13.3 EXPLANATIONS

(a) Background information

Post offices in Italy are subject to local variations. Some open at 8 a.m. to close at 2 p.m. Others close from midday to 2 p.m. and are open until 6 p.m. They are closed on Saturday afternoons and Sundays.

Letter boxes are red and have the inscription POSTE. Sometimes there is a box for mail in town IN CITTÀ and a box for every other destination FUORI CITTÀ.
The postage costs vary frequently because of inflation. It's wise to check when you buy stamps. These can be bought from post-offices or, more frequently, from tobacconists. Outside these shops you read SALI E TABACCHI (lit. salts and tobaccos). Unlike England, post-offices, however small, do not sell goods.

Proverbio: Lontano dagli occhi, lontano dal cuore.
Out of sight, out of mind.

(b) Commands (familiar form with the imperative) – *grammar ref. 65*

These are the endings to form the familiar form of the imperative:

guard + a (1st conj.)	look
scriv + i (2nd conj.)	write
sent + i (3rd conj.)	listen
sped + isci (3rd conj.)	send

This tense is also used to encourage people. In this case, you may add pure after the verb:

Posso guardare questo libro?	May I look at this book?
Guarda pure!	Do look at it! By all means!

Verbs which are irregular in the present tense, are usually irregular in the imperative:

Posso andare?	May I go?
Vai pure! (familiar)	Do go!
Vada pure. (formal)	

(c) Prohibitions (negative form of the imperative) – *grammar ref. 65(c)*

To warn people not to do something with the formal form, you place non in front of the verb:

Signora, non metta una lettera nel pacco.	Don't put a letter in the parcel.

To warn not to do something with the familiar form, (i. e. negative imperative) you use the infinitives of the verbs, placing non in front:

Non andare da sola!	Don't go on your own!
Non mettere ghiaccio nel vino!	Don't put ice in the wine!
Non spedire soldi nelle buste!	Don't send money in the envelopes!

(d) Be choosy (the superlative): il più + adj. – *grammar ref. 46*

To say you want the most . . . , you say il più:

Voglio il più caro.	I want the most expensive.
Mi dia il più grande!	Give me the largest one!

The article and the endings of the adjective vary according to the noun which is implied:

Vorrei la più elegante.	I would like the most elegant one.
Mi dia i più piccoli!	Give me the smallest ones!
Prendo le più basse.	I'll take the lowest.

Equally you may say:

Vorrei quella più elegante.	I would like the most elegant one.
Mi dia quelli più piccoli.	Give me the smallest.
Prendo quelle più basse.	I'll take the lowest.

(e) Addressing shopkeepers

You already know how to ask shopkeepers whether something is available, with the plural form voi (avete ... (8.3(g)). You are implicitly asking the institution. You can use the same plural form with any verb:

Vendete sigarette?	Do you sell cigarettes?

If you use the verb essere, the following adjective must be m pl.:

Siete aperti o chiusi domenica?	Are you open or closed on Sunday?
Siamo chiusi.	We are closed.

(f) Finding out 'until when ...?' fino a quando?

Fino a che ora è aperto?	Until what time is it open?
Fino alle tre.	Until three o'clock.
Non fino alle tre e mezzo.	Not until half past three.

(g) Nel ... (in + the) – *grammar ref. 16*

If followed by a definite article (il, etc.) in always combines with it, in the following way:

Cerca nel portafoglio!	Look in the wallet!
Metti il foglio nella busta!	Put the sheet in the envelope!
Metti zucchero nell'aperitivo?	Do you put sugar in the aperitif?
Includi i soldi nei pacchi?	Do you include the money in parcels?
C'è il bagno nelle camere?	Is there a bath in the rooms?
C'è interesse nello sport?	Is there any interest in sport?

(h) Finding a solution: come faccio? (what do I do?) – *grammar ref. 64*

The infinitive of this form is fare.

Come faccio a spedire dei soldi?	How do I send money? (lit. how do I make to . . . ?)

(i) Find out what postal service to use
To ask for postage rates, you may ask:

Quant'è un francobollo per . . . ?	How much is a stamp for . . . ?

Or say you want a stamp for a particular country:

Mi dia i francobolli per l'Inghilterra.	May I have the stamps for England?

If you know the value of the stamp you want, say:

Mi dia un francobollo da trecento.	May I have a 300 lira stamp?

To indicate postal services, here are common expressions with fare: fa' or fai (familiar order), faccia (polite request):

Faccia un pacco!	Make a parcel.
Faccia una raccomandata!	Send by registered mail.
Fai un pacco raccomandato!	Send a registered parcel.
Fai un espresso!	Send a letter 1st class. (lit. express)

(l) Saying you know how to do things: sapere – *grammar ref. 64*
The English expressions 'I know how to do something' or 'I can do something' are conveyed in Italian with the verb sapere (3.3(g)) followed by the infinitive:

Sai compilare un vaglia?	Can you fill in a postal order? (familiar)
Sa trovare l'albergo?	Can you find your hotel? (formal)

The replies may be:

Sì.	Yes I can.
Sì, lo so compilare, grazie.	Yes, I can fill it in.

13.4 EXERCISES

Exercise 1

Tim is told what to do to send an urgent card. But he checks first to see that he understands properly.

Example: Vai alla posta – Devo andare alla posta?

1. Scrivi il biglietto.
2. Vai in tabaccheria.
3. Compra una busta.
4. Chiedi quant'è per l'Inghilterra.
5. Prendi anche una cartolina.
6. Vai alla posta.
7. Spedisci il biglietto espresso.

Exercise 2

At a dinner-party, McKenzie is encouraged to make himself at home. Can you supply his questions?

Example: Prenda pure! – Posso prendere?

1. Apra pure quella bottiglia!
2. Ascolti pure quel disco!
3. Cerchi pure il suo collega!
4. Fumi pure il suo Toscano!
5. Beva pure un Martini.
6. Prenda pure una birra dal frigo.

Exercise 3

You are looking for a few things in a stationery shop but nothing really as you want.

Example: (buste piccole) Cerco delle buste piccole. Le più piccole sono queste?

un notes basso; della carta sottile; delle cartoline interessanti; una rivista recente; un biglietto grande; della carta da pacco robusta; una biro a buon prezzo.

Exercise 4

There are no vegetables at home. Imagine you are an au pair in Italy and need to ring a friend to ask for advice. Can you say this in Italian?

1. We haven't got crisps.
2. What can I do?

3. In the fridge there are only a few tomatoes.
4. Are the shops still open?
5. At what time do they close?
6. At one o'clock?
7. But how can I manage to get (arrive) there?
8. The car?
9. I haven't got it.

Exercise 5 (revision ch. 3)
In the morning at the hotel. Play McKenzie's role (use the formal form):

Portiere: Buongiorno. Come va?
McKenzie: (Very well, thank you. And you?)
Portiere: C'è un messaggio per lei.
McKenzie: (I don't understand.)
Portiere: C'è un messaggio per lei.
McKenzie: (Ah! Thank you. (he reads it) I must go to the Banca Centrale. Excuse me, to go to this bank, what do I have to take?)
Portiere: Deve prendere il sette.
McKenzie: (Where is the bus stop? How frequent is the bus?)
Portiere: È dietro l'angolo. C'è ogni quarto d'ora.
McKenzie: (Is the tube quicker?)

Exercise 6
At a tobacconist's, get the right stamps:

— Prego.
— (Ask how much a stamp for a postcard costs.)
— Per l'estero o per l'Italia?
— (Say for England.)
— Quattrocento.
— (Say you would like to send an air-mail letter to (for) England. How much is it?)

B

Exercise 7
You are working in an Italian office and need to tell people what to do and what not to do. Use the formal form.

1. Bring today's newspaper, please.
2. Fill in these forms.

3. Don't sign those letters.
4. Write to the Pradella firm.
5. Ring up the Chamber of Commerce; I'll go there in half an hour.
6. Please order two coffees, with milk and with sugar.
7. When you go home, go to the bank and change this money.
8. Prepare these receipts.
9. Send these parcels express.

Exercise 8

At the tobacconist's, Tim meets Laura and tells her what he is doing. Reproduce Tim's conversation in Italian.

I'm looking for some postcards of the town and the surroundings. These are the most interesting ones. I'll take ten postcards and a biro. No, I haven't got the stamps. I need to buy ten stamps for England. I am also buying some writing paper and envelopes. Yes, I'll ask for the strongest ones. They haven't any, but I'll come back later. They are open until seven.

Exercise 9

McKenzie enters a snack bar while waiting for the stationer's to open. He chats with the barman. Reproduce his conversation in Italian.

I'm waiting until half past two. I need wrapping paper and string because I'm sending a parcel to Scotland. It's fragile. It's a vase. But the stationer's is closed. (Perhaps the barman may help.) Have you got some strong paper and some string? How big is the parcel? It's one metre and twenty centimetres high, fifteen centimetres wide. Thank you very much. It's very kind of you. May I offer you an aperitif?

FINDING OUT ABOUT ENTERTAINMENTS; REFUSING INVITATIONS

14.1 DIALOGUES

Dialogue 1 La pagina degli spettacoli

Lucio's mother suggests an evening out.

Mamma: (to everybody) Che cosa fate stasera?
Tim: Lucio, a te piace andare al cinema?
Lucio: A me, sì. Che film danno?
Tim: Guardiamo sul giornale. Guarda la pagina degli spettacoli. Dov'è il giornale di oggi?
Lucio: Ma, non so. Guarda sul tavolo.

(Tim goes through the page. He doesn't understand one word.)

Tim: Che cosa significa prima visione?
Lucio: Sono i film più recenti. E i cinema più cari.
Mamma: Perchè non andate a vedere ''L'albero degli zoccoli'' di Ermanno Olmi? È bellissimo, dicono.
Lucio: (Turns to Carla and Julie) Voi venite?
Carla: Ma, a noi piacciono i film comici. E a voi piacciono di più i film romantici!
Lucio: Testa o croce? (They toss. The girls win.)
Carla: Benone. Allora andiamo a vedere un film comico con Nino Manfredi. (to her mother) Vuoi venire?
Mamma: (laughing) No, grazie. Vengo un'altra volta.

Dialogue 2 In discoteca

After the film, Tim and friends go to a disco.

Franco: (to Carla) Vieni volentieri, in discoteca?
Carla: Io sì. (to the others) E a voi, va?

AGOSTO

1	**Mostra Mercato** "artigiani al lavoro"
	continua sino a settembre la **mostra Gioielli Antichi**
3	**Itinerario agrituristico** nell'entroterra di Desenzano
4	**Concerto** Banda Cittadina-Rivoltella
5	**Crociera** in onore degli ospiti
5	**Concerto** Banda Cittadina
6	**Serata musicale** International Rock
6/8	Tradizionale **"Festa del Lago e dell'Ospite"** organizzata dal Gruppo Folkloristico "Cuori ben Nati" di Rivoltella
12/15	**Mostra** del libro
14/15	**Mostra** Gruppo Pittori del Ponte Bianco alla Veneziana
21	**Regata delle Bisse** in notturna
22	**Spettacolo Pirotecnico**
26	**Crociera** in onore degli ospiti
28/29	**Mostra Mercato** "artigiani al lavoro"
31	**Itinerario agrituristico** nell'entroterra di Desenzano

Lucio: Conoscete una buona discoteca qui vicino?
Franco: Sì. Qui vicino c'è la "Disco rock". È la più frequentata di Milano e è a buon prezzo, dicono.
Julie: Che musica suonano?
Franco: Di pomeriggio, c'è il jux-box. Di sera, c'è l'orchestra in una sala e il jux-box in un'altra.

(After a while in the disco.)

Lucio: Mettiamo un disco di musica lenta. A te va?
Carla: Sì, dai! Sono stanca di tutto questo rock ... Che cosa fai domani ... ?
Tim: (to Julie) Balliamo ancora? Ti piace questa canzone?
Franco: Qualcosa da bere?
Carla: Un frullato con il ghiaccio. A voi, va?
Cameriere: Una birra è compresa nel biglietto d'ingresso.
Carla: Allora tutti una birra!

Dialogue 3
McKenzie and friends are going out too.

Rossi: Andiamo fuori stasera? Venite volentieri?
Bianchi: Io non posso venire. Ho già un appuntamento.
Pardi: Guardiamo la Pagina degli Spettacoli. Uh! C'è un concerto con Claudio Abbado.
Rossi: È il più bravo direttore italiano di oggi, dicono.
Pardi: Oppure alla Piccola Scala, ci sono due solisti. Suonano musiche di Bach. Non viene proprio, Bianchi?
Bianchi: Mi dispiace. Non posso proprio venire. Grazie, un'altra volta.
Rossi: (to McKenzie) Conoscete i Gufi? Cominciano a recitare oggi.
Pardi: (to McKenzie) A lei piace uno spettacolo di cabaret? I Gufi sono i migliori cabarettisti italiani.
McKenzie: Eh, ho paura di non capire tutte le battute. Posso provare.
Pardi: Bene. Telefoniamo e chiediamo a che ora cominciano.
Rossi: Signora, prenoti subito. Beviamo un aperitivo, intanto.

Dialogue 4 Al botteghino
At the box office. McKenzie has not enjoyed the cabaret humour. He wants to make up for it with a musical and invites the Pardis.
McKenzie: Ci sono ancora dei posti per domenica sera?
Impiegata: Che giorno?
McKenzie: Domenica. Il venticinque di questo mese.
Impiegata: Sì. Ci sono ancora dei posti in balconata e delle poltrone.
McKenzie: Le poltroncine sono tutte esaurite?
Impiegata: Sì, sono tutte esaurite per domenica.
McKenzie: Va bene. Mi dia tre biglietti per tre poltrone. A che ora comincia lo spettacolo?

Impiegata: Alle nove in punto. E finisce a mezzanotte. C'è l'orario sui biglietti.
McKenzie: C'è tutti i giorni lo spettacolo?
Impiegata: Sì. Tranne il lunedì.

(At the hotel, he rings up Mrs Pardi)

McKenzie: Che cosa fa domenica pomeriggio? Niente di speciale? Ho tre biglietti per un musical. Venite volentieri a teatro?

14.2 VOCABULARY

Dialogue 1

fate (pl.) (fare)	you do
stasera	tonight
il cinema (m) (pl. inv.)	cinema
il film (m)	film
danno (dare); danno un film	they give; there is a film on
la pagina (f)	page
lo spettacolo (m)	performance; play; show; event
la visione (f)	run (of film)
dicono (dire)	they say
comico-a (pl. -ci; -che)	comic
romantico-a (pl. -ci; -che)	romantic
testa o croce	to toss (lit. head or cross)
venire	to come
vengo (venire)	I come
'L'albero degli zoccoli'	'The tree of the wooden clogs'

Dialogue 2

la discoteca (f)	disco
vieni (venire)	you come (familiar)
volentieri	with pleasure
frequentato-a	attended
suonare	to play (music)
il pomeriggio (m); di-	afternoon; in the afternoon
l'orchestra (f)	orchestra
la sala (f)	hall
lento-a	slow
stanco-a (pl. -chi; -che)	tired
fai (fare)	you do (familiar)
ballare	to dance

ancora	again; once more
la canzone (f)	song
biglietto d'ingresso (m)	admission ticket

Dialogue 3

fuori; andare –	out; to go out
già	already
il concerto (m)	concert
bravo-a	good (professionally)
il direttore (d'orchestra) (m)	conductor
oppure	or
il solista (m)	soloist
viene (venire)	he, she, it comes; you come (formal)
il gufo (m)	owl
recitare	to play (perform)
il cabaret (m) (pl. inv.)	cabaret
il/la cabarettista (m and f)	cabaret performer
aver paura	to be afraid
la battuta (f)	verbal joke

Dialogue 4

la balconata (f)	balcony; dress-circle
la poltrona (f)	stall
la poltroncina (f)	pit-stall
in punto	on the dot
l'orario (m)	timetable
tranne	except
fa (fare)	he, she, it makes; you make, you do (formal)
il teatro (m)	theatre

14.3 EXPLANATIONS

(a) To find out about entertainments and events:

Look in the Pagina degli Spettacoli of the local newspapers and, above all, ask at the Tourist Office to find out what is on. A great number of events are organized everywhere throughout the year.

(b) Asking people about their plans: che cosa fa? – *grammar ref. 64*

For a general question, use the verb fare (irr.) (to do):

Che cosa fai stasera?	What are you doing tonight? (familiar)
Che cosa fa domani?	What are you doing tomorrow? (formal)
Che cosa fate dopo?	What are you doing after? (pl.)

(c) More about piacere (to like)
You know now how to express your likes and dislikes:

Il cinema mi piace.	I like the cinema.
I film inglesi non mi piacciono.	I don't like English films.

This word order is frequently switched round. You put what you like after the verb:

Mi piace il cinema.	I like the cinema.
Non mi piacciono i film inglesi.	I don't like English films.

When you don't repeat what you like, you simply say:

Mi piace.	I like (it).
Non mi piacciono.	I don't like (them).

(d) Contrasting likes and dislikes: a me (to me) – *grammar ref. 47*
If you wish to emphasize or contrast people's tastes, you use these pronouns after the preposition a:

A me piace il cinema, e a te?	I like the cinema, do you? (fam.) (lit. to me appeals the cinema, and to you?)
A lei piace il cabaret?	Do you like the cabaret? (formal)
A voi non piacciono i western?	Don't you like western films?

In reply, you may say:

A noi? Sì.	Yes, we do! (lit. To us? yes!)
A noi piacciono.	Yes, we like them.

(e) Asking people if a proposal suits them – *grammar ref. 47*
You may use the expression that you know, va bene (fine, all right):

A te va (bene)? (familiar) A lei va? (formal) A voi va? (plural)	Is it all right with you? Does it suit you? do you like the idea?

To reply, say:

Sì, a me va bene. Sì, a noi va bene . . .

(f) What's on? che cosa danno? – *grammar ref. 64*
This expression lit. means what do they give? The plural form is used because you are referring to an institution.

Danno un film con Mastroianni.	There is on a film with . . .
Danno un film di Fellini.	There is a film by Fellini.

This expression may be used with films. For plays etc. you say:

Che cosa c'è al Teatro Nuovo?

To indicate il regista (film director) the expression is:
Un film di . . . Equally for novelists and painters: un romanzo di Moravia (a novel by Moravia) un quadro di Modigliani (a painting by Modigliani).

(g) Il . . . più ('the most' . . . + noun) – *grammar ref. 46*
You know how to say 'it's the most interesting': è il più interessante (13.3(d)). If you mention the thing or the person that is most interesting, you use this word order:

È il film più interessante.	It's the most interesting film.
È la discoteca più elegante.	It's the most elegant disco.
Metti la canzone più lenta.	Put on the slowest song.

(h) Rumours: dicono ('they say') – *grammar ref. 64*
To refer to the opinion of critics and people, add dicono (they say) at the end of your sentence:

È una brava attrice, dicono.	She is a good actress, so they say.

(h) Inviting people: vieni? (will you come?) – *grammar ref. 64*
You may use the verb venire (irr.)

Vieni a teatro?	Will you come? Are you coming? to the theatre? (familiar)
Viene fuori stasera?	Would you like to go out tonight? (formal)
Venite con noi domani?	Are you coming with us tomorrow (pl.)

The reply may be:

Sì, vengo.	Yes, I'll come.
Sì, veniamo volentieri.	Yes, we'll come with pleasure.

If you want to add 'with me', etc., you say con me (use the same pronouns as in (d) above).

(i) Declining an offer
Either say:

No, grazie. Mi dispiace.	No, thank you. I'm sorry.

Or say:

Mi dispiace, non posso. Un'altra volta perchè ...	I'm sorry, I can't. Next time, because ...

(j) Addressing people by surname
In dialogue 3, Bianchi is addressed formally but by his surname. It's a common habit in Italy to call colleagues in offices, banks, schools, by their surname only. It is not at all impolite and it's still more usual than to address colleagues by their first names, unless they are also friends. So, don't be surprised and upset.

14.4 EXERCISES

A

Exercise 1
Ask these people what they plan to do on those occasions.
Example: Mrs Rossi/tomorrow. Signora Rossi, che cosa fa domani?

1. Miss Dani/this afternoon.
2. Mr Bianchi/on Sunday.
3. The director/afterwards.
4. Tim/on Friday.
5. Carla/on Wednesday.

Exercise 2
Tim goes to see a film. Play his role.
Impiegata: Prego?
Tim: (Ask for two tickets.)
Impiegata: Per quando?
Tim: (You want them for now.)
Impiegata: Che posti?
Tim: (Ask for the cheapest.)
Impiegata: Duemila lire.
Tim: (Ask at what time the performance starts.)

Exercise 3
(a) Ask people to join you at these places.
Example: Franca/to the cinema—Franca, vieni al cinema?

1. Mr and Mrs Bianchi/to the theatre.
2. Laura/to a fantastic disco.
3. Mrs Pardi/to the office/at four o'clock.
4. Laura and Lucio/to the ice-cream parlour/tonight.
5. Tim/to school by car?

(b) They can't all make it this time. They will come next time. Say this in Italian for each of them.
Example: Non possiamo questa volta. Veniamo la prossima.

Exercise 4
Insist on your opinions!
Example: *Amico*: È il più bello? (film) *Tu*: Sì, per me è il film più bello!

1. È il più divertente? (spettacolo).
2. Sono i più bravi? (cantanti).
3. È il più comico? (musical).
4. È la più romantica? (attrice).
5. Sono le più drammatiche? (canzoni).
6. È il più classico? (concerto).
7. È il più famoso? (complesso).

Exercise 5
Go to the Tourist Office and find out where you can go to spend the evening:

McKenzie: (Good evening.)
Impiegata: Desidera?
McKenzie: (Ask what is on tonight at the local cinemas.)
Impiegata: Ecco la pagina degli spettacoli sul giornale locale.
McKenzie: (Ask if you need to book.)
Impiegata: No! Non deve prenotare. C'è sempre posto.
McKenzie: (Ask if there are other events (spettacolo) in town or in the surroundings.)
Impiegata: Sì, c'è uno spettacolo vicino al lago. È molto bello, dicono.
McKenzie: (Ask if it's entertaining and at what time it starts.)
Impiegata: Guardi questo opuscolo! Ci sono tutte le informazioni.

Exercise 6 (revision ch. 4)
You've applied for a job in Italy. You have been called for an interview. Ready? (You are addressed informally. You are under 20.)

— Come ti chiami? Di nome? E di cognome?
— (Say your name and surname.)
— Di dove sei?
— . . .
— Sai l'italiano?
— (Say you know it a little.)
— Parli francese?
— (Say you do.)
— Dove lavori in Inghilterra?
— (Say you are an office clerk and work for a large firm.)
— Come si chiama la tua ditta?
— (Say your firm is called . . .)
— Quanto resti in Italia?
— (Say you are staying for one year.)
— Conosci il signor Bruni?
— (Say yes, you know Mr Bruni and his family.)

B

Exercise 7
Mr McKenzie is inviting out the Pardis. Can you put the right verbs in the blank spaces?

Che cosa . . . stasera? Perchè non . . . al cinema? . . . un film interessante con Robert de Niro. Il regista è Martin Scorsese. Allora . . . quattro posti al cinema Astra. (It's his turn to be invited now) Domenica? No, non . . . niente di speciale. . . . volentieri a un concerto di Claudio Abbado. . . . invitare anche un collega inglese? A lui . . . molto la musica classica.

Exercise 8
After the performance, Mr McKenzie and his friends talk about music. Translate what they say: (use a me, a lei etc.)

Do you like classical music a lot? Yes. I like it a lot. I have records of Mozart, Bach . . . I like dramatic music. My wife prefers more cheerful classical music. She likes the music of Vivaldi and Monteverdi. Usually I listen to it early in the morning, when I go to my office by car or late in the evening. I often go to concerts. We don't like going to parties (feste) because rock music doesn't suit me. Light music is all right with me but not the noisy kind. I like slow music like the waltz (valzer). I never go with my wife or with (my) friends to a disco. Discos? I don't know where they are. My son and my daughter often dance in discos. My son likes rock music. We prefer the opera or a good laugh with a musical.

Exercise 9
Decline these offers. It will be for next time.

— Vieni a teatro con noi stasera?
— (I'm sorry. I can't come with you (pl.) tonight. Next time.)
— Non puoi venire domani sera?
— (No, I can't. I have to finish some work.)
— Abbiamo dei biglietti per un musical divertentissimo!
— (Thank you. But I really can't come. If I don't finish these letters, I can't leave tomorrow.)
— Ma sono poltrone! E viene anche Laura . . .
— (What time does the performance begin?)
— Alle nove in punto.
— (And what time does it finish?)
— Alle undici e un quarto, circa.
— (It's very late . . . It's funny, they say? Okay! I'll go to the office when the performance ends . . . and you all come with me!)

SAYING WHAT YOU DID SOME TIME BEFORE; TALKING OF THE WEATHER

15.1 DIALOGUES

Dialogue 1 Al ristorante

Mrs Sally McKenzie has arrived and the Pardis take the McKenzies out for a meal.

Mr Pardi: Buonasera. Ho prenotato un tavolo per quattro.
Cameriere: Che nome?
Mr Pardi: Pardi. L'ho prenotato l'altro giorno da Milano.

(They sit down and choose the first course.)

Mr Pardi: (to the waiter) Di primo, quale specialità consiglia ai nostri ospiti?
Cameriere: (to the McKenzies) Avete già preso gli spaghetti alla genovese?
Mr McKenzie: No, non li abbiamo mai presi. Come sono?
Cameriere: Il sugo è fatto di basilico. È squisito.
Mrs Pardi: Sì, ha ragione. Noi li prendiamo sempre quando veniamo.
Mrs McKenzie: (to Mr McKenzie) Sì, prendiamoli anche noi.
Mr Pardi: (to the waiter) Quali vini sono adatti?
Cameriere: Un vino leggero . . . un Cinqueterre.

(While they wait, the conversation turns to the weather.)

Mrs Pardi: (to Mrs McKenzie) Che tempo ha avuto in Inghilterra quest'ultimo mese?
Mrs McKenzie: Uh! Ho avuto brutto tempo per molti giorni. E voi?
Mrs Pardi: Sì, anche noi abbiamo avuto una stagione fredda.

Dialogue 2

The conversation is about the restaurant.

Mr McKenzie: Venite spesso qui?
Mr Pardi: Sì, veniamo spesso. La volta scorsa ho ordinato la cima alla genovese.
Mr McKenzie: È un piatto leggero?
Mr Pardi: No, è un piatto un po' pesante. È vitello arrosto con ripieno di uova, salsicce e funghi.
Mrs Pardi: La cima è squisita. L'ho preparata anch'io qualche giorno fa, quando ho invitato degli amici a pranzo.

(The waiter is ready for the second course.)

Mr Pardi: Di secondo, quali piatti consiglia?
Cameriere: Delle scaloppine al liquore . . . del fegato al burro . . .
Mr McKenzie: Ho già avuto occasione di mangiare il fegato . . .
Mrs McKenzie: (to Julian) Allora prendiamo le scaloppine?
Mr McKenzie: Sì, prendiamole.
Cameriere: Di contorno, con le scaloppine, consiglio insalata rossa.
Mr Pardi: (to the waiter, aside) Porti il conto a me, per favore.

Dialogue 3 In trattoria

Tim and friends enjoy a countryside restaurant.

Lucio: (to the owner) Avete qualcosa di pronto?
Proprietario: Di primo, abbiamo ravioli. Sono fatti in casa. Li ha fatti mia moglie, qualche ora fa.
Lucio: Allora, porti ravioli per quattro.
Proprietario: Di secondo, abbiamo pollo arrosto. I polli sono i nostri. Di contorno, abbiamo zucchine, melanzane . . .
Lucio: Porti quattro polli e quattro porzioni di zucchine.
Cameriere: E da bere? Porto un litro di vino bianco sciolto?

(While they wait, the girls talk about their last holidays.)

Carla: (to Julie) Che tempo hai avuto l'estate scorsa in vacanza?
Julie: Ho avuto sempre un sole splendido. E tu hai avuto bel tempo?
Carla: No, io ho avuto qualche giornata di pioggia.
Lucio: (to the waiter) Porti dell'altro pane, per favore.
Cameriere: Va bene. Porto a te il conto?
Lucio: No, paghiamo alla romana!

HOTEL BARCHETTA

PANE E COPERTO L.1.000
SERVIZIO 15%

ANTIPASTI

Antipasto assortito all'italiana

Prosciutto crudo S. Daniele

Insalata di mare

PRIMI PIATTI

Cannelloni alla Barchetta

Pasticcio di lasagne alla Bolognese

Ravioli alla parmigiana

Spaghetti al pomodoro

Spaghetti alle vongole

Spaghetti al patè d'oliva

PIATTI DEL GIORNO

Pollo novello al forno

Arrosto di vitello

Roast beef all'inglese

Cotoletta alla milanese

Scaloppine ai funghi

Tutti i piatti sono con due contorni

PESCE

Trota salmonata bollita

Filetti di trota dorati

Seppie in umido

FRUTTA E DOLCI

Coppa gelato

Macedonia di frutta

Ananas al maraschino

Frutta di stagione

Formaggi nazionali

VINI

Rosso del Garda

Lugana

minerale

Birra media

Birra grande

Liquori nazionali

Liquori esteri

caffè

Dialogue 4

... the dishes they had on previous occasions.

Tim: Venite spesso in questa trattoria?
Carla: Veniamo qualche volta. La volta scorsa ho ordinato lasagne con i funghi. Le ho gustate moltissimo.
Tim: (to Julie) La mamma di Lucio le ha fatte la settimana scorsa. Buonissime. Le abbiamo mangiate a pranzo e a cena!

Julie: Che vino avete bevuto con le lasagne?
Lucio: Non hai mai assaggiato i nostri vini? Li fa mio papà ogni autunno.
Julie: No, non li ho mai assaggiati. Sono forti o dolci?
Lucio: Sono un po' forti. Sono adatti ai sughi, alla carne . . .
Julie: Sì, hai ragione . . . agli antipasti . . . non ai dolci.
Carla: (to Julie) Ti piace cucinare?
Julie: Sì, soprattutto dolci. Stamattina ho sperimentato una nuova ricetta: la zuppa inglese.
Lucio: Ah, sì! L'ho già mangiata un'altra volta.

15.2 VOCABULARY

Dialogue 1

il primo (m); di –	first course; as –
la specialità (f) (pl. inv.)	speciality
consigliare	to advise
preso (prendere)	taken
gli spaghetti (m pl.)	spaghetti
genovese -e; alla –	of Genoa, from Genoa
il basilico (m)	basil
squisito-a	delicious
aver ragione	to be right
adatto-a	suitable
il tempo (m)	weather
avuto (avere)	had (past participle)
brutto-a	bad (weather); ugly
molti-e	many
la stagione (f)	season

Dialogue 2

scorso-a	last (previous)
la cima (f)	a sort of joint
pesante-e	heavy
il vitello (m)	veal
l'arrosto (m)	roast joint
il ripieno (m)	stuffing
qualche (m and f)	a few
il pranzo (m)	dinner; meal
il secondo (m); di –	second course; as –
la scaloppina (f)	cutlet
il liquore (m); al –	liqueur; alcoholic drink; cooked with –

il fegato (m); – al burro	liver; cooked with butter
l'occasione (f)	occasion; opportunity
il contorno (m); di –	vegetables (at meals); as –
il conto (m)	bill

Dialogue 3

pronto-a	ready
i ravioli (m pl.)	ravioli
il pollo (m); -arrosto	chicken; roast chicken
la zucchina (f)	courgette
la melanzana (f)	aubergine
la porzione (f)	portion
sciolto-a	sold by the glass
l'estate (f)	summer
splendido-a	splendid
bel (bello)	good (weather)
la pioggia (f)	rain
romano-a; alla romana	from Rome; Dutch treat

Dialogue 4

le lasagne (f pl.)	lasagne
gustare	to enjoy something, to taste
la cena (f)	evening meal; supper
assaggiare	to taste
l'autunno (m)	autumn
dolce-e	sweet
la carne (f)	meat
l'antipasto (m)	hors d'oeuvre
cucinare	to cook
soprattutto	above all; most of all
stamattina	this morning
sperimentare	to experiment
la ricetta (f)	recipe
la zuppa inglese (f)	trifle

15.3 EXPLANATIONS

(a) Tips are on no occasion compulsory in Italy. However, there are some conventions. Taxi drivers and porters at railway stations are usually paid the required tariff only. In hotels and restaurants there is a service charge (20% approx.) included in the bill. But porters, bellboys, room-maids, restaurant waiters and hair stylists' assistants ae usually given a tip of 10-15%. Giving tips, you may say 'Per lei' (for you) or 'Tenga pure' (keep the change). La trattoria may be a cheap eating-place or a smart restaurant, both in town or in the countryside.

(b) Saying you did something in the past: (the present perfect; the simple past) – *grammar ref. 66*
To say that something happened in the past, recent or remote, you use the perfect tense (e.g. I have walked) in everyday conversations. The endings of the past participle of regular verbs are the following:

compr – are	ho compr + ato (1st conj.)	I bought
ricev – ere	ho ricev + uto (2nd conj.)	I received
fin – ire	ho fin + ito (3rd conj.)	I finished
*prefer – ire	ho prefer + ito (3rd conj.)	I preferred

Most forms take the verb avere (to have) as auxiliary:

Hai prenotato il tavolo?	Have you booked/did you book the table?
Sì, ho prenotato sei posti.	Yes, I booked six seats.
Signora, ha assaggiato questo vino?	. . . Did you taste this wine?
Signori, avete bevuto bene?	Ladies and gentlemen, did you drink well?

(For the irregular past participles, see the vocabulary lists.)

(c) Expressions referring to the past: (some . . . ago; last)

qualche giorno fa	a few days ago
qualche ora fa	a few hours ago

Notice that qualche is used in front of m and f nouns which are always in the singular.

The word scorso-a (last) with expressions of time usually follows the noun it refers to, agrees with it in gender and number and requires a definite article before the noun:

il mese scorso	last month
la volta scorsa	last time
nei giorni scorsi	in the last days
nelle notti scorse	in the last nights

But with the days of the week there is no article:

lunedì scorso	last Monday

There are other forms for the word 'last' in Italian:

l'ultima volta	last time
l'altra volta	last time

(d) Using object pronouns with the perfect tense – *grammar ref. 69*
The following pronouns are placed, as with the present tense, in front of the verb: mi; ti; lo, la, ci, vi, li, le etc.

Il pullman? Sì, l'ho prenotato ieri.	. . . Yes, I booked it yesterday.

Notice that lo (*it* m) and la (*it* f) are shortened before a vowel or an h.

When there is a direct object before the past participle, the latter becomes m or f, or pl. according to the noun it refers to:

Hai preparato una torta?	Did you prepare a cake?
Sì, l'ho preparata.	Yes, I prepared it.
Hai fatto le lasagne?	Did you make the lasagne?
No, non le ho fatte.	No, I didn't make it.
Avete cucinato gli spaghetti?	Did you cook the spaghetti?
Sí, li abbiamo cucinati.	Yes, we cooked it.

Notice that lasagne and spaghetti are singular only in English – they are plural in Italian.

(e) Quale + noun (which . . .)? – *grammar ref. 76(c)*
You are already familiar with the question qual è? (*4.3(m)*). You also use quale-i to ask 'which . . . ?' 'which . . . one?' 'which ones?'

Quale specialità consiglia?	Which speciality do you advise?
Quali vini preferisce?	Which wines do you prefer?

Or you may use it without a noun:

Mi porti un aperitivo, cameriere.	Waiter, bring me an aperitif.
Quale?	Which one?
Hai preso le mie penne?	Did you take my pens?
Quali? Le biro?	Which ones? The biros?

(f) I nostri, i vostri (our, your, (pl.) ours, etc.) – *grammar ref. 32*
The plural forms of il nostro, il vostro, la nostra, la vostra are i nostri, i vostri, le nostre, le vostre.

Ho le nostre borse ma non le vostre	I have our bags but not yours.

It is important that you remember to combine the definite article with the prepositions a, da, per, in, su, when in front of a possessive adjective.

Hai parlato ai nostri amici?	Di you speak to our friends?
Forse è nelle nostre borse.	Perhaps it's in our bags.

(g) Saying you have already done something: già
You are already familiar with this expression in the present tense:

Ho già un appuntamento.	I already have an appointment.

With the perfect tense, già is placed between the two verbs:

I ravioli? Li ho già assaggiati.	. . . I have already tried them.

Notice the agreement of the past participle (see (d) above).

(h) Saying you have never done something – *grammar ref. 77, 78*
Compare the position of mai (never) with the present tense and with the present perfect:

Il fegato? Grazie, non lo prendo mai.	Liver? I never take it.
Il fegato? Non l'ho mai preso.	Liver? I have never taken it.

(i) Acknowledging someone is right: aver ragione
To acknowledge a statement is true, you say:

Ha ragione	You're right. (formal)
Hai ragione, sì.	You're right. (informal)
È purtroppo vero.	Unfortunately, it's true.

To suggest you do not believe something, you say:

Mi dispiace, non credo.	I'm sorry. I don't think so.

(j) Anche + pronoun (me too) – *grammar ref. 48*

Sei inglese anche tu?	Are you English too?
Sì, sono inglese anch'io.	Yes, I'm English too.
Signora, è inglese anche lei?	Madam, are you English too?

anche noi (we too); anche voi (you too, pl.); anche lui (he too); anche lei (she too); anche loro (they too).

But with expressions such as 'me too', 'you too', etc. you say:

Anche per te un piatto di spaghetti?	For you too a dish of spaghetti?
Anche per lei, signora?	For you too, madam? (formal)
Sì, anche per me.	Yes, for me too.

(k) let's + pronouns
You met this expression (let us . . .) in the last chapter. Any pronoun required is added to the end of the verb:

Li mangiamo?	Shall we eat them?
Mangiamoli!	Let's eat them.
No, non mangiamoli.	Let's not eat them.

(l) Asking what weather people have had – *grammar ref. 66*

Che tempo hai avuto?	What kind of weather did you have? (familiar)
Ho avuto bel tempo.	I had good weather.
Che tempo ha avuto?	What weather did you have? (formal)
Ho avuto brutto tempo.	I had bad weather.

You may also address people with the plural form avete avuto. (It is implied that they had the same weather as a lot of other people.)

Notice that bello, in front of a noun, has an irregular pattern:
Bel tempo; bell'albergo; bello spettacolo; bei bambini etc. – *grammar ref. 41*

Proverbio: L'appetito vien mangiando.
Appetite comes with eating.

15.4 EXERCISES

A

Exercise 1
You have a headache. Kindly refuse these offers.
Example: Non mangia niente?—No, grazie. Ho già mangiato. Un'altra volta.

1. Non assaggia niente?
2. Non beve niente?
3. Non fuma niente?
4. Non ordina niente?
5. Non prende niente?

Exercise 2
Say you have done it before.
Example: Firma queste cartoline. (before) Le ho firmate prima. (Make the changes in the past participles.)

1. Spedisci questa lettera (this morning).
2. Compra quei francobolli (last Monday).
3. Fa quel dolce (a few hours ago).
4. Prepara alcuni panini (last night).
5. Prenota questi posti (a few weeks ago).

Exercise 3
Ask what weather people have had. Use the familiar or formal form according to the indications.
Example: Carla: Questo lunedì?—No, lunedì scorso. Che tempo hai avuto?

1. Signora: Questo mese?
2. Signorina: Quest'anno?
3. Amica: Quest'estate?
4. Direttore: Quest'autunno?
5. Negoziante: Questa settimana?

Exercise 4
Talk about your life in the past.

1. Say you lived in London for three years.
2. Say you started at the International Bank.

3. Say you then worked as a waiter for five months in the countryside.
4. Say you changed (your) job last summer.
5. Say you met your boyfriend some months afterwards.

Exercise 5

You are eating out. Play the customer's role.

Cameriere: Prego?

Cliente: (Say you have already ordered, an hour ago.)

Cameriere: Mi dispiace, può ordinare ancora?

Cliente: (Say you won't take the first course. As a second course, you will take roast chicken, and courgettes. Then you will take some trifle.)

Cameriere: Quale vino ha ordinato?

Cliente: Half a bottle of red wine. (to your friend) Aren't those our friends? (to them) Come here.

Amici: È buona la cucina qui, vero? Prendiamo il pollo.

Cliente: Say they are right. (They order chicken) Say you have had it too. Ask for your bill.

Exercise 6 (revision ch. 5)

You need to change money. Play your role at the bank.

1. Ask how one says 'passport' in Italian.
2. Ask if the bank is open.
3. Ask when it opens.
4. Say you have got it.
5. Ask if you can change the money without a passport.
6. Say you're sorry. You have only a one thousand lira note.

B

Exercise 7

Talk to people about the weather.

Example: Last year/splendid sunshine/on holiday. L'anno scorso ho avuto un sole splendido in vacanza.

1. Last summer/good weather/for only three weeks.
2. Last autumn/a lot of rain/everyday.
3. Last May/not a lot of sunshine/the first week.
4. In the mountains/last week/bad weather/the whole day.
5. Yesterday/here in town/good weather/in the morning/but bad weather/in the afternoon.

Exercise 8
Ask your friend to do as you have done.
Example: (Chiedi di mangiare il pollo arrosto.)—Mangialo anche tu. L'ho mangiato anch'io.

1. Chiedi di provare gli spaghetti al sugo.
2. Chiedi di bere del vino rosso.
3. Chiedi di assaggiare delle zucchine.
4. Chiedi di ordinare dell'altro pane.
5. Chiedi di prendere della carne.

Exercise 9
Say to your friends what you had as presents.
Example: (a pipe) Ho avuto una pipa in regalo tre giorni fa.

1. A cigarette lighter.
2. A large box of chocolates.
3. A leather bag.
4. Some elegant writing paper.
5. Two tickets for the theatre.

Exercise 10
Say when you started, when you finished and how long you worked.
Example: 1 o'clock – 3 o'clock. Abbiamo cominciato alla una, abbiamo finito alle tre. Abbiamo lavorato due ore.

1. 4 o'clock – 7 o'clock
2. midday – 6 o'clock
3. 9 o'clock – 10 o'clock
4. 4.30 – 5 o'clock

REVISION AND SELF-ASSESSMENT TEST FOR CHAPTERS 11-15

A

Exercise 1
Ask for the following services at the hotel. Address people formally.

1. Can you bring me a local newspaper.
2. Can you prepare me two boiled eggs.
3. Can you bring me some more tea.
4. Can you put my bag in the car.
5. Can you prepare my bill (lit. prepare me the bill).

Exercise 2
Supply the questions to fit these answers. Use the formal form.

1. Sì, ho tre figli.
2. No, non ho figlie.
3. La figlia più giovane lavora in banca.
4. No, mio marito non è qui in Italia.
5. Sì, ricevo posta dall'Italia.

Exercise 3
Go to the agency and make these complaints.

1. Say the ticket is rather expensive.
2. Say that the trip is rather short.
3. Say that the coach is not very comfortable.
4. Say you are looking for a less expensive trip.
5. Say that the coach leaves too early.

Exercise 4
Choose the right answer out of each group of three. What would you say if:

1. You want to introduce someone: a) Posso guardare in giro? b) Posso scrivere in stampatello? c) Le posso presentare . . . ?
2. You want a reduction: a) Che cosa significa? b) Come si dice? c) È l'ultimo prezzo?
3. You insist on making an offer: a) Pago io. b) Offro io. c) Anche per lei?
4. You want to know what is on at the cinema: a) Che cosa danno? b) Che spettacolo c'è? c) Che cosa fai?

B

Exercise 5
Play Tim's role in the following dialogue at a prints shop.
Negoziante: Desideri?
Tim: (You are looking for some postcards in colour.)
Negoziante: Ecco qualche cartolina a colori. Va bene?
Tim: (Ask if there are other subjects, with a gondola and the sea.)
Negoziante: Sì, abbiamo queste con il mare e la gondola.
Tim: (Ask if it's really the last price.)
Negoziante: Sì, è proprio l'ultimo prezzo.
Tim: (Say you will take them and ask that he wraps them.)

Exercise 6
Can you match the sentences of group (a) with group (b) to form sensible sequences?

(a)

1. Mi può fare uno sconto?
2. Mi può presentare a quella signorina?
3. Mi può riportare a casa?
4. Mi può telefonare?
5. Mi può comprare quella rivista?

(b)

1. Mi dispiace, ma non conosco quella signorina.
2. No, non posso perchè l'edicola è chiusa.
3. Mi dispiace, ma non ho il suo numero.

4. Mi dispiace, ma abbiamo prezzi fissi.
5. Mi dispiace, ma non ho l'automobile.

Exercise 7

Match the right-hand expressions with the left-hand ones to form sensible statements:

1. Mi piace questo formaggio	perchè è tardi.
2. Studio il tedesco	perchè è molle.
3. McKenzie ha un appuntamento	perchè è nata a Milano.
4. McKenzie noleggia un'auto	ma non è facile.
5. Non è inglese	con la sua collega.

Exercise 8

Find out what people have to do, in Italian. (Use the familiar form)

1. What will you do tonight? Will you go back to Rome?
2. What will you do now? Will you go out for a drink?
3. What will you do in half an hour? Will you ring up your mother?
4. What will you do at the bank? Will you change the money?
5. What will you do? Will you buy it (m)?

Exercise 9

Be adventurous, as in the example:
(noleggiare un'auto)—Non l'abbiamo mai noleggiata. Noleggiamola!

1. Prendere in affitto una camera.
2. Comprare un prodotto dell'artigianato locale.
3. Prenotare due posti per la Scala.
4. Ascoltare questi dischi.
5. Suonare questa musica.

Exercise 10

Give an affirmative reply to these questions.
Example: Sai aprire questa scatola?—Sì, la so aprire.

1. Sai cominciare questa lettera?
2. Sai chiedere un appuntamento?
3. Sai cercare questi indirizzi?
4. Sai prenotare questi posti?
5. Sai parlare italiano?
6. Sai guidare l'automobile?

Exercise 11

Reply according to the indications in brackets.

Example: Quando avete avuto i vostri regali? (ieri) — I nostri? Li abbiamo avuti ieri.

1. Quando avete venduto i vostri libri? (l'anno scorso).
2. Quando avete pagato la vostra camera? (due giorni fa).
3. Quando avete avuto il vostro appuntamento? (un'ora fa).
4. Quando avete preparato i vostri pacchi? (una settimana fa).
5. Quando avete assaggiato i vostri dolci? (un momento fa).

Every exercise done correctly in 20 minutes is worth 10 points.
In 30 minutes, it is worth 5 points.
Above 70 points: lei è bravissimo!
Between 35 and 70: lei è bravo!
Under 35: va così, così.

TALKING OF WHERE YOU HAVE BEEN; DRESSING UP

16.1 DIALOGUES

Dialogue 1 **In un negozio di scarpe**

Sally McKenzie is taken out shopping by Mrs Bini.

Bini: (rings her up) . . . Dovrei fare delle spese. Mi accompagna?
McKenzie: Sì, l'accompagno volentieri.
Bini: Dove la incontro? All'uscita del cinema Odeon? Dovrei comprare delle scarpe, così mi consiglia anche lei.

(They meet on the dot and look at the shop windows)

Bini: Da Galtieri, ho già visto delle scarpe che mi piacciono.
McKenzie: È già entrata a provarle?
Bini: No, sono stata prima da Gerosa. Sono una cliente e qualche volta mi fanno lo sconto. Ma non hanno le scarpe che cerco.
McKenzie: È stata a vedere in un grande magazzino?
Bini: Sì, sono stata circa quindici giorni fa. Ma le scarpe nuove non sono ancora arrivate.
McKenzie: Di che colore le vuole?
Bini: O blu o grigie o marroni.
McKenzie: Dovrei comprare delle scarpe anch'io.

Dialogue 2

They enter

Bini: (to the assistant) Vorrei vedere quelle scarpe blu che sono in vetrina.
Commessa: Quali, signora? Quelle eleganti o quelle sportive?
Bini: Quelle eleganti, con il tacco alto.

Commessa: Che numero porta?
Bini: Il trentasette.

(The assistant brings them)

Bini: Sì, mi vanno bene. Le prendo. Le incarti pure.
McKenzie: Le stanno molto bene.
Bini: Ho già avuto un modello uguale, della stessa marca.
McKenzie: È stata contenta?
Bini: Sì, sono stata molto contenta. Sono durate tanto tempo, quelle scarpe.
Commessa: (to Mrs McKenzie) Signora, non le serve niente?
McKenzie: Sì, un paio di stivali. Ha qualche modello nuovo?
Commessa: Che numero? Trentanove? Proviamoli.
McKenzie: (tries them on) Mi sembrano un po' stretti. Mi porti un altro numero, più grande.

'Quelle eleganti o quelle sportive?'

Dialogue 3 In un grande magazzino
In a department store. Tim and his friends need smart shirts for a party.

Tim: (rings up Julie and Laura) Dovrei andare a comprare una camicia con Lucio. Perchè non ci accompagnate? E ci aiutate?

Julie: Va bene. Dove vi incontriamo? Vi aspettiamo davanti al grande magazzino Dansta.

(They meet and go in.)

Tim: (to an assistant) Scusi, dov'è il reparto di abbigliamento per uomo?

Commesso: Al secondo piano. La scala mobile è di fronte.

Tim: (upstairs) Vorrei vedere una camicia per me.

Commesso: Come la vuoi? Di cotone? Di nylon?

Tim: No. Una più bella. Di lino o di seta pura.

Commessa: Che taglia porti?

Tim: Mi sembra il trentotto, per il collo. Posso provarla? (he tries it on) Come mi sta?

Tim: Mi sembra un po' stretta.

Commesso: No! È la tua taglia. È di moda. Ti sta bene.

Tim: Va bene. La prendo. La incarti, per favore.

Dialogue 4

At home they dress up for the party.

Mamma: (to all of them) Dove siete stati?

Lucio: Siamo stati a comprare una camicia per Tim. Per stasera.

Mamma: Io sono un po' stanca. Mi riposo un momento.

Julie: (looks at the watch) Siamo andati e ritornati in un'ora.

Mamma: Faccio una doccia, così mi rilasso un po'. E tu, Julie?

Julie: Mi riposo qui in poltrona e poi mi cambio. E lei, signora, che cosa si mette stasera?

Mamma: Mi metto un vestito lilla a quadretti. E Tim, che cosa si mette?

Julie: Si mette un vestito scuro.

Mamma: Non è un po' fuori moda? Adesso, qui in Italia è di moda la giacca bianca.

Julie: Sì, ho visto. Ma Tim non ce l'ha.

(Lucio enters)

Lucio: Vado a cambiarmi e a farmi la barba. E voi non andate a farvi belle?

Mamma: Sì, adesso vado a vestirmi e a truccarmi. Tra mezz'ora sono pronta.

16.2 VOCABULARY

Dialogue 1

la scarpa (f)	shoe
dovrei (dovere)	I should; I ought to
la spesa (f); fare le spese	shopping; to go –
accompagnare	to go with (to accompany)
la	you (formal)
l'uscita (f)	exit
visto (vedere)	seen
entrare	to enter; to go in
il/la cliente (m and f)	customer
stato-a (essere)	been
il grande magazzino (m)	department store
marrone-e	brown

Dialogue 2

sportivo-a	casual
il tacco (m) (pl. -chi)	heel
portare	to wear
andare bene	to fit
stare bene (irreg.)	to suit
il modello (m)	model
uguale-e	identical; equal
lo stesso (m) la stessa (f)	the same
contento-a	pleased
servire; che cosa le serve?	to serve; can I help you?
il paio (m) (pl. paia) (f)	pair (pairs)
lo stivale (m)	boot
provare	to try on
sembrare	to seem; to look
stretto-a	narrow, tight

Dialogue 3

la camicia (f)	shirt
aiutare	to help
davanti a	opposite
il reparto (m)	department
l'abbigliamento (m)	clothes
la scala mobile (f)	escalator
il lino (m)	linen
la seta (f)	silk
la taglia (f)	size

il collo (m)	neck
di moda	fashionable

Dialogue 4

stanco-a (pl. -chi; -che)	tired
riposarsi	to rest
la doccia (f); fare la –	shower; to take a –
rilassarsi	to relax
la poltrona (f)	armchair
cambiarsi	to change dress
mettersi	to put on (a dress)
il vestito (m)	dress; suit
lilla (pl. inv.)	lilac
il quadretto (m); a quadretti	small check; with small checks
scuro-a	dark
fuori moda	out of fashion
la barba (f); farsi la –	beard; to shave
farsi bello-a	to make oneself pretty
vestirsi	to get dressed
truccarsi	to make up

16.3 EXPLANATIONS

(a) Background information

Clothes	England	10	12	14	16	18
sizes	Italy	36	38	40	42	44
Ladies'	England	3½	4	5	6	6½
shoes	Italy	36	37	38	39	40
Men's	England	8	9	10	11	
shoes	Italy	42	43	44	45½	
Collar	England	14½	15	15½	16	17
size	Italy	37	38	39	41	43

(b) Saying you should do something: dovrei

To say you should do something (I should, I ought to), you use the verb dovere (irr.) in the conditional tense + the infinitive:

Dovrei fare delle spese.	I should do some shopping.
Dovrei comprare una camicia.	I ought to buy a shirt.
Che cosa devi fare oggi?	What do you have to do today?
Dovrei studiare italiano.	I should learn Italian.

(c) Inviting people: la, ti (pronouns) – *grammar ref. 49*
When you are talking to a person and refer to him or her with a pronoun following the verb (I meet you), you use la (formal) or ti (familiar):

Carla, ti accompagno.	Carla, I'll go with you.
Signor Rossi, la incontro qui.	Mr Rossi, I'll meet you here.
Signora Rossi, la incontro qui.	Mrs Rossi, I'll meet you here.

Notice that these pronouns precede the verb. Remember that la (object pronoun) also means 'it' (f sing.) and 'her' (12.3(e)).

Quella borsa? La prendo.	That bag? I take it.
Quella signora? La incontro ogni giorno.	That woman? I meet her every day.

(d) Other pronouns referring to people – *grammar ref. 49*
If you are talking to more than one person, use vi:

Signori, vi incontro là.	Gentlemen, I meet you there.

The answers may be:

Va bene, mi trova là.	Fine, you'll find me there.
Va bene, ci troviamo là.	Fine, we'll find each other (us) there.

Referring to people, the direct object pronouns are:

Lo vedo, stasera.	I'll see him tonight.
La vedo dopo.	I'll see her afterwards.
Li incontro a casa.	I'll meet them (m) at home.
Le incontro a casa.	I'll meet them (f) at home.

(e) Che (relative pronoun: which, that, who) – *grammar ref. 55*
Che is used to refer both to people and things, either masc. or fem., plural or sing.:

Le scarpe che sono in vetrina.	The shoes which are in the window.
Il manifesto che ho visto.	The poster which I saw.
La ragazza che ti ho presentata.	The girl that I have introduced to you.

In Italian the relative pronoun is used even when in English it may be omitted:

Gli stivali che ho provati.	The boots I tried on.

The past participle following che may agree with the preceding direct object:

La ragazza che ti ho presentata.	The girl I have introduced to you.

(f) Saying you've gone, arrived etc.: the past tense with essere – *grammar ref. 66–8*

To describe actions in the past, with some verbs you need the verb essere as auxiliary. Some of these verbs are: andare, venire, entrare, partire, restare, arrivare, uscire:

Lucio, sei entrato in quel negozio?	Lucio, did you go into that shop? Have you entered that shop?

With verbs which take essere, the past participle agrees with the subject:

Dove sei andata, Carla?	Where did you go Carla?
Dove siete andati, ragazzi?	Where did you go, boys?
Le scarpe non sono arrivate.	The shoes haven't arrived.
Le scarpe sono durate.	The shoes have lasted.

(g) Saying where you have been: the past tense with essere – *grammar ref. 67, 68*

To say you have been in or to a place, you say sono stato-a (lit. I am been). Unlike English, to form the past of essere, you also use essere as an auxiliary. The past participle stato (been) agrees with the subject:

Professore, è stato a Londra?	. . . have you been to London?
No, non sono mai stato.	No, I have never been.
Ragazze, siete state a Firenze?	Girls, have you been to Florence?
Ragazzi, siete stati in banca?	Boys, have you been to the bank?
No, non siamo ancora stati.	No, we haven't yet been.

(h) Saying you went to do something: sono stato a + infinitive

Talking of the present, you say:

Vado a telefonare.	I'm going to phone.

Talking of the past, you may use the verb essere or the verb andare:

Sono andato a vedere quella vetrina.	I went to see that shop window.
Sono stato a comprare del pane.	I have been to buy some bread.

(i) Pronouns after the infinitive – *grammar ref. 51*

When you use any pronoun after an infinitive, you remove the last vowel of the infinitive and add the pronoun to it: provare + lo = provarlo

Quelle scarpe? Sono entrata a provarle.	Those shoes? I went in to try them on.
Quel manifesto? Sono stata a comprarlo.	That poster? I have been to buy it.

(j) Le, ti (to you) – *grammar ref. 49*

In previous dialogues (12.3(e)) you have seen that le refers to f pl. nouns (people or things). Prendo quelle scarpe? Sì, le prendo – yes, I take them.

Le is also used when you talk to a person and refer to him or her. Il cinema le piace? – Do you like films? (lit. does the cinema appeal to you?) Here are some more examples taken from the dialogues:

Le scarpe le vanno bene?	Do the shoes fit you? (lit. do the shoes go well to you?)
Le stanno bene.	They suit you. (Lit. they stay well to you)
Le serve qualcosa?	Do you need anything? (lit. does anything serve to you?)

If you address people familiarly, you use ti:

Ti stanno bene.	They suit you.
Ti vanno bene?	Do they fit you?
Ti serve una penna?	Do you need a pen?

(k) Expressing an opinion tentatively: mi sembra (I think)

Le scarpe sono strette, mi sembra.	The shoes are narrow, I think. (lit. it seems to me).

You may put this expression at the end of your sentence, as in the example above. Or you may say:

La giacca mi sembra stretta.	The jacket seems tight to me.

In this position, you use mi sembrano if the object is plural:

Le scarpe mi sembrano strette.	The shoes look narrow to me.

(l) Reflexive verbs – *grammar ref. 54*

There are verbs which always require a reflexive pronoun in front of them. The infinitive forms of these verbs (the forms which are listed in dictionaries) are the following:

cambi – ARSI (1st conj.); mett – ERSI (2nd conj.); vest – IRSI (3rd conj.). Addressing a question, you say:

Ti riposi subito? (familiar)	Are you going to rest (yourself) immediately?
Si riposa? (formal)	Are you resting (lit. yourself)?
Vi riposate? (plural)	Are you resting (yourselves)? / Are you going to rest?

To reply, you say:

Sì, mi riposo subito.	Yes, I'll rest (lit. myself) immediately.
No, non ci riposiamo subito.	No, we shan't rest immediately (lit. ourselves)

To refer to other people, you say:

Carla si cambia?	Is Carla changing? (lit. Is Carla changing herself?)
Carla e Lucio si cambiano?	Carla and Lucio, are they changing? (lit. Are they changing themselves?)

(m) Words

Entrare is always followed by in: Entriamo nel grande magazzino? Do we enter the department store?

16.4 EXERCISES

A

Exercise 1
Say you ought to do it too, as in the example:
Dovrei fare delle spese. – Dovrei farle anch'io.

1. Dovrei vedere quel film!
2. Dovrei provare quella camicia.
3. Dovrei fare un regalo.
4. Dovrei prendere un taxi.
5. Dovrei cambiare un assegno.

Exercise 2
These are Lucio's mother's questions to her son. Fill in the blanks. Use the verbs essere or avere, as necessary:

— Perchè . . . ritornato senza rivista?
— Ma, Lucio, . . . stato dal giornalaio?
— . . . comprato quella rivista che ti . . . chiesta (asked)?
— Non l' . . . trovata?
— Perchè non . . . andato all'edicola?
— . . . venduto tutte le riviste?
— . . . comprato un altro giornale?

Exercise 3
Tim meets a friend at the coach station. Play the friend's role.

Tim: Ciao! Non ti vedo da molto! Dove sei stato?
Amico: (He says he has been to the university of Turin.)
Tim: E Giulia, la tua amica?
Amico: (He says that his friend has been on holiday in France.)
Tim: È andata da sola?
Amico: (He says she left with a few friends.)
Tim: Quando ritorna?
Amico: (He says she has already come back.)

Exercise 4
You feel undecided, like Hamlet. Say you don't know what to do, as in the example:
Ti vesti? – Ma! Mi vesto o non mi vesto?

1. Ti trucchi?
2. Ti riposi?
3. Ti rilassi un po'?
4. Ti fai la barba?
5. Ti metti il vestito rosso?

Exercise 5
Say how things are according to you. You have to supply the opposite of the adjective suggested.
Example: È larga questa camicia? – No, mi sembra un po' stretta.

1. È scura questa borsa?
2. Sono sportivi questi stivali?
3. Sono a buon prezzo queste giacche?
4. È piccola questa camicia?
5. È corto questo vestito?
6. È chiaro questo tappeto?

Exercise 6 (revision ch. 6)
Play McKenzie's role in the bookshop.

Libraio: Prego?
McKenzie: (Say you would like an Italian-English dictionary.)
Libraio: Un'edizione tascabile o un vocabolario più grande?
McKenzie: (Say you would like a good edition, but not very expensive.)
Libraio: I vocabolari sono su questo scaffale.
McKenzie: (Say you would also like to see some books in Italian but easy . . . short stories or a short novel.)

B

Exercise 7
What your friend has to do, you did yesterday.
Example: Dovrei fare delle spese. – Io le ho fatte ieri.

1. Dovrei fare dei ravioli.
2. Dovrei fare delle lasagne.
3. Dovrei fare una telefonata a Londra.
4. Dovrei fare del pollo arrosto.
5. Dovrei fare dei frullati.

Exercise 8
Decline the offers that people make to you, as in the example: Devo spedire quella lettera per te? No, grazie, l'ho spedita ieri. Use essere or avere as an auxiliary, as required.

1. Devo andare in banca per te?
2. Devo comprare dei francobolli per te?
3. Devo guardare una camicia per te ai grandi magazzini?
4. Devo ritornare all'Ente Turismo per te?
5. Devo andare in libreria per te?
6. Devo prendere un giornale inglese, per te?

Exercise 9
Play Mr McKenzie's role when he meets some Italian acquaintances.

Amici: Come va?
McKenzie: (Say very well, thank you. Ask about them. Ask what they are doing there.)
Amici: Siamo appena ritornati dalla Sicilia.
McKenzie: (Ask when they left.)
Amici: Siamo partiti quindici giorni fa.
McKenzie: (Ask whether they went by car.)
Amici: Sì, siamo andati in auto.
McKenzie: (Ask whether their son went (use venire) with them.)
Amici: Sì, nostro figlio è venuto con noi.
McKenzie: (Ask whether their daughter too went with them.)
Amici: No, nostra figlia è restata a casa.

Exercise 10
You are late. Reply you will do everything immediately.
Example: Ti cambi? – Mi cambio subito!

1. Ti vesti?
2. Ti fai la barba?
3. Ti metti la giacca?
4. Ti trucchi?
5. Ti vesti?

Exercise 11
Put these questions to your friends (they are girls).

1. Have you never been to England?
2. When have you been to London?

3. Did your friend come with you?
4. When did you come back?
5. Did you stay long in England?

DESCRIBING WHAT YOU USED TO DO; TALKING OF A MISADVENTURE

17.1 DIALOGUES

Dialogue 1

Mrs McKenzie tells Mrs Bini what she used to do at the seaside last year.

Bini: Ha voglia di un caffè? Fermiamoci a prenderlo.
McKenzie: Sì, sediamoci qui fuori e guardiamo la gente che passa.

(They sit and talk)

Bini: Come si è trovata l'anno scorso al mare in Liguria?
McKenzie: Molto bene. Era sempre sereno e il mare era sempre calmo.
Bini: La spiaggia era molto affollata?
McKenzie: No, non era molto affollata. Gli alberghi non erano esauriti.
Bini: C'era gente simpatica in albergo?
McKenzie: Sì. Facevamo delle gite in compagnia tutti i giorni.
Bini: Faceva il bagno tutti i giorni?
McKenzie: Sì, ogni mattina alle otto, prima della colazione. Prendevo il sole tutta la mattina e passavo il pomeriggio in gita.
Bini: Aveva la spiaggia privata?
McKenzie: Sì, avevo la spiaggia privata.

Dialogue 2

Mrs McKenzie tells her of her misadventure.

McKenzie: Ah, ora le racconto la mia disavventura!
Bini: Niente di grave, spero.

McKenzie: Una mattina, non mi sono sentita bene. Avevo mal di testa e avevo una leggera febbre.

Bini: Ha chiamato il dottore?

McKenzie: No, sono andata in farmacia. Il farmacista mi ha domandato:

Farmacista: 'Che cosa si sente? Ha mal di testa? Ha febbre? È molto rossa. Ha preso molto sole?'

Bini: Un colpo di sole?!?

McKenzie: Sì, proprio. Ho preso un colpo di sole!

Bini: Ma come ha fatto?

McKenzie: Un pomeriggio sono andata fuori in motoscafo, senza cappello, senza niente . . . e ho preso il sole in testa per tutto il pomeriggio . . .

Bini: Vicino all'acqua, il sole non sembra caldo, vero?

McKenzie: Eh, sì. Ha ragione.

Bini: E adesso come sta?

McKenzie: Adesso, sto bene, grazie.

'Faceva il bagno tutti i giorni?'

Dialogue 3

Tim and friends are at a party. He talks of what he used to do at the camping-site last year.

Amico: Tim, siediti un momento. Come ti sei trovato l'anno scorso in campeggio al mare?

Tim: Mi sono divertito molto! Era sereno tutti i giorni e il mare era sempre calmo.
Amico: Il campeggio era molto affollato? C'era molta gente?
Tim: No, il campeggio era quasi vuoto. Era bassa stagione.
Amico: Era attrezzato bene? Aveva tutte le comodità?
Tim: Sì, avevo tutte le comodità . . . docce, servizi. Era pulito.
Amico: Avevi degli amici con te o eri solo?
Tim: Eravamo in quattro. Tutti inglesi.
Amico: Dove mangiavate?
Tim: Cucinavamo a turno. Ogni giorno compravamo mezzo chilo di pane, chili di frutta, etti di salame . . . uova . . .
Amico: C'era la spiaggia vicino al campeggio?
Tim: Sì, c'era una spiaggia bella, pulita e il mare era calmissimo . . .

Dialogue 4

Tim now tells him of his misadventure with his motor bike.

Tim: Ah, ti racconto la mia disavventura con la moto.
Amico: Non ti sei fatto male, spero.
Tim: No. Il dieci maggio, un lunedì, mi sono fermato a un distributore. Ho fatto il pieno di benzina. Ho controllato freni, acqua e olio. Poi sono ripartito a tutto gas.
Amico: E hai rotto la moto!
Tim: No! Ho rotto il portafoglio!! Dietro una casa la polizia è uscita all'improvviso!
Polizia: Documenti, prego. Sei in contravvenzione per eccesso di velocità.
Amico: Non sapevi che nei paesi la velocità è di cinquanta chilometri?
Tim: Non lo sapevo, ora lo so.

17.2 VOCABULARY

Dialogue 1

fermarsi	to stop (oneself)
sedersi	to sit
la gente (f sing.)	people
passare	to pass; to spend
trovarsi; -bene	to be; to be well
era (essere)	it was
sereno-a	cloudless, clear

calmo-a	calm
la spiaggia (f) (pl. -ge)	beach
affollato-a	crowded
simpatico-a (pl. -i, -che)	friendly
facevamo (fare)	we used to do; we used to make
faceva (fare) (formal)	you used to do
la compagnia (f); in –	company; together with
il bagno (m); fare il –	to swim; to take a swim
prendere il sole	to sunbathe
privato-a	private

Dialogue 2

raccontare	to tell (a story)
la disavventura (f)	misadventure
grave-e	serious
sperare	to hope
sentirsi	to feel
il mal di testa (m)	headache
la febbre (f)	temperature, fever
chiamare	to call
la farmacia (f)	chemist shop
il/la farmacista (m)	chemist
domandare	to ask
il colpo (m); – di sole	a stroke; a sun stroke
il motoscafo (m)	motorboat
il cappello (m)	hat
la testa (f)	head
caldo-a	hot; warm
stare bene	to be all right, to feel well

Dialogue 3

il campeggio (m); in –	camping site; camping
divertirsi	to enjoy oneself
vuoto-a	empty
attrezzato-a	equipped
la comodità (f) (pl. inv.)	comfort
la doccia (f)	shower
il servizio (m)	convenience, service
pulito-a	clean
eri (essere)	you were (familiar)
eravamo (essere)	we were
cucinare	to cook
il turno (m); a –	turn; in turn

il chilo (m)	kilo
l'etto (m)	hectogram; 3 oz. approx.

Dialogue 4

la moto (f) (pl. invar.)	motor bike
farsi male	to hurt oneself
il distributore (m)	petrol station
la benzina (f); fare –	petrol; to get some petrol
pieno-a; il pieno (m); fare il –	full; fullness; to fill up
controllare	to check
il freno (m)	brake
l'olio (m)	oil
il gas (m); a tutto –	gas; at great speed
rotto-a (rompere)	broken
la polizia (f)	police
uscire	to go out, to get out
all'improvviso	suddenly
il documento (m)	document
la contravvenzione (f)	fine
la velocità (f)	speed

17.3 EXPLANATIONS

(a) Background information

In case of emergency, ask for first aid: IL PRONTO SOCCORSO. If you need a doctor, say ho bisogno di un dottore.

Remember that there is a convention among the EEC countries for free medical treatment. Ask your local Department of Health and Social Security for the form E 111 well before you leave.

(b) Requests with reflexive verbs – *grammar ref. 54*

When you ask people to do something, using the imperative form (*13.3(b); (7.3(b)*), if you use a reflexive verb, you usually add the reflexive pronoun to the *end* of the verb:

fermiamo + ci	siedi + ti

Signora, fermiamoci.	Mrs. . . . let's stop.
Sediamoci un momento.	Let's sit for a moment.
Tim, siediti.	Tim, sit down.

But, with the formal form (*12.3(d)*) the pronoun goes in front of the verb:

Si sieda (irreg.), signora.	Take a seat, madam.

(c) Saying what you did in the past, with a reflexive verb – *grammar ref. 67*

Carla, ti sei fermata in banca?	Carla, did you stop at the bank?

As you see, reflexive verbs require the auxiliary **essere** in the present perfect. The reflexive pronoun precedes both parts of the verb and the past participle agrees with the subject. Here are more examples:

Signora, come si è trovata in Italia?	Madam, how did you get on in Italy? (formal)
Tim, ti sei trovato bene?	Tim, did you get on well? (familiar)
Vi siete divertiti?	Did you enjoy yourselves? (pl.)

The answers may be:

Sì, mi sono divertito.	Yes, I enjoyed myself.
No, non ci siamo divertiti.	No, we did not enjoy ourselves.

Referring to other people:

La signora si è cambiata?	Did the lady change (her dress)?
Le signore si sono cambiate?	Did the ladies change (their dresses)?

(d) Saying what the weather was like: essere – the imperfect – *grammar ref. 71*

Era sereno.	It was cloudless.
Il mare era calmo.	The sea was calm.
C'era molto sole.	There was a lot of sun.
Non c'erano nuvole.	There were no clouds.

Era, erano are forms of the past tense of the verb **essere**. This tense is called the imperfect. You use it to describe what the weather was like:

Era freddo o era caldo?	Was it hot or cold?

(e) Describing what something was like: the imperfect – *grammar ref. 71*

You also use the imperfect of essere to describe states or conditions in the past:

Com'era la spiaggia?	What was the beach like?
La spiaggia era affollata.	The beach was crowded.
Gli alberghi erano esauriti.	The hotels were all booked.
C'era solo un campeggio vuoto.	There was only one camping-site vacant.

(f) Describing your routine in the past: the imperfect, 1st, 2nd, 3rd conj. – *grammar ref. 71*

To describe what you used to do in the past, what your habits were, you use the imperfect:

In Italia mangiavo tutti i giorni gli spaghetti.	In Italy I used to eat spaghetti every day.

Note, however, that single actions in the past are conveyed in the perfect tense:

Ma un giorno o due ho mangiato ravioli.	But on one or two days I ate ravioli.

Compare the description of a routine in the past in dialogues 1 and 3 with the description of *one* event in the past in dialogues 2 and 4.

Here are some examples to show you the pattern of the imperfect: 1st conj. (andare)

Dove andavi ogni giorno?	Where did you go every day? (familiar)
Dove andava ogni giorno?	Where did you go every day? (formal)
Andavo sempre alla spiaggia.	I went every day to the beach.

2nd conj. (prendere)

Prendevi il sole tutto il giorno? (familiar)	Did you sunbathe the whole day?
Prendeva il sole? (formal)	Did you sunbathe?
Prendevo il sole di mattina.	I sunbathed in the morning.

3rd conj. (uscire)

Uscivi ogni sera? (familiar)	Did you go out every evening?
Usciva ogni sera? (formal)	Did you go out every evening?
Uscivo ogni sera.	I went out every evening.

For the plural forms, see *grammar ref. 71.*

(g) Fare: the imperfect – *grammar ref. 72*
The imperfect of fare is formed with the stem fac-, fac + evo, etc.:

Facevi molti bagni?	Did you swim a lot? (familiar)
Che cosa faceva di solito?	What did you usually do? (formal)
Facevo il bagno ogni giorno.	I took a swim every day.

But, one day:

Non *ho fatto* il bagno.	I did not have a swim.

(h) Informing people (pronouns: to you) – *grammar ref. 49*
Some verbs which tell or inform people require the pronoun equivalent to 'to you' (le or ti). In English, 'to' is often omitted.

Le consiglio.	I advise you. (formal)
Le dico.	I tell you. (formal)
Le telefono.	I ring you up. (formal)
Ti scrivo.	I write to you. (familiar)
Ti parlo.	I talk to you. (familiar)

If you refer to someone else, you say:

Gli scrivo.	I write to him.
Le scrivo.	I write to her.

(i) Talking of your health
The key question is: come sta? – (formal) Come stai? (familiar). Here are the most frequent replies if you are not well:

Non sto bene.	I'm not feeling well, I'm not well.
Mi sento male.	I feel sick.
Non mi sento bene.	I don't feel well.
Mi sono fatto male al piede.	(I've hurt myself + the part of the body) I've hurt my foot

Other common expressions need the verb to have, as in English:

Ho mal di testa.	I have headache.
Ho una febbre leggera.	I have a slight temperature.
Ho mal di denti.	I have toothache.

(j) Saying you didn't feel well in the past: imperfect
To describe the general state of your health in the past, you use the imperfect:

Non mi sentivo bene quella mattina.	I didn't feel well that morning.
Avevo mal di testa.	I had a headache.

(k) Prima di (before)
The word prima (before) requires di after it, if followed by a noun, a pronoun or a verb:

prima della colazione	before breakfast
prima di me	before me
prima di andare	before going

(l) Niente di + adj.
You are already familiar with qualcosa di bello (something beautiful). Similarly, niente (nothing) requires di after it, if followed by an adjective:

Niente di grave, spero.	Nothing serious, I hope.
Non c'era niente di divertente.	There was nothing pleasant.

(m) Words
La gente è simpatica – people are friendly. Unlike English la gente is a singular feminine noun, requires sing. verbs and a singular feminine adjective.

17.4 EXERCISES

A

Exercise 1
Play Mrs McKenzie's role at the doctor's.

Dottore: Buongiorno. Che cosa si sente, signora?
McKenzie: (Say you don't feel well. You have a headache.)
Dottore: Ha febbre?
McKenzie: (Say you have a low temperature, you think.)
Dottore: Ha mangiato molto a pranzo?
McKenzie: (Say you have eaten a light dinner.)
Dottore: È stata sulla spiaggia questa mattina?
McKenzie: (Say you have been on the beach the whole morning.)
Dottore: Ha preso il sole tutta la mattina?
McKenzie: (Say, yes, you sunbathed for four hours.)
Dottore: Ha preso troppo sole. Adesso deve riposarsi.

Exercise 2
Play Tim's role at a petrol station.

Tim: (Say good morning. Ask to fill up the motor bike.)
Benzinaio: Ecco. Tutto bene i freni? L'olio?
Tim: (Ask to check the brakes and the oil.)
Benzinaio: Tutto a posto.
Tim: (Ask if he has checked also the water, please.)
Benzinaio: Sì, ho controllato anche l'acqua.
Tim: (Ask how much it is.)
Benzinaio: Cinquemila lire in tutto.
Tim: (Say thank you and goodbye.)

Exercise 3
Answer the following questions relating to dialogue 1.

1. Come si è trovata la signora McKenzie l'anno scorso al mare?
2. Com'era il cielo? E com'era il mare?
3. La spiaggia era affollata? E gli alberghi erano tutti esauriti?
4. Com'era la gente in albergo?
5. Che cosa faceva la signora McKenzie tutti i giorni?
6. A che ora faceva il bagno?
7. Aveva la spiaggia privata?

Exercise 4
Tell your friends about your holidays, in Italian.

Every day I stopped at the coffee bar where I took a chocolate-flavoured ice-cream. Then I went to the beach, sunbathed for the whole day. In the afternoon, I took a swim. Then I went back to the hotel. And every evening, after dinner, I went out with friends to dance at a disco. Yes, people were very friendly. And the weather was beautiful.

Exercise 5
Reply you will do it. Use the formal or familiar form as in the examples:
a) Quando mi insegni? (to a friend) Ti insegno subito.
b) Quando mi racconti? (to your boss) Le racconto subito.

1. Quando mi telefoni? (to your friend).
2. Quando mi scrivi? (to your boss).
3. Quando mi dici sì? (to your girlfriend).
4. Quando mi mostri il catalogo? (to your boss).

Exercise 6 (revision ch. 7)
Tell people what you and your friend like to eat and drink:

1. At breakfast we usually drink tea with milk, without sugar.
2. Yes, we prefer an English breakfast.
3. No, we don't understand Italian a lot.
4. At breakfast we usually eat two slices of toasted bread, some jam and butter and honey.
5. Are the crisps good?
6. We feel like having a glass of draught beer.
7. Are the bottles large? Are they expensive?

B

Exercise 7
Say you did it not just once, but every day.
Example: Hai fatto un bagno solo? – No, lo facevo tutti i giorni.

1. Hai preso il sole un giorno solo?
2. Hai fatto il bagno un giorno solo?
3. Sei andata a ballare una volta sola?

4. Sei uscita con il tuo ragazzo una volta sola?
5. Sei entrata in quel ristorante una volta sola?

Exercise 8

Reproduce the conversation of Mrs Bini and Mrs McKenzie, in Italian:

We stopped to drink a coffee. We sat outside and looked at the people. Mrs McKenzie told me that (mi ha detto che) she was fine last year at the seaside in Liguria. The sky was blue and the sea was calm. Every day she took a trip somewhere together with other people. Those people were very friendly. But one day she had a misadventure. Nothing serious. One morning she had a headache and she had a temperature. She went to a chemist's shop. The chemist asked her how she felt, if she had a temperature: 'One afternoon, I went out in a motorboat, without a hat, without anything . . . ' And the chemist told me: 'Madam, you must rest for a day or two, you have had (ha preso) a sun stroke.'

Exercise 9

Play Lucio's role in telling Tim's misadventure:

Mamma: (to Lucio) Come si è trovato, Tim, l'anno scorso?
Lucio: (Camping? He enjoyed himself very much.)
Mamma: Com'era il campeggio?
Lucio: (The camping site was well equipped with all comforts and conveniences.)
Mamma: Era pulito?
Lucio: (It was very clean.)
Mamma: Dove mangiavano ogni giorno?
Lucio: (Every day they cooked in turn. They bought half a kilo of bread, half a pound of salame, eggs . . .)
Mamma: Tutti i giorni?
Lucio: (Except one day. On a Monday (un lunedì) they went to a local trattoria near the beach. They ate roast veal, tomatoes, aubergines . . .)
Mamma: Non hanno ordinato il primo?
Lucio: (No, they all had hors d'oeuvre.)

Exercise 10

Give the right direction and the right time as in the examples:
a) È dopo la stazione? – No, è prima della stazione.
b) Vieni dopo le tre? – No, vengo prima delle tre.

1. È dopo l'albergo Firenze?
2. Vieni dopo le due?
3. È dopo l'edicola?
4. È dopo la cartoleria?
5. Vieni dopo Carla?

TALKING OF THE PAST; TALKING OF WHAT YOU WERE DOING ONE DAY

18.1 DIALOGUES

Dialogue 1 I passatempi

Mr McKenzie is invited to play tennis. But . . .

McKenzie: Sa giocare a cricket?

Rossi: No. Non so giocare a cricket. Perchè non giochiamo a tennis? C'è un campo qui vicino.

McKenzie: Eh! Una volta giocavo a tennis, quando avevo vent'anni!

Rossi: Via! È ancora giovane e in forma. Andiamo!

McKenzie: Allora giocavo non solo a tennis, ma anche a rugby. Oggi gioco a cricket; qualche volta, di rado, gioco a golf.

Rossi: Quali erano i suoi passatempi preferiti?

McKenzie: Ma, io non facevo molti sport da ragazzo. Mia moglie sì. Nuotava tutti i giorni, senza nessun maestro.

Rossi: Non aveva altri passatempi?

McKenzie: Da bambino facevo collezione di francobolli.

Rossi: Ne aveva molti?

McKenzie: Sì. Mi ricordo che li avevo nella mia camera e li guardavo ogni sera.

Rossi: E non li ha più?

McKenzie: No, non ho più nessun album.

Dialogue 2 Dai vigili urbani

Mrs McKenzie has lost her wallet and goes to the police.

McKenzie: Buongiorno. Sono una turista straniera. Ho bisogno del suo aiuto. Ho perso il portafoglio.

Vigile: Dove lo teneva? Non lo teneva nella borsa?

'Facevo collezione di fotografie'

McKenzie: Non mi ricordo. Forse era nella borsa o nelle tasche.
Vigile: Quando si è accorta che non l'aveva più?
McKenzie: Mi sono accorta mezz'ora fa.
Vigile: Dov'era? Che cosa faceva?
McKenzie: Ero seduta ai giardini pubblici e chiacchieravo con un mio conoscente. Guardavamo gli altri turisti che passavano.
Vigile: Di che colore era il portafoglio?
McKenzie: Era marrone. Era grande così (she makes a gesture).
Vigile: Che cosa aveva dentro nel portafoglio?
McKenzie: Non mi ricordo più bene. Circa trentamila lire e una mia vecchia foto.
Vigile: E i suoi documenti? Dove li teneva?
McKenzie: (she smiles) Li portavo addosso.

Dialogue 3 Gli animali

Tim and his friends talk about their pets.

Carla: Hai degli animali a casa in Inghilterra?
Tim: Vuoi dire dei . . . "pets"? Come si dice "pets" in italiano?
Lucio: Non c'è nessuna parola in italiano per "pets". Si dice animali.

Tim: (laughing) No, non ho nessun animale, nè tigri nè leoni. Ma da bambini, io e mio fratello avevamo due cani: due labrador.
Carla: Vi piacevano di più i cani o i gatti?
Tim: I cani. A te piacevano di più i gatti?
Carla: Avevo due gatti, fino a due anni fa. Erano neri. Erano bellissimi e affettuosi.
Tim: Mi ricordo che i nostri cani ci accompagnavano a scuola.
Carla: Come si chiamavano i tuoi cani?
Tim: Si chiamavano Black e White. Avevano il pelo lucido.
Carla: I nostri gatti avevano gli occhi verdi.
Tim: Erano un maschio e una femmina?
Carla: Sì, erano un maschio e una femmina.

Dialogue 4 In lavanderia

Tim takes a pair of trousers to the dry cleaner's.

Tim: Buongiorno. Volevo far pulire questi calzoni.
Proprietaria: (perplexed) Che macchia è? È unto?
Tim: Non lo so. Ho visto la macchia mentre mangiaro.
Proprietaria: Che cosa mangiavi?
Tim: Mangiavo degli spaghetti al sugo e bevevo del vino.
Proprietaria: Non è nè una macchia di sugo nè di vino.
Tim: Forse, mentre scendevo dal tram . . . o mentre aggiustavo la moto.
Proprietaria: È come gomma . . .
Tim: Ah! Sì . . . forse mentre misuravo la pressione delle gomme.
Proprietaria: Sono pronti per domani. Va bene?
Tim: Veramente, avevo premura. Ne avevo bisogno stasera.
Proprietaria: Va bene. Ritorna tra due ore e sono pronti.
Tim: Grazie. Buongiorno.
Proprietaria: Ciao.

18.2 VOCABULARY

Dialogue 1

giocare	to play
il cricket (m); giocare a –	cricket; to play –
il tennis (m)	tennis
il campo (m)	ground; field
una volta	once upon a time; once
la forma (f); in –	shape; fit, on form.
il rugby (m)	rugby
di rado	rarely

il golf (m)	golf
i suoi (m pl.); le sue (f pl.)	his, her; hers; your (formal); yours (formal)
il passatempo (m)	pastime; hobby
nuotare	to swim
nessun-a	no . . .
il maestro (m); la maestra (f)	teacher; coach
la collezione (f)	collection
ricordarsi	to remember
che	that
non . . . più	no . . . longer
l'album (m) (pl. invar.)	album

Dialogue 2

il/la turista (m and f)	tourist
l'aiuto (m)	help
perso (perdere)	lost (to lose)
tenere (irreg.)	to keep
accorto (accorgersi)	realized
seduto-a	sitting, seated
il giardino (m)	garden
pubblico-a (pl. -i -che)	public
chiacchierare	to chat
il/la conoscente (m and f)	acquaintance
così	like this
quanti-e	how many
vecchio-a	old
addosso	on oneself (lit: on one's back)

Dialogue 3

l'animale (m)	animal
voler dire; che cosa vuoi dire? (familiar)	to mean; what do you mean?
la parola (f)	word
nè . . . nè	neither . . . nor
la tigre (f)	tiger
il leone (m)	lion
da	as, when
il cane (m)	dog
il gatto (m)	cat
affettuoso-a	loving
il pelo (m)	fur
lucido-a	shiny

l'occhio (m)	eye
il maschio (m)	male
la femmina (f)	female

Dialogue 4

la lavanderia (f)	dry cleaner's
pulire; far –	clean; to have cleaned
i calzoni (m pl.)	trousers
la macchia (f)	stain
l'unto (m)	grease
mentre	while
aggiustare	to mend
la gomma (f)	rubber; tyre
misurare	to measure
la pressione (f)	pressure
veramente	actually
avere premura	to be in a hurry

18.3 EXPLANATIONS

(a) Background information

In case of serious accidents, ring or ask for 113 'il centotredici'. To report a theft go either to the police station—LA POLIZIA—or to the municipal police—I VIGILI URBANI—which exist even in small places.

(b) Saying what you used to do a long time ago: imperfect

– grammar ref. 71

To say what you used to do once, you use the 'imperfect':

Una volta, giocavo. Ma ...	Once upon a time I used to play. But ...
Oggi sono vecchio	Nowadays, I am old

To indicate the time of your youth, you say:

Da giovane	As a young man, woman
Da ragazza	When I was a girl
Io e Carla avevamo due cani da bambini.	Carla and I had two dogs when we were children.

(c) Saying how old you were: avere, the imperfect – *grammar ref. 71*

You remember that to express your age, you say you have so many years: ho trentadue anni – I am thirty-two years old. To say how old you were in the past, you use the 'imperfect' of avere:

Quando avevo vent'anni . . .	When I was twenty . . .
Allora avevo due anni.	At that time I was two.

(d) I suoi – i tuoi (your, yours plural) – *grammar ref. 32–3*

The plural forms of the possessive adjective and pronoun il suo and la sua is i suoi and le sue:

Quali sono i suoi passatempi?	Which are your pastimes? (formal)
Questi soldi sono i suoi?	Are these banknotes yours?
Sono le sue figlie?	Are they your daughters?
Queste foto, sono le sue?	These photos, are they yours?

You use i suoi and le sue to refer to a third person too:

Questi calzoni sono di Lucio?	Are these Lucio's trousers?
Sì, sono i suoi.	Yes, they are his.
Queste giacche sono di Carla?	Are these jackets Carla's?
Sì, sono le sue.	Yes, they are hers.

The familiar form in the plural is i tuoi – le tue:

Sono le tue queste vecchie scarpe?	Are these old shoes yours?
Questi calzoni, sono i tuoi?	Are these trousers yours?

(e) Molti, molte (many, a lot)

Molti is used to refer to masc. plural nouns:

Avevi molti francobolli?	Did you have many stamps?
Sì, ne avevo molti.	Yes, I had a lot (of them).

Molte is used to refer to feminine plural nouns:

Da piccola, andavi molte volte a Londra?	As a small child, did you often go to London? (lit. many times)

Molte volte?	Many times?
Sì, molte.	Yes, many.

(f) Nessun, nessuna (no . . . + noun) – *grammar ref. 77, 78*

Read these sentences. There are two ways of translating them:

Non ho nessun libro.	I have no book; I haven't any books.
Non c'è nessuna parola.	There is no word; there aren't any words.
Non faccio nessuno sport.	I practise no sport; I don't . . . any sport.

As you notice, unlike English, a) the word following **nessun** is always sing.; b) **nessun** requires **non** in front of the verb; c) the ending changes according to the noun following it.

un album	nessun album
uno sport	nessuno sport
una parola	nessuna parola
un'amica	nessun' amica

(g) Non . . . più (no longer, any longer)

As above (f), one Italian expression is equivalent to two English ones:

Non ho più nessun album.	I haven't an album any longer. I no longer have an album.

(h) Mi ricordo che (I remember that . . .)

The word linking many verbs (to tell, to know, to realize) with the following sentence, is translated in Italian with **che**.

Mi ricordo che avevo un cane.	I remember that I had a dog.
Tim ha detto che era bel tempo.	Tim said that the weather was fine.

(i) Describing physical details (in the past): imperfect

Describing physical and moral details, or social characteristics—either temporary or permanent—referring to the past, you use the imperfect:

Il gatto aveva gli occhi verdi.	The cat had green eyes.
Era una signora ricca.	She was a rich lady.
Era un uomo elegante.	He was elegant (he used to be smart).

(j) Saying what you were doing: imperfect – *grammar ref. 71*
The English past tense I was (do) + ing, they were (do) + ing is conveyed in Italian with the imperfect:

Mentre mangiavo . . .	While I was eating . . .
Che cosa facevi?	What were you doing?
Guardavo la gente.	I was watching people.

(k) Nè . . . nè (neither . . . nor) – *grammar ref. 78*
Like nessun (see (f) above), this expression too requires non in front of the verb:

Non avevo nè leoni nè tigri.	I had neither lions nor tigers.
Non è nè di sugo nè di vino.	It is neither of sauce nor of wine.

(l) Ero seduto (I was sitting) (lit. I was seated)
Sedersi is an irreg. verb. The expression I was sitting is conveyed with ero seduto. This last word agrees in gender and number with the subject:
Carlo e Franca erano seduti.
Carla era seduta.

(m) Un mio amico (a friend of mine) – *grammar ref. 35*
If the noun you refer to is masculine, you say:

Un mio conoscente è arrivato	An acquaintance of mine has arrived.
Due miei amici sono in Italia.	Two friends of mine are in Italy.

If it is feminine, you say:

Ho perso una mia foto	I lost a photo of mine
due mie foto	two photos of mine

(n) Saying what you wanted in the past: volere, the imperfect
In most cases, you use the imperfect with the verb volere if you refer to the past:

Volevo il suo aiuto.	I wanted your help.

Proverbio: Altri tempi, altri costumi.
Other times, other customs.

18.4 EXERCISES

A

Exercise 1

Say that you used to do it, but you don't do it any longer.
Example: Sai giocare a tennis?—Giocavo a tennis una volta. Non gioco più.

1. Sai giocare a cricket?
2. Sai giocare a golf?
3. Sai giocare a rugby?
4. Sai nuotare?
5. Sai suonare musica classica?
6. Sai recitare?
7. Sai parlare francese?

Exercise 2

Julie and Carla talk about their pets. Play Julie's role.

Carla: Hai degli animali a casa in Francia?
Julie: (Say yes, you have a cat and a dog.)
Carla: Sono vecchi o giovani?
Julie: (Say the cat is young, the dog is old. He is fifteen years old. And you, Carla, do you have a cat? A dog?)
Carla: Non ho nessun gatto, adesso. Avevo due gatti fino a due anni fa.
Julie: (Ask what they were like.)
Carla: Erano belli. Avevano il pelo lungo. E i tuoi animali?
Julie: (Say the dog is brown with loving, deep brown eyes. The cat's fur is black, long. The eyes are green.)
Carla: Come si chiamano?
Julie: (Say they are called Mimi and Mumu.)

Exercise 3

Mrs McKenzie is at a dry cleaner's. Play her role.

— Buongiorno, desidera?
McKenzie: (Say you wanted to have this shirt cleaned.)
— Per quando?
McKenzie: (Say for tomorrow, you are in a hurry.)
— Che macchia è?
McKenzie: (Say you don't know. You were making some sandwiches. Perhaps it was butter . . . or while you were getting dressed and you were putting on make up . . .)

Exercise 4
Mrs McKenzie is at the police station. She has lost her bag. Play her role:

McKenzie: (Say good morning. Say you have lost your bag.)
Vigile: Quando l'ha persa?
McKenzie: (Say you lost it half an hour ago.)
Vigile: Dove?
McKenzie: (Say at the department store in (of) Milan road. Say you were trying on some shoes with a friend (f). Say that when you finished, the bag was no longer there.)
Vigile: Che cosa aveva dentro?
McKenzie: (Say you had fifty pounds, approximately.)
Vigile: Il suo nome . . . prego.
McKenzie: (Say your name . . .)

Exercise 5
Complete these questions inserting molti or molte, as suitable:

1. Avevi—studenti nella tua scuola?
2. C'erano—professori?
3. Studiavi—ore alla settimana?
4. Ti sei fermato—giorni a Milano?
5. Avevi—amiche a Milano?

Exercise 6 (revision ch. 8)
Order more of the following things at the restaurant, as in the example:
(birra) Per me, dell'altra birra, per favore. È buonissima.

1. mozzarella
2. prosciutto crudo
3. formaggio tenero
4. vino rosso

5. macedonia
6. insalata condita
7. sugo
8. acqua minerale
9. gelato alla frutta
10. frullati
11. pizze ai funghi

B

Exercise 7
How would you end these sentences if you were addressing the question to the people in brackets?
Example: (to Carla) Questi stivali sono i tuoi?

1. (to Lucio) Queste scarpe sono . . . ?
2. (to Lucio) Questi calzoni sono . . . ?
3. (to Mr McKenzie) Queste camicie sono . . . ?
4. (Mr McKenzie) Queste giacche sono . . . ?
5. (Lucio) Questi soldi sono . . . ?
6. (to Mr McKenzie) Questi documenti sono . . . ?
7. (to Carla) Queste riviste sono . . . ?

Exercise 8
This is Tim's last composition in class. Can you too write it in Italian?

1. When I was a child, I lived in a large house in (the) countryside.
2. I liked playing in the garden or at home with little cars.
3. I had two large dogs. They were called Black and White. They had long, shining fur. Their eyes were brown.
4. I liked going to school because I liked my teacher, but I did not like what we used to eat.
5. When I was twelve, I started playing tennis. I also liked swimming. My sister was quieter. She used to read, to play (the) music. She was always very smart, because my mother made her dresses.

Exercise 9
Say, in Italian, what Mr McKenzie said to the police.

This morning I went out of the hotel Turin about eight o'clock. I had my briefcase with me. I put (ho messo) it in (the) car. While I was driving towards the office, I stopped in front of a newspaper kiosk. I got out (sono sceso) and I went to buy a newspaper. While I was buying it and I was paying for it, a man entered my car and took (ha preso) my briefcase. What do I have to do?

Exercise 10

While you were doing ... (say this in Italian).

1. While I was watching the windows of a shoe shop ...
2. While I was filling up with petrol ...
3. While I was talking with an acquaintance of mine ...
4. While I was sitting at the bar with a friend (m) of mine ...
5. While I was taking the tram with a colleague (f) of mine ...
6. While I was getting off the tube with many parcels ...

Exercise 11

People are trying to borrow things from you. Refuse, as in the example:

Hai dei libri inglesi?—Mi dispiace, non ho nessun libro inglese.

1. Hai dei rotocalchi nuovi?
2. Hai delle cartoline di Milano?
3. Hai dei gettoni del telefono?
4. Hai dei fogli e delle buste?
5. Hai una biro?

Exercise 12

Reproduce, in Italian, the conversation over the phone between Mr Rossi and Mr McKenzie. Use the formal form.

1. Can you play tennis?
2. Why don't we play tennis this afternoon?
3. Where do I meet you?
4. Very well, I'll meet you outside your office, at 3.30.
5. No, I used to play rugby when I was twenty. Now I play golf. Yes, I used to like every sport.

ORGANISING DEPARTURES; FAREWELLS

19.1 DIALOGUES

Dialogue 1

Mr McKenzie will leave in a week's time for Amalfi with his wife. He is talking to Miss Dani about it.

Dani: Quando partirà con sua moglie per Amalfi?
McKenzie: Partirò tra una quindicina di giorni. Andrò direttamente a Napoli, se ci sarà posto in vagone letto.
Dani: E per arrivare a Amalfi?
McKenzie: Per arrivare a Amalfi, prenderò un battello.
Dani: Che cosa farà se non ci sarà nessun posto in vagone letto?
McKenzie: Prenderò il rapido delle 7.50 in prima classe che arriva a Roma alle 13.48.
Dani: Quanto tempo ci vuole da Roma a Napoli?
McKenzie: Ci vogliono circa tre ore. Se il treno sarà in orario a Roma, sarò a Napoli alle cinque, circa.
Dani: Ci sarà subito la coincidenza?
McKenzie: Se ci sarà subito la coincidenza, proseguirò. Altrimenti mi fermerò qualche giorno a Roma, forse.
Dani: Quanto tempo starà a Amalfi?
McKenzie: Starò quindici giorni. Ma se ci sarà bel tempo, starò di più.

Dialogue 2

Mrs McKenzie bids farewell to Mrs Pardi. After the fortnight in Amalfi, it's time to go back to London.

Pardi: Allora le è piaciuto questo soggiorno?
McKenzie: Sì, grazie. Mi è piaciuto moltissimo. La ringrazio tanto di tutto. È stata molto gentile e ospitale.

Pardi: Quando avrà un po'di tempo, mi scriva.
McKenzie: Senz'altro. E l'aspetto a Londra tra non molto.
Pardi: A che ora arriverà a Londra, di preciso?
McKenzie: Se l'aereo non sarà in ritardo, arriveremo a Londra alle otto.
Pardi: Chi sarà a aspettarvi all'aeroporto?
McKenzie: Mia sorella ci aspetterà con la sua auto.
Pardi: Quanti chilometri ci sono dall'aeroporto a casa?
McKenzie: Ci sono circa trenta chilometri.
Pardi: Quanto tempo ci vuole per attraversare Londra?
McKenzie: Ci vogliono circa quaranta minuti.
Pardi: Avrà qualche giorno per riposarsi prima di cominciare il lavoro?
McKenzie: Avrò qualche giorno, spero. Fino a domenica prossima.

Dialogue 3

Tim will go back to London in a fortnight. He is talking about it to Lucio's mother.

Mamma: Allora ritornerai in treno?
Tim: Se gli aeroporti saranno in sciopero, ritornerò con un accelerato.
Mamma: Un accelerato?? Hai detto con un accelerato?
Tim: Sì, così osserverò adagio il paesaggio delle Alpi.
Mamma: Ma fino a dove arriverai con l'accelerato?
Tim: Arriverò fino al confine francese. Poi prenderò un espresso, se ci sarà subito la coincidenza.
Mamma: Quanto tempo ci vuole da Milano a Basilea in accelerato?
Tim: Non lo so. Non importa. Non ho premura.
Mamma: E che cosa farai, se non troverai la coincidenza?
Tim: Mi fermerò da alcuni amici, per alcuni giorni, poi prenoterò una cuccetta fino alla Manica.
Mamma: Chi sono questi amici?
Tim: Sono ragazzi svizzeri che studiano a Londra.

Dialogue 4 Alla stazione

At the station, Tim is saying farewell to Lucio's family.

Mamma: Tim, salutami tanto, tanto, i tuoi genitori.
Tim: Lo farò senz'altro.
Mamma: Non dimenticarti di telefonare quando arriverai a casa.

'Quando partirà per Amalfi?'

Tim: Telefonerò subito, appena arriverò.
Mamma: Ti aspettiamo l'anno prossimo per un altro soggiorno.
Tim:: La ringrazio tanto di tutto. È stata molto gentile con me.
Mamma: E non dimenticarti l'italiano! Lo parli bene, adesso!
Tim: (to Lucio) Allora, tra quanti giorni ti rivedo a Cambridge?
Lucio: Tra diciotto giorni, due ore, trenta minuti! Se l'aereo non sarà in ritardo.
Carla: (to Tim) Allora ti è piaciuto questo mese in Italia?
Tim: Mi è piaciuto moltissimo. Mi sono proprio divertito. Grazie di tutto.
Carla: Quando avrai tempo, manda qualche cartolina, o scrivi!
Tim: Senz'altro, ti manderò molte cartoline. Grazie della compagnia e arrivederci all'anno prossimo.

19.2 **VOCABULARY**

Dialogue 1

l'aeroporto (m)	airport
una quindicina (f)	a fortnight
andrò (andare)	I will go
direttamente	directly
sarà (essere)	it will be

il vagone (m); -letto	carriage; sleeping-car
per	in order to
il battello (m)	boat
ci vuole – ci vogliono (volerci)	it requires
il treno (m)	train
in orario (m)	in time
sarò (essere)	I will be
la coincidenza (f)	connection
proseguire	to proceed
altrimenti	otherwise
stare	to stay

Dialogue 2

il soggiorno (m)	stay
ringraziare di	to thank for
tanto	so much
ospitale-e	hospitable
avrà (avere)	he, she, it will have; you will have (formal)
senz'altro	undoubtedly
di preciso	precisely
in ritardo	late
chi?	who?
attraversare	to cross
avrò (avere)	I will have

Dialogue 3

saranno (essere)	they will be
lo sciopero (m); in-	strike; on-
l'accelerato (m)	slow train
detto (dire)	said; told
osservare	to observe
adagio	slowly
le Alpi (f pl.)	Alps
il confine (m)	border
l'espresso (m)	direct train
la cuccetta (f)	couchette, berth
la Manica (f)	the Channel

Dialogue 4

salutare	to greet
dimenticarsi	to forget
appena	as soon as

rivedere	to see again
grazie di	thank you for
avrai (avere)	you will have (familiar)
mandare	to send

19.3 EXPLANATIONS

(a) Background information

If you want to plan the route of a journey by train, you may go to a travel agency or ask the porter of your hotel or the landlady of your boarding-house. If you want to work it out yourself, buy a pocket timetable in a stationer's shop. Ask for L'Orario Ferroviario. There is one for winter (27th September – 22nd May) and one for summer.

Types of train: TEE is a luxury inter-city train. First class only. Reservation and an additional fare are required. Rapido is a first class inter-city with an additional fare. Espresso is a fast train. Diretto is a train which stops at all towns of any size or importance. Accelerato is not a quick train (the name is misleading!). It stops at every station. All trains have first and second class prima e seconda classe, except the TEE and some Rapidi. If you risk missing a train, you may get on without previously purchasing a ticket. On the train, you will have to pay a surcharge of 50%.

(b) The future: 1st and 2nd conj. – *grammar ref. 73*

Actions in the immediate future are often expressed, as you know, with the present tense (4.3(f)). Actions in a more distant future are expressed with the future tense. To form it, you replace the ending of the infinitive by the endings below. The 1st and the 2nd conj. (arrivare, prendere) have the same endings:

Quando arriv + erai?	When will/shall you arrive? When are you going to arrive? (familiar)
Quando arriv + erà?	When will you arrive? (formal)
Che treno prend + erete?	What train will you take? (pl.)

To reply, you say:

Arriv + erò stasera.	I shall arrive tonight.
Prend + eremo il treno delle 8.	We'll take the 8 o'clock train.

Referring to a singular noun, you say:

Arriv + erà tra non molto?	Will it arrive in a short time? Will it be here before long?

For the plural:

Arriv + eranno con il rapido?	Will they arrive with the inter-city?

Notice: if you refer to a means of transport by the time of its departure or arrival, you say:

Il treno della una	The 1 o'clock train
Il battello delle due	The 2 o'clock boat

(c) The future: 3rd conj. – *grammar ref. 73*

The following endings apply to all verbs of the 3rd conj. including verbs such as *preferire (*4.3(k)*).

Con che treno part + irai?	On what train will you leave? (familiar)
Da che marciapiede part + irà?	From what platform will you leave? (formal)

The reply may be:

Part + irò con quello delle otto.	I'll leave on the 8 o'clock (one).
Part + iremo poco dopo.	We shall leave a bit later.

Referring to other things or to other people, you say:

Mia moglie prosegu + irà.	My wife will carry on.
Le sue valigie prosegu + iranno.	Her suitcases will be forwarded. (lit. will follow)

(d) Andare: the future – *grammar ref. 73*

Andare (to go) does not follow a regular pattern:

Andrai con il treno delle dieci?	Will you go on the 10 o'clock train? (familiar)
Andrà in auto?	Will you go by car? (formal)

Your answer is:

No, non andrò nè in auto, nè in treno.	No, I won't go either by train, or by car.

(e) Saying that if there is . . . you will . . . – *grammar ref. 73*

When a sentence with the future tense, is linked to a sentence starting with if, this sentence too is expressed in the future.

Se ci sarà la coincidenza, proseguirò subito.	If there is (lit. will be) a connection, I will proceed immediately.
Se ci saranno scioperi, non partirò	If there are strikes (lit. will be strikes) I won't leave.

(f) Indicating your aim: per + infinitive (in order to . . .)

E per arrivare a Amalfi?	And to get to Amalfi?
Prenderò un battello per arrivare.	I'll take a boat to get there.

As you know, to ask how to go to a place you say: Per andare in via Roma? (*see 3.3(b)*). Similarly, you use per + the infinitive of the verb when you ask how to do something or reply to such a question, as in the previous example.

(g) Saying how long it takes

To ask how long it takes to do something, you say:

Quanto ci vuole?	How long does it take? (lit. how long does it want there.)

In reply you say:

Ci vuole un'ora.	It takes one hour.
Ci vogliono due ore.	It takes two hours.

You use the plural (vogliono) if you answer with a plural noun.

(h) Saying that when you have time . . . – *grammar ref. 73*

The word quando (when) requires the future tense if used to describe a future action:

Quando avrò tempo, scriverò.	When I have time (lit. I will have time), I shall write.
Quando farò qualche giorno di vacanza, andrò a Londra.	When I have a few days' holiday, I will go to London.

(i) Avere: future tense – *grammar ref. 73*
Avere has an irregular pattern in the future tense:

Avrai tempo domani?	Will you have time tomorrow? (familiar)
Avrà bisogno di me?	Will you need me? (formal)
Avrete occasione di venire?	Will you have an opportunity of coming? (pl.)

To reply, you say:

Non avrò tempo domani.	I will not have time tomorrow.
Sì, avremo occasione di venire.	Yes, we shall have an opportunity of coming.

(j) Saying you have enjoyed it: mi è piaciuto
To ask whether people have enjoyed something, you use piacere: (for the construction of this verb, see ch. 11 and 12).

Ti è piaciuto questo film?	Did you enjoy this film? (familiar)
Le è piaciuto questo libro?	Did you enjoy this book? (formal)

But if what you enjoyed is feminine or plural, you say:

Mi è piaciuto questo film, ma non mi è piaciuta l'attrice.	I enjoyed this film, but I did not like the actress.
Mi sono piaciuti tutti questi film.	I enjoyed all these films.

(k) Chi (who?) – *grammar ref. 76(c)*
To find out who someone is, you say:

Chi è quel signore là?	Who is that gentleman there?
Chi sono quei ragazzi?	Who are those boys?

(l) Quanti? Quante? (how many?) – *grammar ref. 76(b)*
Like molti (many), this word, which also describes a quantity, has a masculine and a feminine form, according to the word it refers to:

Quanti chilometri ci sono fino a Milano?	How many miles is it to Milan? (lit. there are)
Quante volte sei stato a Londra?	How many times have you been to London?
Non so quanti sono gli studenti.	I don't know how many students there are. (lit. How many are the students?)

19.4 EXERCISES

A

Exercise 1
Here is a shortened version of McKenzie's dialogue. Can you fill in the gaps? It is based on dialogue 1.

Dani: Quando . . . per Amalfi?
McKenzie: . . . tra una quindicina di giorni.
Dani: Quanto tempo . . . da Roma a Napoli?
McKenzie: . . . circa tre ore.
Dani: Ci . . . subito la . . . ?
McKenzie: Se ci sarà . . . la coincidenza . . .
Dani: Quanto tempo . . . a Amalfi?
McKenzie: . . . quindici giorni. Ma se . . . bel tempo, starò . . . .

Exercise 2
You have enjoyed a lot of things. Say it as in the example.
Ti è piaciuto questo soggiorno? – Sì, mi è piaciuto molto. Grazie di tutto.

1. Ti è piaciuto questo spettacolo?
2. Ti è piaciuta questa gita?
3. Ti sono piaciuti questi giornali?
4. Ti è piaciuto questo giornale?
5. Ti è piaciuto questo viaggio?
6. Ti è piaciuta questa festa?

Exercise 3
Say what you will do if . . .

1. If there is a seat, I will leave immediately.
2. If there is a connection, I shall proceed.
3. If there is a strike, I will not take the train. I will go by car.
4. If there is good weather, I will stay longer.
5. If I have time, I will write.
6. If I have time, I'll go and see Mrs Bianchi.

Exercise 4
Say when you will do it.
Example: Quando partirai? (Una quindicina di giorni) Partirò tra una quindicina di giorni.

1. Quando arriverai? (venti giorni).
2. Quando sarai a casa? (tra due ore).
3. Quando partirai? (un'ora).
4. Quando telefonerai? (una settimana).
5. Quando ritornerai? (un mese).

Exercise 5
It takes longer than people think. (More than one hour in each case.)
Say it as in the example:
Quanto tempo ci vuole? Più di due ore? – No, ci vogliono più di tre ore.

1. Quanto tempo ci vuole? Più di otto ore?
2. Quanto tempo ci vuole? Più di sette ore?
3. Quanto tempo ci vuole? Più di dieci ore?
4. Quanto tempo ci vuole? Più di tre ore?
5. Quanto tempo ci vuole? Più di cinque ore?

Exercise 6 (revision ch. 9)
Go to a tobacconist's and ask these questions.

1. Where can I buy some beer?
2. Where is that shop?
3. How far away is it?
4. Give us a packet of twenty cigarettes.
5. May I have those with filter?
6. Give us also some telephone tokens.
7. How much is a token?
8. Sorry, I have no change.

B

Exercise 7
Your friend is leaving. Ask him these questions in Italian:

1. How many kilometres are there from here to Amalfi?
2. How many hours does it take?
3. How many rolls shall I buy?
4. How many kilos of fruit do I buy?
5. How many days are you going to be away?
6. How many suitcases do you have?

Exercise 8
Ask who those people are, as in the example:
(amici) Chi sono? Sono i tuoi amici?–(amico) Chi è? È il tuo amico?

1. amiche
2. professore
3. ospiti
4. compagne
5. colleghi
6. direttore
7. clienti
8. figlie

Exercise 9
Match one phrase on the right with one on the left to form meaningful sentences.

Se avrò bisogno,	sarò contenta.
Se avrò premura,	farò un viaggio più comodo.
Se avrò sete,	arriverò prima.
Se avrò la coincidenza,	mi fermerò di più.
Se avrò un posto in treno,	chiederò un tuo consiglio.
Se avrò un appuntamento,	prenderò un taxi.
Se avrò bel tempo,	prenderò la birra nel frigo.

Exercise 10
Change these formal farewells to familiar ones.
Example: È stato molto gentile. – Sei stato molto gentile.

1. Le è piaciuto il mese a Milano?
2. La ringrazio di tutto.
3. La ringrazio tanto.

4. È stata molto gentile.
5. Sua moglie è stata molto ospitale.
6. Mi saluti i suoi figli.
7. Mi saluti gli amici.
8. Le scriverò senz'altro.
9. Non si dimentichi di noi.

Exercise 11

Go with Mr McKenzie to a travel agency. Ask the questions in Italian

1. I want to go (take a journey) to Amalfi with my wife. What trains are there?
2. I want to leave in the morning.
3. Is there an inter-city train so that I do not have to change?
4. How much is the ticket?
5. How long before do I have to book?
6. With this direct train, when do we arrive in Rome?
7. Is there a connection immediately?
8. Is this train usually on time?

PRIVATE LETTERS, BUSINESS LETTERS

20.1 DIALOGUES

A

Letter 1

Mrs McKenzie writes to Mrs Pardi to thank her for her kindness.

3-4-'83

Gentile signora,

desidero ringraziarla dei giorni piacevoli che abbiamo passati a casa sua. Abbiamo fatto buon viaggio e domani ricominciamo a lavorare. Spero di rivederla presto a Londra. La ringrazio di nuovo di tutto.

Cordiali saluti a lei e a suo marito,
Sally McKenzie

Letter 2

Here's Tim letter to Carla to thank her for the hospitality of her family.

5-4-'83

Cara Carla,

ti ringrazio tanto della compagnia e dell'aiuto durante il mio soggiorno a Milano. Ringrazia di nuovo tutta la tua famiglia anche a nome dei miei genitori. Salutami tutti gli amici e arrivederci all'anno prossimo.

Affettuosi saluti a te e a Lucio
Tim

B

Letter 3

Here is a more detailed letter from Mrs McKenzie to Mrs Pardi.

10-4-'83

Gentile signora,

desidero ringraziarla di nuovo della simpatica ospitalità e della affettuosa compagnia fatta a me e a mio marito. Spero di poter presto ricambiare quando farà una gita in Inghilterra. Il nostro viaggio è andato bene anche se non c'era nessuno a aspettarci all'aeroporto. Oggi mio marito comprerà il libro che lei desiderava e glielo spedirà subito. I vostri regali sono stati molto graditi dai miei figli che ringraziano vivamente e scriveranno a parte. Stiamo ricominciando la vita di ogni giorno. Ho trovato i miei fiori molto belli e anche sulle mie piante in giardino si vedono già i primi boccioli. Ho fatto una foto e gliela spedirò.

Spero di rivederla presto o di ricevere sue notizie tra non molto.

Cordiali saluti anche a nome di mio marito,
Sally McKenzie

Letter 4

Tim writes a letter to Carla.

6-4-'83

Cara Carla,

il mio viaggio è andato molto bene. Non mi sono fermato a Basilea perchè non c'era nessuno dei miei amici. I miei dischi e le mie stampe sono arrivate intatte. Sto ricominciando la vita di tutti i giorni. Un mio amico mi ha detto che i dischi e i manifesti che desideri si trovano in una galleria d'arte a Chelsea. Te li manderò subito.

Ti ringrazio molto di nuovo della simpatica ospitalità di tutta la famiglia e della tua compagnia (e anche dell'aiuto con il mio italiano!). Spero di vedere Lucio presto a Londra.

Ringrazia ancora i tuoi genitori, salutami tutti gli amici e arrivederci all'anno prossimo,

affettuosi saluti
Tim

'Mi ricordo del Lago di Garda . . . '

Business Letters

Letter 5

Asking for addresses of hotels in Italy.

10-1-'83

(indirizzo del mittente)

Spett. Ente Turismo,

gradirei ricevere un elenco aggiornato delle pensioni e degli alberghi della vostra città o dei dintorni, con relativi prezzi, per la prossima estate.

In attesa di una vostra gentile risposta,

porgo distinti saluti

(la firma)

Letter 6

Replying to an advertisement in a newspaper.

(indirizzo del mittente)

14-2-'83

Spett. Ditta,

rispondo al vostro annuncio sul Corriere di Sondrio del 12-2-'83 relativo a un posto part-time di guida turistica con conoscenza dell'italiano. Allego il mio curriculum vitae e sarò lieto di spedire, se necessario, i nomi di due persone per eventuali lettere di referenze.

Distinti saluti
(la firma)

20.2 VOCABULARY

Letter 1

piacevole-e	pleasant
ricominciare	to start again
sperare di	to look forward to, hope to.
rivedere	to see again; to meet again
presto	soon
cordiale-e	warm; friendly
il saluto (m)	greeting

Letter 2

durante	during
a nome	on behalf

Letter 3

l'ospitalità (f)	hospitality
ricambiare	exchange
anche se	even if
nessuno	nobody
glielo-a	it to him; it to her
gradito-a	welcome; appreciated
da	by
vivamente	with warmth
a parte	apart
la vita (f)	life
il fiore (m)	flower
la pianta (f)	plant
il bocciolo (m)	bud

Letter 4

intatto-a	unbroken
detto (dire, irreg.)	said; told
la galleria d'arte (f)	art gallery
te li (familiar)	them to you

Letter 5

Spett. (abbr. of Spettabile)	Dear (respected)
gradirei (gradire)	I would like to; I would be grateful
aggiornato-a	up to date
relativo-a	in relation to
l'attesa (f); in –	waiting
la risposta (f)	answer
porgo (porgere, irreg.)	to give
distinto-a	distinguished

Letter 6

l'annuncio (m)	advertisement
relativo-a; – a	relative; in relation to
il posto (m)	job
la guida (f)	guide
turistico-a (pl. -ci, -che)	related to tourists
la conoscenza (f)	knowledge
allegare	to enclose
necessario-a	necessary
una persona (f)	person
eventuale-e	eventual
la referenza (f)	reference

20.3 EXPLANATIONS

(a) How to start a letter

You write the date on the right of the page in figures, as in the examples. You may write the name of the sender on the left of the page or under your own signature. You may add the address of the receiver, if you wish, but it's not compulsory. There is no all-purpose word such as 'Dear'.

A formal letter may start with these words:

Gentile signora	Dear Madam or
Egregio signore	Dear Sir

A letter to friends may start with these words:

Caro Tim	Dear Tim
Cara Carla	Dear Carla
Carissimo-a	My dear . . .

A business letter starts like this:

Spett. Ditta; Spett. Agenzia; Spett. Ente Turismo.
Spett. Ditta is the most common as is the English 'Dear Sir'. Spett. is the short form of 'spettabile' (respected), a form never used in its full length.

(b) How to end a letter
There is no general expression equivalent to the English 'Yours faithfully' or 'Yours sincerely'.
For a formal or a business letter, you may use these expressions:

Porgo distinti saluti	(lit. I give you my distinguished greetings)
Voglia gradire distinti saluti	(lit. I wish you to accept ...)
'Distinti saluti	

Cordiali saluti is less formal, somewhat equivalent to the English 'Yours' not followed by 'sincerely' but only by the signature.

To a friend you may say:

Cari saluti; Carissimi saluti; Affettuosi saluti.
These expressions are equivalent to the English "best wishes, love, lots of love".

Notice that in a business letter people are addressed with the 2nd person plural (voi ... vi), and the verbs are in the 2nd person plural. The idea is that you are addressing an institution and not an individual:

Spett. Ditta,
vi scrivo ... (I write to you); in risposta alla vostra lettera (in reply to your letter) etc.; vogliate mandarmi (send me).

(c) How to thank people at the end of a letter
Here are some expressions which are very often used in Italian but rarely used in English correspondence. To end a letter simply with 'distinti saluti' (yours sincerely, faithfully) sounds rather abrupt to an Italian:

La ringrazio e porgo distinti saluti
La ringrazio di tutto – ti ringrazio di tutto
In attesa di una vostra risposta, vi ringrazio . . .

To speed up matters, you may say: in attesa di una vostra sollecita risposta ringrazio e porgo distinti saluti. (Sollecita is a formal polite way of saying 'hasten'.)

To ask for further details or information, say: gradirei ricevere ulteriori (further) informazioni; gradirei ricevere ulteriori dettagli (details).

(d) I miei, le mie (my, mine, plural) – *grammar ref. 32*

The plural forms of the possessive adj. and pronouns il mio and la mia are i miei and le mie:

I miei fiori sono molto belli.	My flowers are very nice.
Ci sono boccioli sulle mie piante.	There are buds on my plants.

(e) Il loro, la loro (their, theirs) – *grammar ref. 32*

If you use the possessive adj. and pronoun il loro (their, theirs) remember that loro is an invar. word, but the definite article before it varies and agrees with the noun it refers to:

Il loro soggiorno è stato piacevole.	Their stay was pleasant.
La loro compagnia è simpatica.	Their company is nice.
I loro genitori sono inglesi.	Their parents are English.
Le loro famiglie sono scozzesi.	Their families are Scottish.

(f) Nessuno (nobody, no-one) – *grammar ref. 78*

The word nessuno requires non before the verb:

Non c'era nessuno all'aeroporto.	{ There was nobody at the airport. There wasn't anybody at the airport.

But if you want to be emphatic, you start your sentence with nessuno; in this case non is omitted:

Nessuno è venuto alla stazione.	Nobody came to the station.

(g) Glielo, te lo (combination of direct and indirect pronouns) *– grammar ref. 50*

If the pronouns le (to you, formal) or ti (to you, informal) are used with another pronoun (lo, la, li, le: it, them), they change in the following way:

Mi dia *il nome* di un albergo.	Can you give me the name of a hotel?
Glielo do subito, signore.	I'll give it to you, at once, sir.
Mi dia *una birra*, per piacere.	Can you give me a beer, please?
Gliela do subito.	I'll give it to you, at once.
Mi porti *quelle buste*!	Bring me those envelopes!
Gliele porto subito.	I'll bring them to you immediately.
Mi spedisca *quei vaglia*, per favore.	Please send me those money orders.
Glieli spedisco subito.	I'll send them to you immediately.

Similarly, ti changes into te lo, te la, te li, te le. But the two words *never* combine to form one:

Spediscimi quella lettera!	Send me that letter!
Te la spedisco ora.	I'll send it to you now.

(h) Saying you are in the process of doing something: sto legg-endo

To emphasize what you are doing at this very moment, you may use the verb stare (*grammar ref. 64*) in the following way:

Sto leggendo un libro interessante.	I am reading an interesting book.
Sto guardando questa borsa.	I am looking at this bag.
Sto partendo con questo treno.	I am leaving by this train.

The verb following stare takes one of these endings according to the conjugation:

1st conj.	**2nd conj.**	**3rd conj.**
andare and + ando	leggere legg + endo	partire part + endo

(i) Using an impersonal subject: si vede, si vedono – *grammar ref. 79*

You already know expressions such as come si dice in italiano? (*5.3(b)*) (lit. how does one say it in Italian?).

The word si (without the accent!) is used when the subject is unspecified.

Dove si vede Piazza S. Marco?	Where can one see St Mark's Square.
Dove si prende il treno per Padova?	Where does one get the train to Padua?

If the object is plural, the verb is plural too:

I programmi si trovano sul giornale.	The programmes can be found in the newspaper.
I biglietti si vendono dal tabaccaio.	Tickets are sold at the tobacconist's.

20.4 EXERCISES

A

Exercise 1

Address a letter to the hotel manager. Say you would like to book one double bedroom with bathroom, for a fortnight. Say you would like to know how much it costs. End the letter with formal greetings.

Exercise 2

Address a letter to a new Italian friend. Thank her for her company on behalf of you and your boyfriend. Say you had a good journey back and that you hope to see her in England. End the letter with familiar greetings to her and her mother.

Exercise 3

You have a job as an au pair with an Italian family. Write about your arrival. Address the letter to Mrs ... Say you will arrive at Milan airport next Tuesday at twelve o'clock. You will take the coach to the air-terminal. Then you will ring up. Say the weather in England is awful and you know that it is nice in Italy. End the letter formally.

Exercise 4
You are under pressure from everybody. Say that you *are* doing these things. Follow this model:
Sei andata alla spiaggia? – Sto andando!

1. Hai telefonato?
2. Sei andato in lavanderia?
3. Hai cercato quel numero?
4. Hai scritto (scrivere) alla tua amica?
5. Hai preparato la pizza?

Exercise 5
You are back from Italy and you write about everything. Put the correct form of i miei or le mie in front of the words:

. . . fiori . . . piante . . . dischi . . . manifesti . . . amiche . . . colleghi . . . genitori . . . gatti . . .

Exercise 6
Tim rings up Carla from London. Can you reproduce the same conversation, in the formal form, between Mrs Pardi and Mrs McKenzie?

Tim: Pronto? Carla? Sono Tim.
Carla: Telefoni dall'Inghilterra?
Tim: Sì. Ti telefono perchè ti voglio ringraziare del piacevole soggiorno a Milano e della tua compagnia.
Carla: Hai fatto buon viaggio?
Tim: Sì, grazie.
Carla: Io ho trovato due belle stampe di Milano e Lucio te le porterà.
Tim: Ti ringrazio di nuovo di tutto. Saluti a tutti. Ciao.
Carla: Salutami la tua famiglia. Ciao.

Exercise 7 (revision ch. 10)
Friends want to find out your plans. Reply according to the suggestions in brackets, as in the example:
Andate sui laghi? – (in montagna, al mare) Noi andiamo in montagna, loro vanno al mare.

1. A che ora partite? (alle due, alle due e mezzo)
2. Che pullman prendete? (il pullman delle due, il pullman delle tre)
3. A che ora arrivate? (alle quattro, alle otto)
4. A che ora ritornate? (alle dieci, alle dieci e mezzo)

5. Che cosa leggete? (un romanzo di Alberto Moravia, un racconto di Italo Calvino)
6. Quanto restate in montagna? (un mese, un mese e dieci giorni)

B

Exercise 8
Put these questions in Italian.

1. Ask if there is anybody there.
2. Ask if they haven't any Russian dictionary.
3. Ask if there isn't any chocolate.
4. Ask if there isn't anybody who speaks English.
5. Ask if there are no trains for Rome.
6. Ask if the shop never opens at two o'clock.

Exercise 9
Use each one of the following words to build up a sentence according to the example:
dischi: I miei dischi sono qui. Te li porto subito.

le foto; i bicchieri; la cartella; la penna; i libri; la giacca; le camicie.

Do the same according to this example:
i fogli – Vuole i miei fogli? Glieli do adesso.

Exercise 10
Write this letter in Italian.

Dear Madam,
I write in reply to your advertisement of January the 8th in the *Giornale di Como* for an au pair (alla pari) job. I am twenty years old. I worked with an Italian family in Rome last summer. At present I'm working as a shop assistant in a large department store in London. I would like to spend (the) next summer in Italy in your town. I would be grateful if I could have further information about the job. I like children and I can send you letters of reference if necessary. (Express your hopes for a reply and end the letter formally).

Exercise 11
And now write this letter in Italian to an Italian friend of yours in England.

Dear Laura,

I have been in Italy for a week. I like my job. The family is nice. There is the mother, the father and two young children. The boy is eight, the girl is five. From my room one can see the whole town and the lake. Italy is a very interesting country: stamps are bought at the tobacconists', and bus tickets are sold at newsagents'. Seats for coaches cannot be booked. People always eat (one eats) salad with oil and vinegar and they drink (one drinks) coffee all the time! People eat between one and two o'clock and between eight and nine in the evening. Then one goes out to the cinema or the theatre. It's two o'clock at night. I too have been to the cinema.

REVISION AND SELF ASSESSMENT TEST FOR CHAPTERS 16-20

Exercise 1 (2 points for each correct sentence)
Revise ch. 15. Here is a conversation between Tim and his friends at the restaurant. Fill in the missing words.

Tim: Venite spesso in questa trattoria?
Carla: . . . qualche volta. La volta scorsa ho . . . lasagne con i funghi. Le . . . moltissimo.
Tim: (to Julie) La mamma di Lucio . . . fatte la settimana scorsa. Le . . . a pranzo e a cena!
Julie: Che vino . . . con le lasagne?
Lucio: Non . . . mai . . . i nostri vini? . . . fa mio papà ogni autunno.
Carla: (to Julie) Ti piace cucinare?
Julie: Sì. Stamattina . . . sperimentato una . . . . . . : la zuppa inglese.

Exercise 2 (4 points for each correct answer)
Revise ch. 16. You are looking for a shirt. Put these questions in Italian:

1. Ask where you find shirts.
2. Say you want to see a shirt.
3. Say yes, it's for you.
4. You want cotton, not nylon.
5. Say your size is . . .
6. Ask if you can try it on.
7. Say it's slightly too small.
8. Ask to try on another one.
9. Say that this one is fine.
10. Ask if they have a red shirt like this one.

11. Ask how much it is.
12. Say it's fine. You'll take it.
13. Say thank you and goodbye.

Exercise 3 (3 points for each correct answer)
Revise ch. 17. Mrs McKenzie is in a doctor's surgery. Can you supply the doctor's questions, if these are Mrs McKenzie's answers?

Mrs McKenzie: Non mi sento bene, dottore.
Dottore: . . .
Mrs McKenzie: Ho mal di testa.
Dottore: . . .
Mrs McKenzie: Non ho febbre. No, non ho mangiato molto a pranzo.
Dottore: . . .
Mrs McKenzie: No, non ho bevuto della birra molto fredda.
Dottore: . . .
Mrs McKenzie: Ieri pomeriggio sono andata fuori in motoscafo.
Dottore: . . .
Mrs McKenzie: Sì, ho preso molto sole.

Exercise 4 (2 points for each correct sentence)
Transform dialogue 1 in chapter 17 into a conversation about a holiday now. *For example*: Come si è trovata l'anno scorso al mare in Liguria? – Come si trova quest'anno al mare in Liguria?

1. Era sempre sereno?
2. Il mare era sempre calmo?
3. La spiaggia era molto affollata?
4. Gli alberghi erano esauriti?
5. C'era gente simpatica in albergo?
6. Faceva il bagno tutti i giorni?

Exercise 5 (4 points for each correct sentence)
Revise chapter 18
After a month in Italy, tell your friends how things seemed to you the day of your arrival.

1. There was a friend (m) of mine at the station.
2. I was tired and I wanted to relax.
3. My friend took me to a small hotel near the station.
4. The town seemed noisy but interesting.

5. The hotel was clean.
6. The next morning I went to the school where I met my Italian teacher. She was called Paola Marazzelli.

Exercise 6 (2 points for each correct sentence)
Revise chapter 19. Ask about the train leaving at the time indicated in brackets. Put the question according to the example:
(8 o'clock) Scusi, da che marciapiede parte il treno delle otto?

1. (9.25)
2. (10.10)
3. (5.10)
4. (6.35)
5. (12.40)
6. (7.10)
7. (2.20)
8. (6.20)

Exercise 7
Revise chapter 20. Put the following questions according to this model: Ask where tickets are sold. – Dove si vendono i biglietti?

1. Ask where seats for the theatre can be booked.
2. Ask where you can buy postcards.
3. Ask where you can find a cheap hotel.
4. Ask where you can take a bus for Venice Avenue.
5. Ask where you can buy some good wine.

More than 100 marks: bravissimo! bravissima!
Between 70 and 100 marks: hai fatto un buon lavoro. Bene.
Below 65 marks: così, così. So, so.

II REFERENCE MATERIAL

TRANSLATIONS OF THE DIALOGUES IN CHAPTERS 1-5

CHAPTER 1 INTRODUCTIONS; BREAKING THE ICE; GOODBYES

Dialogue 1

Pardi: Excuse me, are you Mr McKenzie?
McKenzie: Yes. I am Julian McKenzie. Are you Mrs Pardi?
Pardi: Yes. Good morning. How do you do?
McKenzie: How do you do? (They shake hands.)
Pardi: Welcome. Did you have a good journey? (Lit. everything fine on the journey?)
McKenzie: Yes. Thank you. Everything (was) fine.
. . . .
McKenzie: Excuse me, Mrs Pardi, what's that? (lit. what is it?)
Pardi: It is the Castle of the Sforzas.
McKenzie: It is very beautiful!

Dialogue 2

Pardi: Miss Dani, good afternoon. May I introduce to you Mr McKenzie? (lit. I introduce to you . . .) Mr McKenzie, Miss Dani . . .
Dani: How do you do?
McKenzie: How do you do? (They shake hands.)
Pardi: (to McKenzie) May I introduce to you the film director, Luigi Bianchi?
Bianchi: Pleased to meet you.
McKenzie: Pleased to meet you.
Dani: Are you in Italy on business or on holiday?
McKenzie: Oh no! I'm not here on holiday. I'm here on business unfortunately.
Bianchi: Are you here with your family or (are you) on your own?
McKenzie: I'm here on my own.
Pardi: Mr McKenzie, may I introduce you to Dr Rossi?
McKenzie: Pleased to meet you.
Rossi: How do you do?
Pardi: Dr Rossi is not Italian, he is Swiss.
Rosssi: (to McKenzie) Are you English?
McKenzie: No! No! I'm not English. I'm a Scot. The firm is English. It's in London. . . .

Dani: Good evening, everybody. See you tomorrow.
McKenzie: Good evening, Miss Dani. See you tomorrow.

Dialogue 3
Lucio: Excuse me, are you Tim Yeats?
Tim: Yes.
Lucio: I am Lucio Pardi.
Tim: Hallo!
Lucio: Hallo! Welcome! (They shake hands.) Did you have a good journey?
Tim: Yes. Thank you. Everything was fine.
. . .
Tim: Excuse me, Lucio, what is that?
Lucio: It's the church of San Babila.
Tim: It's very beautiful!

Dialogue 4
Lucio: Carla . . . Tim . . . Tim . . . . Roberto, Carla's boyfriend . . .
Carla and Roberto: Hallo! Welcome!
Tim: Hi! (They shake hands.)
Roberto: Are you here in Milan to study or on holiday?
Tim: I'm here to study, unfortunately!
Lucio: Is Julie here?
Roberto: No, she is not here. (To Tim) Julie is Carla's French friend.
Julie: (arriving) Here I am, here I am (lit. I am here). Hallo everybody.
Lucio: Hallo! Are you on your own or with Maria?
Julie: I'm on my own.
Roberto: Julie, let me introduce to you Tim, the English student (who is) Lucio's guest.
Tim: Hallo!
Julie: Hallo! . . .
Roberto: Cheerio, Tim. See you tomorrow.
Tim: Cheerio, Roberto. See you soon.

CHAPTER 2 BOOKING ACCOMMODATION; ASKING THE WAY IN TOWN

Dialogue 1 At the Tourist Office
Clerk: Hallo.
Tim: Good morning. Is there a youth hostel here in Milan?
Clerk: Yes. There is a very large youth hostel.
Tim: Is there a place for a week?
Clerk: No. It's fully booked.
Tim: Well . . . (is there) an inexpensive boarding house? (lit. a boarding house not very expensive). It's for a foreign student.
Clerk: Well . . . There is an inexpensive boarding house in 3, Verdi Road. It is the pensione Florence.
Tim: Is there a single room from next Monday?
Clerk: Yes. A single room . . . yes, there is (one). (It's) six thousand liras a night.
Tim: Is breakfast included?

Clerk: No. It's not included. Your name? (lit. what name?)
Tim: What name? Ah! Steve Lloyd (spelling it) ...

Dialogue 2 In the street

Tim: Excuse me, which way to Verdi Road, please?
Boy: Pardon? Which road?
Tim: Which way to Verdi Road, please?
Boy: It's in the centre. Near the university.
Tim: Is it far?
Boy: No. Keep straight on as far as Garibaldi square.
Tim: Thank you. Cheerio. ... Excuse me, where is Verdi Road, please?
Boy: It's immediately here on the right where there is a bank. Then keep straight on (and) turn left (lit. on the left).
Tim: ... So, immediately here on the left ...
Boy: No! No! Immediately on the right. Then keep straight on ...
Tim: Oh, yes. Thank you.
Boy: Don't mention it. Cheerio.
Tim: ... On the right, keep straight on, on the left.

Dialogue 3 In the street

McKenzie: Good morning, Miss Dani.
Dani: Good morning, Mr McKenzie. Is everything all right?
McKenzie: Yes, thank you. Everything is all right. Excuse me, Miss Dani (can you tell me) where there is a hotel near here, please?
Dani: First or second class?
McKenzie: First class. And not very noisy.
Dani: There is a first class hotel in Turin Road.
McKenzie: Where is Turin Road?
Dani: The first on the right. Then go straight on and, at the end of the road, (take) the second on the left.
McKenzie: Thank you very much. Goodbye.
....
McKenzie: Excuse me, where is the Hotel Trieste?
Traffic Warden: Straight on, after the station.
McKenzie: Thank you. Thank you very much.

Dialogue 4 At the hotel

Receptionist: Good morning, sir. Can I help you?
McKenzie: Good morning. Have you got a double bedroom with bath, please? (lit. is there ... ?)
Receptionist: For how long? For a night?
McKenzie: No. For a week. From next Saturday.
Receptionist: Yes. We have a vacant bedroom from next Saturday.
McKenzie: How much is it a night?
Receptionist: One hundred thousand liras a night.
McKenzie: And is there air conditioning?
Receptionist: Yes. There is air conditioning, TV ...
McKenzie: That's fine. Is breakfast included or not?
Receptionist: It's not included. Your name, please?
McKenzie: Sally and Julian McKenzie.
Receptionist: Thank you. Goodbye.
McKenzie: Goodbye.

CHAPTER 3 ASKING ABOUT TRANSPORT IN TOWN; COURTESIES

Dialogue 1 At the tube station

McKenzie: Good morning, excuse me . . .
Policeman: Yes, can I help you?
McKenzie: (I want to go) to San Giuliano. Can I get there by tube?
Policeman: No, there isn't a tube as far as San Giuliano. It only goes to Bologna square.
McKenzie: And then what must I take?
Policeman: From Bologna Square you change and take a number seven (bus).
McKenzie: And does the seven go straight to San Giuliano?
Policeman: No, then you'll have to take a coach, number 8.
McKenzie: And how often does the coach run? (how often is there?)
Policeman: Every half hour.
McKenzie: The tube, the bus, and (then) a coach every half hour! A taxi! A taxi, please! It will be quicker!
Policeman: Yes, you're right! Time is money.

Dialogue 2 At the taxi rank

McKenzie: Good morning. Are you free?
Taxi driver: Yes, good morning. Where to?
McKenzie: To San Giuliano, please. Do you know where it is?
Taxi driver: Yes, I know.
Taxi driver: (approaching San Giuliano) What's the address?
McKenzie: The address is 3 Verona Road. It's the Pradella company.
Taxi driver: Oh, yes. I know it. It's this building here on the left, after the traffic lights.
McKenzie: How much is that?
Taxi driver: Ten thousand liras.
McKenzie: (He hands over the money) Here you are. Thank you. Goodbye.
(McKenzie entering the building meets an old acquaintance)
Businessman: Good morning, Mr McKenzie. How are you?
McKenzie: Fine. Thank you. How are you?
Businessman: Not too bad, thank you. Is all well at home?
McKenzie: Yes, fine. Thank you.

Dialogue 3 At the bus stop

Tim: Good morning.
Taxi driver: Where do you want to go?
Tim: To the International School, please. Excuse me, can you tell me how much it will cost, please?
Taxi driver: Well, two thousand, three thousand . . . approximately.
Tim: Pardon?
Taxi driver: Two thousand, three thousand . . .
(Tim thinks it's too expensive and looks for a bus)
Tim: No . . . thank you . . . Excuse me . . . Can you tell me where I can catch a bus to Venice Avenue, please?
Taxi driver: There is the number twelve.
Tim: Where is the bus stop for the number twelve, please?
Taxi driver: It's just here round the corner. Opposite the Bologna hotel.

Tim: And where can I buy the ticket?
Taxi driver: You go to an 'edicola'.
Tim: What's that?
Taxi driver: It's a 'giornalaio'. Do you know what that is?
Tim: Yes, I know. Goodbye. Thanks a lot.
Taxi driver: Cheerio.

Dialogue 4 At the bus stop
Tim: Excuse me, please. How often does the number twelve run?
Young girl: Every quarter of an hour.
(The number twelve arrives and Tim gets on. After a while he checks.)
Tim: Excuse me, doesn't the number twelve go to Venice Avenue?
Lady: No, it doesn't.
Tim: Where is the best bus stop for me to get off then? The next one?
Lady: No, you must get off here. At this stop, at the traffic lights.
(Tim gets off at the stop and asks a young girl.)
Tim: Excuse me, can you tell me which bus goes to Venice Avenue?
Young girl: The number fifteen goes as far as Paris Avenue which is near the stadium.
Tim: Where is the bus stop?
Young girl: It's right here. But the tube is more convenient.
Tim: Could I walk there?
Young girl: (she laughs) Well, yes, straight on! When you get to the end of Genoa Avenue, turn left . . . then immediately right, then left . . .
Tim: Thank you, goodbye.
Tim takes out his pocket dictionary and looks up the expression *never mind*. He reads pazienza! But at the school he is cheered up by Julie.
Julie: Hallo, Tim. How are you?
Tim: Fine, thanks. Everything all right?
Julie: Yes. Thank you. Not too bad.

CHAPTER 4 GETTING TO KNOW OTHER PEOPLE; TALKING ABOUT YOURSELF

Dialogue 1
Teacher: (to a student) What's your name?
Student: My name is Ivan.
Teacher: What's your friend's name?
Ivan: She is called Dolores Suarez.
Teacher: (to Ivan) Ivan, where are you from?
Ivan: I'm Russian. I come from Moscow.
Teacher: And where does your friend come from?
Ivan: She is Spanish.
Teacher: (to Dolores) Dolores, are you from Madrid?
Dolores: No. I come from a little village near Madrid.
Teacher: (to Julie) Julie, can you speak Italian well?
Julie: No. I can't speak it well.
Teacher: Do you have a good knowledge of French?
Julie: Yes, I know it well.
Teacher: Why are you in Italy?
Julie: Because I want to speak Italian well.

Dialogue 2 After the interval

Teacher: Hans, what's your favourite sport?
Hans: My favourite sport is swimming.
Teacher: Juan, who's your favourite actress?
Juan: My favourite actress is Ornella Muti. She's Italian.
Teacher: (to another student) Who's yours?
Student: I prefer Jane Fonda.
Teacher: Do you know Italian well?
Student: No, I don't. But I understand it a little.
Teacher: How long are you staying in Italy?
Student: I beg your pardon? I don't understand (the teacher explains).
Student: Ah! I am staying for a month here in Milan. Then I'll go to Florence.
Teacher: (to Ivan) And you, when are you going back to your country?
Ivan: I'm leaving in a month.
Teacher: In Moscow, do you work or are you a student?
Ivan: I work. I am a teacher of Russian.
Teacher: And where do you work?
Student: I work for an Italian firm in Paris.

Dialogue 3 In an office

McKenzie: Good morning. I have a meeting with the assistant-director.
Receptionist: Your name, please?
McKenzie: Julian McKenzie. I am from Avonex of London.
Receptionist: Please sit down. (He rings up.) Second floor.
Assistant-director: (he welcomes him at the door) Welcome! Have you met my colleague, Franco Marconi?
Marconi: (shaking hands) How do you do? I often go to England.
McKenzie: Pleased to meet you.
Assistant director: Mr McKenzie, would you like to begin with this catalogue? I'm expecting Luca Briato.
McKenzie: Yes, I would like to place an order straight away.
(After a while and after other transactions)
McKenzie: It's alright. I'll ask London to confirm it.
Assistant director: (pointing to a pen on the table) Signor McKenzie, is this pen yours?
McKenzie: Uh! Yes. Thank you. It's mine.

Dialogue 4 A business lunch

Rotondi: Is this folder yours?
McKenzie: No. It isn't. (Pointing to his neighbour) Perhaps it's his.
Rotondi: (offering a cigarette) Do you smoke?
McKenzie: Yes, thank you. It's my favourite brand.
Rotondi: What firm do you work for?
McKenzie: I work for Avonex, in London. Whom do you work for?
Rotondi: For Sampiro International.
McKenzie: Is it a limited company?
Rotondi: Yes, it's a limited company.
McKenzie: Where's its headquarters?
Rotondi: It's in Paris, with a branch in New York. How long are you going to stay in Italy?

McKenzie: I'll be here for a month. But I'll be back again soon. Are you from Milan?
Rotondi: Yes, I'm from Milan. But I live in Paris.
McKenzie: When are you going back?
Rotondi: I'm leaving this evening or I might stay on until tomorrow.

CHAPTER 5 CHANGING MONEY; MAKING TELEPHONE CALLS

Dialogue 1 At the currency exchange office
Tim: I have to change. How do you say in Italian . . . a "traveller's cheque".
Lucio: It is called 'traveller's cheque' or 'assegno da viaggio'.
Tim: Do you know when the currency exchange office closes?
Lucio: Yes, it closes at noon, but I don't know when it opens again.
Tim: (at the exchange office). Good morning.
Clerk: Can I help you?
Tim: I must cash a traveller's cheque, please.
Clerk: Here is the form. Have you got your passport?
Tim: Yes . . . (he can't find it). I'm sorry, but I haven't got it with me.
Clerk: Haven't you got your passport?
Tim: No, I really haven't . . . Just a moment . . . No, no. But can't I cash a traveller's cheque without a passport.
Clerk: No, I'm sorry.
Tim: Ah, I have my driving licence. Is it all right?
Clerk: No, I'm sorry. I can't. You must come again.

Dialogue 2 At the phone in a coffee bar
Tim: Good morning. May I have a telephone token, please?
Barman: Here's the token. Are you calling a local number? (here in town?)
Tim: Yes. How much is it? A hundred liras? (He hands him a large banknote.)
Barman: Yes. Haven't you got any change? Have you got a thousand liras note?
Tim: No. I'm sorry.
(Tim inserts the phone token and dials.)
Lucio: Hallo?
Tim: Is that Lucio? Hallo. It is Tim (lit. I am Tim) Do you have a spare moment?
Lucio: Yes, sure!
Tim: I haven't got my passport! And I can't cash my traveller's cheque.
Lucio: Of course not. Where is your passport?
Tim: In my bedroom. Can you come here?
Lucio: Where are you?
Tim: I am at the Bar Italia in Bologna.
Lucio: I'll be there shortly.
Tim: All right. Thanks. You are a real friend.

Dialogue 3 At the bank
McKenzie: Good morning. I need to cash a traveller's cheque.
Banker: Very well. Do you have your passport?

McKenzie: Yes. Here it is.
(The British passport sparks off a conversation)
Banker: I have a son in England.
McKenzie: Is he working or studying?
Banker: He's studying English in a school for foreigners. He needs to learn it for work.
Banker: Here's the form. You have to sign here please.
McKenzie: What's the rate of exchange for the pound today?
Banker: Two thousand liras. Really, the lira is coming down!
McKenzie: May I speak with the bank manager, please?
Banker: Do you have an appointment?
McKenzie: I'm sorry, I don't.
Banker: Well, in this case you can't do it today. Is tomorrow all right?
McKenzie: All right. Tomorrow.

Dialogue 4 At the Public Telephone Office
McKenzie: Good morning. I need a telephone token, please.
Telephonist: Is it a local call or a trunk call?
McKenzie: I'm phoning locally but I don't know the number.
Telephonist: The directory is behind there.
McKenzie: How much is it? One hundred liras?
Telephonist: Yes.
(McKenzie pays with a five thousand liras note.)
Telephonist: Don't you have any change?
McKenzie: No, I'm sorry. I have a two thousand liras coin, though.
Telephonist: All right. Here's 200, 300, 400, 500, 1000, 2000.

(There is no reply and McKenzie comes back)

McKenzie: They are not answering (lit. He doesn't answer). It is the Chamber of Commerce. Does anybody know when it closes?
Telephonist: It closes at midday. You have half an hour.
McKenzie: Thank you. Good morning.
Telephonist: Good morning.

KEY TO THE EXERCISES

CHAPTER 1 INTRODUCTIONS; BREAKING THE ICE; GOODBYES

A

Exercise 1

(i)
— Le presento il signor McKenzie.
— Piacere.
— Tutto bene in viaggio?
— Sì, grazie. Tutto bene.
— Buonasera, signor McKenzie.
— Buonasera.

(ii)
— La signorina Dani, il signor McKenzie.
— Piacere.
— Molto lieta. È qui in vacanza o per lavoro?
— Per lavoro.
— È qui solo o con la famiglia?
— Sono qui solo.

(iii)
— È la signora Bruni?
— Sono Tim Yeats.
— Piacere.
— Lucio è qui?
— Ciao, Lucio!

Exercise 2

1. Tutto bene? Sì, grazie.
2. Sei scozzese? Sì. Sono scozzese.
3. Scusi, è solo? No, sono con la famiglia.

Exercise 3

— Sei qui solo a Milano? Sì, sono qui solo.
— Sei qui in Italia per studio? Sì, sono qui in Italia per studio.

— Sei Tim Yeats? Sì, sono Tim Yeats.
— Sei inglese? Sì, sono inglese.

B

Exercise 4

1. La chiesa di San Babila è bella? Sì. È molto bella.
2. Il signor McKenzie è a Milano per lavoro o per studio? È a Milano per lavoro.
3. La famiglia McKenzie è a Milano? No. La famiglia McKenzie non è a Milano.
4. Julie è l'amica di Tim? No. Julie non è l'amica di Tim.
5. Julie è svizzera? No, Julie non è svizzera.
6. Il regista Bianchi è francese? No. Il regista Bianchi non è francese.
7. Sei italiano? No. Non sono italiano.

Exercise 5

Sono Julian McKenzie, l'amico scozzese di Maria Pardi. Tutto bene a Londra. A domani *or* Arrivederci a domani.

Exercise 6

—È il signor Gardi?—Sì. Sono il signor Gardi.—Sono Tim Yeats. Buongiorno. Sono a Milano con la famiglia di Lucio Bruni.—Sei solo?—Sì. Sono solo. La famiglia è a Londra.—Sei qui in vacanza?—No. Non sono qui in vacanza. Sono qui per studio.—Tutto bene in viaggio?—Sì, grazie.—Arrivederci/Ciao, Tim—Arrivederci, signor Gardi.

Exercise 7

il signor; il viaggio; il castello; il regista; il lavoro; il dottore; il ragazzo; l'amico; l'amica; l'Italia.

CHAPTER 2 BOOKING ACCOMMODATION; ASKING THE WAY IN TOWN

A

Exercise 1

Mamma: Ciao, Tim. Allora, c'è un ostello qui a Milano?
Tim: Sì, c'è un ostello della gioventù.
Mamma: C'è un posto da lunedì prossimo?
Tim: No. È tutto esaurito.
Mamma: E allora, c'è una pensione non molto cara?
Tim: Sì. C'è una pensione non molto cara in via Verdi.
Mamma: È libera per una settimana?
Tim: Sì. È libera per una settimana.
Mamma: La colazione è inclusa?
Tim: No. La colazione non è inclusa.

Exercise 2

Portiere: Buongiorno.
Tim: Buongiorno.

Portiere: Prego?
Tim: C'è una camera singola?
Portiere: Con bagno?
Tim: Sì. Con bagno.
Portiere: Per quanto tempo?
Tim: Per una settimana, da lunedì.
Portiere: Che nome, prego?
Tim: Steve Lloyd.
Portiere: Grazie.
Tim: Prego.

Exercise 3
McKenzie: Scusi, per piacere . . .
Vigile: Prego?
McKenzie: Dov'è via Garibaldi, per piacere?
Vigile: È verso via Mazzini.
McKenzie: È a destra o a sinistra?
Vigile: No. È sempre dritto.
McKenzie: È dopo una banca e un albergo grande?
Vigile: Sì.
McKenzie: Molte grazie. Buongiorno.

Exercise 4
Scusi, per l'università? Scusi, per piazza Garibaldi? Scusi, per lo stadio di San Siro? Scusi, per l'albergo in via Trieste? Scusi, per l'Ente Turismo?

B

Exercise 5
una stazione; un'università; una piazza; una pensione; un bagno; una settimana; una via; un nome; una strada; un'amica.

Exercise 6
Dove c'è un ostello della gioventù qui vicino? Dove c'è una camera singola qui vicino? Dove c'è una pensione qui vicino? Dove c'è una chiesa qui vicino?

Exercise 7
Luca: È qui vicino?
Tim: No. Non è qui vicino.
Luca: Verso l'Ente Turismo?
Tim: No. In piazza Roma, a destra.
Luca: In via Venezia?
Tim: Sì. In via Venezia.
Luca: A sinistra c'è l'albergo Italia?
Tim: Sì. C'è l'albergo Italia.
Luca: E poi?
Tim: Poi la prima a sinistra e poi la terza a destra.
Luca: È via Roma?
Tim: Sì. È via Roma.
Luca: Scusa, che numero?
Tim: Il numero 8.

Luca: Grazie. Ciao. Arrivederci.
Tim: Ciao. Arrivederci.

Exercise 8
Qui è la stazione Vittoria. Subito a destra, c'è un albergo. È l'albergo Vittoria e c'è una banca. Dopo la prima strada a destra, c'è una banca e un ufficio turismo. A sinistra, c'è una pensione non molto cara. È sei sterline per una camera singola per notte. Non c'è bagno, non c'è la televisione, non c'è l'aria condizionata. La colazione inglese è inclusa!

CHAPTER 3 ASKING ABOUT TRANSPORT IN TOWN; COURTESIES

A

Exercise 1

1. Buongiorno, signor McKenzie. Come va?	Bene, grazie. E lei?
Tutto bene all'albergo?	Sì. Grazie. Non c'è male.
2. Ciao, Lucio. Come va?	Bene, grazie. E tu?
Tutto bene all'università?	Bene, grazie. Non c'è male.
3. Buongiorno, signora. Come va?	Bene, grazie. E lei?
Tutto bene a casa?	Sì. Grazie. Non c'è male.
4. Ciao, Carla. Come va?	Bene, grazie. E tu?
Tutto bene in ditta?	Sì. Grazie. Non c'è male.

Exercise 2
1. Scusi.
2. Dov'è l'hotel Trieste?
3. C'è la metropolitana?
4. Che cosa devo prendere?
5. Devo cambiare?
6. L'autobus numero sette va dritto fino a corso Venezia?
7. Dove devo scendere?
8. Dov'è la fermata dell'autobus?

Exercise 3
Tassista: Buongiorno.
McKenzie: Devo andare a Milano.
Tassista: Che indirizzo?
McKenzie: In via Garibaldi.
Tassista: Che numero?
McKenzie: Undici.
Tassita: Diecimila.
McKenzie: Ecco a lei. Grazie. Buongiorno.

Exercise 4
Che autobus va in via Garibaldi? Che autobus va in corso Venezia? Che autobus va in via Verona? Che autobus va in piazzale Firenze?

Exercise 5
Tim: Buongiorno. Scusi?
Signore: Prego?

Tim: C'è la metropolitana per San Siro?
Signore: No. Non c'è la metropolitana per San Siro.
Tim: C'è un autobus?
Signore: Sì. C'è un autobus.
Tim: Va dritto fino a San Siro?
Signore: No. Non va dritto fino a San Siro.
Tim: Dov'è la fermata?
Signore: La fermata è proprio qui di fronte.

B

Exercise 6

1. Ogni quanto c'è? — (g) C'è ogni quarto d'ora.
2. Che indirizzo? — (e) Via Garibaldi 3.
3. C'è un ostello? — (f) No, non c'è un ostello.
4. Quant'è? — (d) Tremila lire.
5. Per quanto? — (a) Per un giorno.
6. A sinistra? — (c) Sì, a sinistra.
7. Dove va? — (b) Va verso piazza Roma.

Exercise 7

1. Ma non c'è un autobus? No. Non c'è un autobus.
2. Ma non c'è un taxi? No. Non c'è un taxi.
3. Ma il sette non va in via Torino? No. Non va in via Torino.
4. Ma non c'è ogni ora? No. Non c'è ogni ora.
5. Ma l'indirizzo non è via Trento 10? No. L'indirizzo non è via Trento 10.
6. Ma non c'è il bagno? No. Non c'è il bagno.

Exercise 8

Pardi: Buongiorno, signor McKenzie. Come va?
McKenzie: Molto bene. Grazie.
Pardi: Tutto bene a San Giuliano?
McKenzie: Sì. Grazie. Tutto bene.
Pardi: Dove deve andare?
McKenzie: Devo andare in via Cavour.
Pardi: Non sa dov'è?
McKenzie: No. Non lo so. È qui vicino?
Pardi: Sì. È la prima a sinistra.
McKenzie: Allora, vado a piedi.

Exercise 9

Roberto: Ciao! Tim. Dove vai?
Tim: Vado allo stadio.
Roberto: A piedi? Ma sai dov'è?
Tim: Sì. Lo so. È molto lontano.
Roberto: C'è la metro e c'è il tram numero cinque. Va dritto allo stadio.
Tim: Bene. Grazie. Ciao.
Roberto: Ciao.

CHAPTER 4 GETTING TO KNOW OTHER PEOPLE; TALKING ABOUT YOURSELF

A

Exercise 1
No. Sono uno studente. No. Sono un vice-direttore. No. Sono un portiere. No. Sono un vigile. No. Sono un tassista. No. Sono un uomo d'affari. No. Sono un impiegato. No. Sono un'impiegata. No. Sono una segretaria.

Exercise 2
Steve: C'è una camera singola per Steve Lloyd?
Signora: Sì. Sei tu? Sei l'amico di Tim Yeats?
Steve Lloyd: Sì.
Signora: Parli italiano?
Steve: Un poco. Molto poco.
Signora: Di dove sei?
Steve: Di Cambridge.
Signora: Studi all'università di Cambridge?
Steve: No. Studio all'università di Londra.
Signora: Resti a Milano per una settimana?
Steve: Sì. Resto per una settimana.

Exercise 3
Signore: È inglese?
McKenzie: No. Sono di Edinburgo.
Signore: Ah! Sa bene l'italiano!
McKenzie: Lo so un poco.
Signore: È in Italia per lavoro?
McKenzie: Sì. Lavoro per una ditta di Londra.

Exercise 4
Amico: Come ti chiami?
Tim: Mi chiamo Tim Yeats.
Amico: Di dove sei?
Tim: Sono inglese.
Amico: Conosci bene l'Italia?
Tim: No. Un poco.
Amico: Ma capisci l'italiano?
Tim: Capisco un poco. Ma non lo parlo.
Amico: Dove abiti?
Tim: Abito a Cambridge.
Amico: Preferisci Londra o Cambridge?
Tim: Preferisco Cambridge.

Exercise 5
L'Italia? È il mio paese preferito! Il castello di Warwick? È il mio castello preferito! Il nuoto? È il mio sport preferito! Via Veneto? È la mia via preferita!

B

Exercise 6
1. Sì. Riparto domani. Devo ripartire domani.
2. Sì. Aspetto la segretaria. Devo aspettare la segretaria.
3. Sì. Scendo qui. Devo scendere qui.
4. Sì. Resto fino a giovedì. Devo restare fino a giovedì.

Exercise 7
1. Scendi qui? Scendo qui ogni sera!
2. Vai alla Scuola Internazionale? Vado alla Scuola Internazionale ogni sera!
3. Riparti per San Giuliano? Riparto per San Giuliano ogni sera!
4. Incontri Carla? Incontro Carla ogni sera!
5. Vai a piedi? Vado a piedi ogni sera!

Exercise 8
1. È tua questa penna? No. Non è mia. La mia è più bella.
2. È tuo questo catalogo? No. Non è mio. Il mio è più piccolo.
3. È tua questa cartella? No. Non è mia. La mia è più grande.
4. È tuo questo denaro? No. Non è mio. Il mio è inglese.

Exercise 9
McKenzie: Dove lavora?
Signore: Lavoro a Roma.
McKenzie: Ogni quanto ritorna a casa?
Signore: Ritorno a casa ogni settimana.
McKenzie: Preferisce Milano o Roma?
Signore: Preferisco Milano.
McKenzie: È più rumorosa Roma o Milano?
Signore: È più rumorosa Roma.
McKenzie: Arrivederci.
Signore: Arrivederci. A domani.

Exercise 10
Signore: Conosce l'Italia?
McKenzie: Sì. Conosce l'Italia. Preferisce Roma.
Signore: Come si chiama?
McKenzie: Si chiama Sally.
Signore: Lavora a Londra?
McKenzie: Sì. Lavora a Londra.
Signore: È scozzese?
McKenzie: Sì. È scozzese.

CHAPTER 5 CHANGING MONEY; MAKING TELEPHONE CALLS

A

Exercise 1
Come si dice 'the driving licence' in italiano? Si dice la patente.
Come si dice 'a telephone token' in italiano? Si dice un gettone.

Come si dice 'the signature' in italiano? Si dice la firma.
Come si dice 'the church' in italiano? Si dice la chiesa.
Come si dice 'to walk' in italiano? Si dice andare a piedi.
Come si dice 'a quarter of an hour' in italiano? Si dice un quarto d'ora.
Come si dice 'the traffic lights' in italiano? Si dice il semaforo.
Come si dice 'I'm sorry' in italiano? Si dice mi dispiace.

Exercise 2
Quando apre e quando chiude questo ufficio cambi? Quando apre e quando chiude questa ditta? Quando apre e quando chiude questa scuola? Quando apre e quando chiude questa edicola? Quando apre e quando chiude quest'ostello? Quando apre e quando chiude questa banca? Quando apre e quando chiude quest'albergo?

Exercise 3
Lucio: Tim, hai il passaporto?
Tim: Non ce l'ho.
Lucio: Ma non devi cambiare un assegno?
Tim: Ho la patente.
Lucio: Puoi cambiare un assegno senza il passaporto?
Tim: Non lo so. Ma non so dov'è il passaporto.
Lucio: Non lo sai?
Tim: Forse è in camera.
Lucio: Hai moneta?
Tim: Ho un pezzo da mille lire.
Lucio: Ma non devi fare un'interurbana?
Tim: Sì. Devo fare un'interurbana.
Lucio: Allora, hai bisogno di moneta!

Exercise 4
Può chiedere una camera? Può andare in banca?
Può cambiare un assegno? Può firmare un modulo?
Può parlare con la mia segretaria? Può telefonare a Londra?
Può restare fino a domani? Può ripartire lunedì?
Può verificare questo numero?

Exercise 5
Ho bisogno di un albergo. Devo restare qui un mese.
Ho bisogno di un taxi. Devo andare al posteggio.
Ho bisogno d'un pullman. Devo andare a Venezia.
Ho bisogno di una camera. Devo andare in un albergo.

B

Exercise 6
Che cosa deve cambiare Tim? Deve cambiare un assegno da viaggio.
Quando chiude l'ufficio cambi? Chiude a mezzogiorno.
Tim ha il passaporto? No. Non ha il passaporto.
Tim deve ritornare all'ufficio cambi? Sì. Deve ritornare.
Dove ha il passaporto Tim? Ha il passaporto in camera.
Dov'è Tim quando telefona? È al bar.
Quant'è un gettone? È cento lire.

Exercise 7

Banchiere: Ah! Hai il passaporto?
Tim: Sì. Ho il passaporto.
Banchiere: Hai bisogno di cambiare l'assegno da viaggio?
Tim: Sì. Ho bisogno di cambiare l'assegno da viaggio.
Banchiere: Allora, il passaporto, prego.
Tim: Eccolo.
Banchiere: mille, duemila, tremila, quattromila, cinquemila, seimila, settemila, ottomila . . .
Tim: mille, duemila, tremila, quattromila, cinquemila, seimila, settemila, ottomila . . .
Banchiere: Va bene?
Tim: Sì. Va bene. Grazie.
Banchiere: Arrivederci.

Exercise 8

Oggi ho un appuntamento con un amico. Si chiama Franco Lugli. Ma non posso andare. Aspetto un'interurbana da Londra. E non posso telefonare a Franco perchè non ha il telefono. Abita vicino all'albergo Flora. Devo prendere un taxi subito.

Note: Key to revision exercises are together on pages 307–13.

CHAPTER 6 ORDERING DRINKS; ASKING FOR ADVICE IN SHOPS

A

Exercise 1

Vorrei un gelato alla frutta, per favore.
Vorrei due bicchieri di latte, per favore.
Vorrei tre succhi di frutta, per favore.
Vorrei una scatola di biscotti, per favore.

Exercise 2

Scusi, mi dia un altro gelato alla frutta, per favore.
Scusi, mi dia un altro succo di frutta, per favore.
Scusi, mi dia un altro gelato alla cioccolata, per favore.
Scusi, mi dia un altro bicchiere di latte, per favore.

Exercise 3

Scusi, ci sono altri album di Battisti?
Scusi, ci sono altri vocabolari italiani?
Scusi, ci sono altri romanzi inglesi?
Scusi, ci sono altri racconti americani?
Scusi, ci sono altri gettoni?

Exercise 4

1. Scusi, dove sono i taxi? I taxi sono lì fuori.
2. Scusi, che cosa sono? Sono amaretti di Saronno.
3. Scusi, di dove sono questi studenti? Questi studenti sono di Parigi.

4. Scusi, ci sono negozi aperti? Sì, ci sono negozi aperti.
5. Scusi, che cosa sono? Sono racconti contemporanei.
6. Scusi, ci sono tavoli liberi? Sì, ci sono tavoli liberi.

Exercise 5
un romanzo americano;
un albergo caro;
una pensione completa;
autori contemporanei;
cantanti folcloristici;
musica folcloristica;
una strada rumorosa;
un gelato buono.

B

Exercise 6
Ciao! Non c'è male, grazie, e tu? Una gelateria, vicino alla scuola. No, non da solo, con altri studenti stranieri. Non sono tutti inglesi. Oh, sì. Anche uomini d'affari stranieri, francesi, americani, . . . No, non un succo di frutta. Gli altri—gelati, bicchieri di latte, frullati. No, non a casa, in un negozio di dischi. Non vicino alla stazione. È il negozio dopo l'università. Sì, il tredici fino a Piazza Garibaldi e poi a piedi. No, non di musica classica, musica folcloristica. Sì, due album di cantanti italiani famosi. Sono molto belli. Sono Battisti e De André. No! Non ventimila lire! Sedicimila lire! Non sono molto cari. Sì, ci sono i testi dietro la copertina. Va bene. Arrivederci.

Exercise 7
Via Montenapoleone. È una strada italiana molto famosa. Va da via Manzoni a piazza San Babila. Di fronte c'è la Scala. Non lontano, a destra, c'è il Duomo, la chiesa molto bella di Milano. A destra o a sinistra di questa strada—non lo so bene—c'è il British Council—. L'indirizzo è via Manzoni 18. Un palazzo di via Montenapoleone è la casa di un autore famoso, un poeta, il Premio Nobel Eugenio Montale. Ci sono negozi, alberghi di prima categoria, ma non ci sono autobus. La metro è lì vicino. C'è una stazione della metropolitana in piazza San Babila e ci sono due autobus in via Manzoni.

CHAPTER 7 DOING THINGS WITH OTHER PEOPLE; INSISTING ON PAYING

A

Exercise 1
Sì, grazie. Prendiamo due caffè.
Sì, grazie. Prendiamo due tè.
Sì, grazie. Prendiamo due cappuccini.
Sì, grazie. Prendiamo due bicchieri di latte.
Sì, grazie. Prendiamo due birre alla spina.
Sì, grazie. Prendiamo due aperitivi lisci.
Sì, grazie. Prendiamo due amari con ghiaccio.
Sì, grazie. Prendiamo due succhi di frutta.

Sì, grazie. Prendiamo due cioccolatini.
Sì, grazie. Prendiamo due aranciate.

Exercise 2
Hai voglia di prendere qualcosa? Di un frullato?
Hai voglia di prendere qualcosa? Di un tè?
Hai voglia di prendere qualcosa? Di un aperitivo?
Hai voglia di prendere qualcosa? Di un Martini rosso?
Hai voglia di prendere qualcosa? Di un caffè con latte senza zucchero?
Hai voglia di prendere qualcosa? Di alcune olive?
Hai voglia di prendere qualcosa? Di alcune patatine?
Hai voglia di prendere qualcosa? Di un bicchiere di latte freddo?

Exercise 3
1. Purtroppo, non restiamo mai un mese in Italia.
2. Mi dispiace, non mangiamo mai frutta a colazione.
3. Non andiamo mai in ufficio a piedi.
4. Eh, no. Non compriamo mai libri cari.
5. Non ascoltiamo mai la televisione.
6. Non leggiamo mai racconti tradotti.
7. Non parliamo mai francese a casa.

Exercise 4
Due biglietti, per favore.
Due birre, per favore.
Due camere singole, per favore.
Due aranciate, per favore.
Due gelati, per favore.
Due dischi, per favore.
Due moduli, per favore.
Due penne, per favore.
Due scatole di cioccolatini, per favore.
Due pacchetti di patatine, per favore.
Due sterline, per favore.

Exercise 5
McKenzie: Signor Rossi, ha voglia di un caffè?
Rossi: Sì, grazie. Ho proprio voglia di un caffè.
McKenzie: Con latte?
Rossi: No, grazie. Senza latte.
McKenzie: Prende zucchero?
Rossi: No, grazie. Non prendo zucchero.
McKenzie: Un caffè, per piacere.
Rossi: Pago io, per favore.
McKenzie: No, no. Offro io.
Rossi: Grazie. Molto gentile.

B

Exercise 6
Comincio con il tè. Latte, ma non zucchero. Poi prendo due fette di pane tostato con burro, salato, se posso, e marmellata. Prendo anche yogurt alla

frutta, un succo di frutta, due fette di pancetta e una salsiccia. No, grazie. Non prendo pomodori.

Exercise 7
Ho bisogno di alcune birre.
Ho bisogno di alcune aranciate.
Ho bisogno di alcuni bicchieri.
Ho bisogno di alcune olive.
Ho bisogno di alcuni dischi.
Ho bisogno di alcune bottiglie di acqua minerale.
Ho bisogno di alcuni biscotti.
Ho bisogno di alcuni gelati.
Ho bisogno di alcuni Martini.
Ho bisogno di alcuni analcolici.

Exercise 8
— Ci sono due camere singole con bagno?
— Restiamo per tre settimane.
— Ripartiamo mercoledì prossimo.
— Aspettiamo due colleghi.
— Quando chiude l'albergo?
— Arriviamo tra due ore.

Exercise 9
Dove vai? Vado a imparare inglese.
Dove vai? Vado a studiare italiano.
Dove vai? Vado a lavorare in Inghilterra.
Dove vai? Vado a aprire il negozio.
Dove vai? Vado a chiudere l'ufficio.
Dove vai? Vado a prendere l'autobus.
Dove vai? Vado a cambiare il denaro.
Dove vai? Vado a bere un bicchiere di acqua.

Exercise 10
Oggi, come ogni giovedì, comincio con una colazione leggera. Un tè, con latte, senza zucchero. La mia colazione favorita è fatta di un uovo sodo e una fetta di pane. Poi, con due amiche, vado a piedi alla SIP dove lavoro. Non prendiamo l'autobus perchè l'ufficio non è lontano. Parlo francese, inglese e tedesco e ogni ora ascolto cento interurbane. Firmo circa cento moduli. A mezzogiorno, l'ufficio chiude e ritorniamo a casa. Lì preparo . . .

CHAPTER 8 ORDERING MEALS; SAYING SOMETHING IS VERY GOOD

A

Exercise 1
1. Anche per noi. Due caffè, per favore.
2. Anche per noi. Due tè, per favore.
3. Anche per noi. Due analcolici, per favore.

4. Anche per noi. Due birre, per favore.
5. Anche per noi. Due pizze al prosciutto, per favore.

Exercise 2

(i) Buongiorno, avete dell'insalata?
Buongiorno, avete del formaggio?
Buongiorno, avete del latte?
Buongiorno, avete del burro?
Buongiorno, avete della marmellata?
Buongiorno, avete delle salsicce?
Buongiorno, avete delle uova?
Buongiorno, avete delle aranciate?

(ii) Scusi, avete dell'altra insalata?
Scusi, avete dell'altro formaggio?
Scusi, avete dell'altro latte?
Scusi, avete dell'altro burro?
Scusi, avete dell'altra marmellata?
Scusi, avete delle altre salsicce?
Scusi, avete delle altre uova?
Scusi, avete delle altre aranciate?

Exercise 3

— Buongiorno, signorina, desidera?
— Quant'è quel salame?
— Mille lire il pacchetto.
— Prendo due pacchetti.
— Poi? Del prosciutto? Del formaggio?
— Com'è quel formaggio?
— È buonissimo.
— Mi dà una fetta di quel formaggio?
— Ecco una fetta. È buona?
— È buonissima!

Exercise 4

Mi dà della marmellata. Poi prendiamo del miele e dell'acqua minerale. Vorrei anche della frutta e dei pomodori.
Vorrei fare un regalo. Ma sono indeciso. Avete dei libri inglesi tradotti? Posso vedere dei vocabolari italiani? Scusi, ci sono delle edizioni tascabili?
Scusi, ci sono delle pensioni qui vicino? E dei telefoni? Sa se ci sono dei negozi aperti?

Exercise 5

Scusi, come sono queste arance? Sono buonissime o buone?
Scusi, come sono queste acciughe? Sono buonissime o buone?
Scusi, come sono questi biscotti? Sono buonissimi o buoni?
Scusi, come sono questi cioccolatini? Sono buonissimi o buoni?
Scusi, come sono questi dolci? Sono buonissimi o buoni?
Scusi, come sono questi formaggi? Sono buonissimi o buoni?
Scusi, come sono questi funghi? Sono buonissimi o buoni?
Scusi, come sono questi gelati? Sono buonissimi o buoni?

Scusi, come sono questi limoni? Sono buonissimi o buoni?
Scusi, come sono queste marmellate? Sono buonissime o buone?
Scusi, come sono queste salsicce? Sono buonissime o buone?

B

Exercise 6
Quale? Quel direttore lì?
Quale? Quella filiale lì?
Quale? Quella banca lì?
Quale? Quel catalogo lì?
Quale? Quella firma lì?
Quale? Quell'albergo lì?
Quale? Quel banchiere lì?
Quale? Quella camera di commercio lì?

Exercise 7
Pardi: Com'è questa birra? È buona?
McKenzie: È buonissima.
Rossi: Va bene questo formaggio?
McKenzie: Questo formaggio va bene. È tenerissimo.
Pardi: Va tutto bene, allora?
McKenzie: Va benissimo.

Exercise 8
1. La signora Pardi ordina dell'insalata e del prosciutto crudo.
2. No, il signor McKenzie non prende un piatto di prosciutto cotto.
3. Prende un panino al prosciutto crudo e un'insalata.
4. Sì, il signor McKenzie mangia l'insalata senza olio.
5. Il signor Rossi prende un panino al salame e della frutta.

Exercise 9
Questa pizza non è buona. È senza acciughe.
Questo latte è ghiacciato. Desideriamo un bicchiere di latte non ghiacciato.
Sì, abbiamo il Martini rosso e il Martini bianco.
Alcuni formaggi italiani sono molli, ma questo non è molle.
Questa città è splendida. Ma questo albergo è molto rumoroso.
Mi dispiace, questi tavoli non sono liberi.

Exercise 11
A casa non mangio mai molto. Sono solo (*or* sola) a mezzogiorno. Se sono con una collega prepariamo dei panini (*or* alcuni panini) con del prosciutto cotto o del formaggio. O mangiamo un piatto di insalata con delle fette di formaggio e alcune (*or* delle) fette di pomodori. Poi prendiamo uno yogurt alla frutta o una macedonia di frutta o dei (*or* alcuni) biscotti. Non mangio mai del pane e non bevo mai del vino o della birra perchè sono a dieta. Qualche volta bevo un succo di pomodoro o un succo di frutta. Se sono con una collega ascoltiamo alcuni (*or* dei) dischi di musica classica: autori inglesi, italiani o tedeschi. Poi beviamo un caffè e dopo un'ora vado con la mia collega alla SIP. Se non vado a casa, vado in una gelateria o a una tavola calda. C'è una tavola calda famosa vicino al mio ufficio.

CHAPTER 9 ASKING PERMISSION; EXPRESSING YOUR WISHES

A

Exercise 1
Laura: Buongiorno.
Tabaccaio: Buongiorno. Prego?
Laura: Ha delle sigarette inglesi?
Tabaccaio: No, mi dispiace. Non ho delle sigarette inglesi.
Laura: Mi dia delle sigarette italiane.
Tabaccaio: Ecco delle sigarette italiane.
Laura: È un pacchetto con filtro?
Tabaccaio: Sì. È un pacchetto con filtro.
Laura: Mi dia un pacchetto da dieci.
Tabaccaio: Va bene. Un pacchetto da dieci.
Laura: Grazie. Arrivederci.
Tabaccaio: Arrivederci e grazie.

Exercise 2
Mamma: Ha delle riviste straniere?
Giornalaio: No, non ho delle riviste straniere, mi dispiace.
Mamma: Ha dei quotidiani stranieri?
Giornalaio: Sì. Ho dei quotidiani stranieri.
Mamma: Quanto costa il *Times*?
Giornalaio: Il *Times* costa millecinquecento lire.
Mamma: E quanto costa il *Guardian*?
Giornalaio: Il *Guardian* costa duemila lire.
Mamma: Mi dia questi due.
Giornalaio: Ecco a lei questi due.
Mamma: Quant'è in tutto?
Giornalaio: In tutto è tremilacinquecento lire.

Exercise 3
Signora, posso fumare?
Signora, posso ascoltare dei dischi?
Signora, posso guardare la televisione?
Signora, posso prendere del latte?
Signora, posso prendere il suo libro?
Signora, posso prendere il giornale di Lucio?

Exercise 4
Vuoi della birra?
Vuoi delle riviste inglesi?
Vuoi dei fiammiferi?
Vuoi un'aranciata?
Vuoi un rotocalco a colori?
Vuoi due pellicole?
Vuoi un dolce al cioccolato?
Vuoi un'antologia di racconti?

Exercise 5
Vuole ordinare un frullato e un panino?
Vuole andare alla stazione?
Vuole aspettare qui in ufficio?
Vuole ritornare questa sera?
Vuole trovare quell'indirizzo?
Vuole provare quel numero di telefono?

B

Exercise 6
Può provare in libreria.
Può provare dal giornalaio.
Può provare dal tabaccaio.
Può provare in un negozio di dischi.
Può provare in gelateria.
Può provare alla SIP.

Exercise 7
Dove possiamo trovare un bar?
Dove possiamo trovare una banca aperta?
Dove possiamo trovare alcuni giornali stranieri?
Dove possiamo trovare una fermata di autobus?
Dove possiamo trovare alcuni biglietti nuovi?
Dove possiamo trovare una pizza alla napoletana?
Dove possiamo trovare un giornale di sinistra?
Dove possiamo trovare del tabacco forte?

Exercise 8
Professore: Fumi, Julie?
Julie: No, grazie, non fumo.
Professore: Fumi, Tim?
Tim: No, grazie, non fumo. Ma ho voglia di provare una sigaretta italiana.
Professore: Avete dei fiammiferi?
Yvonne: Io ho dei fiammiferi.
Professore: Ivan, che cosa prendi? Caffè o aranciata?
Ivan: Ho bisogno di un bicchiere di acqua fresca.
Professore: Tim, allora vai a comprare il regalo per il vice-direttore della scuola, oggi?
Tim: Mi dispiace, ma non posso andare oggi. Devo guardare alcune (delle) riviste di politica dal giornalaio.
Professore: Hai bisogno anche di alcuni quotidiani?
Tim: Sì. Grazie. Può portare quei quotidiani a scuola, per piacere?
Professore: Certo. Va bene.
Tim: Molte grazie.

Exercise 9
In ufficio è vietato fumare. Se voglio fumare vado fuori. Fumo circa dieci sigarette ogni giorno. Ma le sigarette non sono forti, sono leggerissime. Spesso compro sigarette francesi con filtro. Un pacchetto costa circa cinquanta penny. Il mio vice-direttore, invece, fuma la pipa. Quando non devo

lavorare molto, porto da casa un quotidiano o una rivista di moda e guardo le fotografie. A casa, invece, leggiamo libri di politica e romanzi di autori contemporanei.

Exercise 10
Per favore, ci dia l'indirizzo dell'Ente Turismo.
Per favore, ci dia il numero di telefono di un posteggio di taxi.
Per favore, ci dia il numero dell'autobus per andare in via Roma.
Per favore, ci dia il nome di una tavola calda dove possiamo mangiare bene.
Per favore, ci dia il giornale di oggi.

CHAPTER 10 ORGANISING THE WEEKEND; TELLING THE TIME

A

Exercise 1
Tim: Dove va questo pullman?
Impiegato: Questo pullman va a Venezia.
Tim: Quando parte?
Impiegato: Parte alle sette.
Tim: Quando arriva?
Impiegato: Arriva alle otto.
Tim: Quando ritorna?
Impiegato: Ritorna a mezzanotte.
Tim: Quando è il prossimo?
Impiegato: Il prossimo è alle nove.
Tim: Che ora è?/Che ore sono?
Impiegato: Sono le tre.

Exercise 2
Tim: Vorremmo delle informazioni.
Impiegato: Dove volete andare?
Tim: In montagna o al mare.
Impiegato: Volete visitare una città o dei paesi?
Tim: Ci dia degli opuscoli, per favore.
Impiegato: Ecco gli opuscoli.
Tim: Scusi, dov'è la Valtellina?

Exercise 3
McKenzie: Vorremmo noleggiare un'auto, per favore.
Impiegato: Ecco gli opuscoli.
McKenzie: In queste tariffe è compresa la benzina?
Impiegato: No, non è compresa la benzina.
McKenzie: È compresa l'assicurazione? E sono compresi i chilometri?
Impiegato: Sì, è tutto compreso.

Exercise 4
Julie: Vorrei prenotare un posto sul pullman Milano-Venezia.
Impiegato: Per quando?

Julie: Per lunedì prossimo.
Impiegato: Solo andata?
Julie: No, andata e ritorno per mercoledì mattina.

Exercise 5

1. No. Preferiamo prendere la colazione a mezzogiorno e mezzo.
2. No. Preferiamo noleggiare l'automobile alle quattro.
3. No, preferiamo riportare l'automobile alle cinque.
4. No, preferiamo visitare il castello alle undici e dieci.
5. No, preferiamo arrivare alle otto e venti.

B

Exercise 6

1. Preferisci andare alle cinque e mezzo o vuoi andare alle sei e mezzo?
2. Preferisce cominciare alla una o vuole cominciare alle due?
3. Preferisce prendere l'autobus alle sette e mezzo o vuole prendere l'autobus alle otto e mezzo?
4. Preferisci preparare uno spuntino alle quattro o vuoi preparare uno spuntino alle cinque?
5. Preferisce finire il lavoro alle due meno un quarto o vuole finire il lavoro alle tre meno un quarto?
6. Preferisce aprire l'ufficio alle tre e venticinque o vuole aprire l'ufficio alle quattro e venticinque?

Exercise 7

1. No, partiamo lunedì.
2. No, finiamo il lavoro domenica.
3. No, ritorniamo mercoledì mattina presto.
4. No, vogliamo visitare il Castello Sforzesco venerdì sera.
5. No, desideriamo arrivare giovedì alle undici.

Exercise 8

1. Abbiamo voglia di qualcosa di fresco.
2. Abbiamo bisogno di qualcosa di caldo.
3. Abbiamo voglia di qualcosa di liscio.
4. Abbiamo bisogno di qualcosa di caro.

Exercise 9

Sabato Roberto e Carla vanno da qualche parte per il fine settimana. Non so dove. C'è un festival di musica contemporanea a Brighton. Vorrei andare con alcuni amici che hanno un'auto veloce. Ma la benzina è cara. Se vado in pullman il biglietto andata e ritorno costa solo cinque sterline. Ma devo partire la mattina presto, alle sei e mezzo. I pullman partono per il mare tra le sette e le otto. E devo restare tutto il giorno a Brighton. Il primo pullman parte la sera alle nove meno venti e non arriva qui fino a mezzanotte quando non ci sono autobus per ritornare a casa e così devo prendere un taxi. Ho bisogno di un amico/un'amica. Se lui/lei può pagare il viaggio, io posso portare dei panini con il . . . salmone!

Exercise 10
La mamma e la sorella di Lucio chiedono a Tim dove va sabato. Vogliono sapere quanto dura il viaggio e quando finisce il Carnevale di Venezia. Chiedono da dove partono i pullman e vogliono vedere gli opuscoli del Carnevale.

CHAPTER 11 TALKING ABOUT ITALY AND ENGLAND; TALKING ABOUT YOUR FAMILY

A

Exercise 1
Tu e Carla, da quanto tempo siete qui?
Siamo qui da tre giorni.
Quando partite?
Partiamo il 29 marzo. Oggi che giorno è?
È il 15 marzo.

Exercise 2
McKenzie: Le piace abitare in campagna?
Rossi: No, mi piace abitare in città.
McKenzie: Perchè?
Rossi: Perchè i negozi piacciono a mia moglie, le automobili piacciono a mio figlio.
McKenzie: Io preferisco la campagna. Ma anche la montagna mi piace e anche i laghi mi piacciono.

Exercise 3
Tim: Ti piace la scuola?
Studentessa: La scuola mi piace molto e anche i professori mi piacciono.
Tim: Abiti con una famiglia o in pensione?
Studentessa: Mio padre lavora a Milano.
Tim: Allora sei qui con tuo papà e tua mamma?
Studentessa: Abito/Vivo con mio padre e mia sorella. Mio fratello insegna all'università di Parigi.
Tim: Da quanto tempo studi italiano?
Studentessa: Studio italiano da sei mesi.
Tim: Trovi l'Italia cara?
Studentessa: Trovo l'Italia a buon prezzo.

Exercise 4
1. La cucina italiana è più saporita.
2. Questo sole è più caldo.
3. Questo mare è meno freddo.
4. Gli italiani sono meno tranquilli.
5. I prezzi sono come i prezzi inglesi.
6. Le città inglesi sono meno frenetiche.
7. Questo cielo è più azzurro.

Exercise 5
The Italian football team is the best. (Gli azzurri is the name of the Italian national football team because the national uniform for sport activities is bright blue.)

Exercise 6
Buonasera.
Buonasera.
Sono . . .
Ben arrivato-a
È il signor Rossi?
Sì, sono il signor Rossi. Le presento la signora Franchi.
Piacere.
Piacere. Tutto bene in viaggio?
Sì, grazie. A domani.

B

Exercise 7
Mia madre (mia mamma). Mia mamma è inglese. È nata in un piccolo paese in campagna. La campagna le piace ancora perchè è verde e tranquilla. Ma adesso lavora in una città grande e rumorosa. Lavora lì da tre mesi. La sua giornata comincia alle sette di mattina quando prepara la nostra colazione per tutta la famiglia. La sua colazione è leggera. Beve solo un succo di frutta e mangia una fetta di pane. Finisce con un tè senza zucchero. Il suo lavoro le piace. Lavora in un negozio di libri in centro. Tutto le piace lì: i libri, i suoi colleghi. Ma anche suo marito e la sua famiglia le piacciono. Preferisce mio fratello perchè è molto divertente e allegro.

Exercise 8
Dani: Come si chiama?
McKenzie: Si chiama Sergio Frattini.
Dani: È giovane?
McKenzie: Non è molto giovane. Ha cinquant'anni. Anche sua madre e suo padre sono di Verona.
Dani: E sua moglie?
McKenzie: È più giovane. Ma è meno divertente.
Dani: E Verona? Le piace?
McKenzie: Verona è molto bella (bellissima). È una città fantastica. È meno frenetica di Milano.
Dani: Le piace l'Arena?
McKenzie: Sì, certo. Ma ha altre opere d'arte belle. La mia chiesa preferita è San Zeno!

Exercise 9
1. Scusi, la banca è ancora chiusa?
2. Da quanto tempo aspetta?
3. È straniero/a?
4. Da quanto tempo è in Italia?
5. È sposato/a?
6. Che ora è (che ore sono?) per favore?

7. Grazie.
8. Ha dei figli?

CHAPTER 12 SHOPPING: DESCRIBING GOODS; BARGAINING

A

Exercise 1

Cameriere: Ecco la sua pizza.
Pignolo: Mi dispiace, ma è un po' grande.
Cameriere: Va bene questa?
Pignolo: Il sugo di pomodoro è un po' salato. Mi dia delle patatine.
Cameriere: Ecco. Tutto bene?
Pignolo: Sono un po'crude e il caffè è un po' freddo.
Cameriere: Ecco il conto . . . Questo è salato!
Pignolo: È l'ultimo prezzo?
Cameriere: Mi dispiace, sono prezzi fissi.
Pignolo: Niente di meno?
Cameriere: Mi dispiace, no.

Exercise 2

1. Quanto costa quel tappeto rosso e quant'è grande?
2. Quanto costa questo vaso bianco e quant'è grande?
3. Quanto costano quei portacenere gialli e quanto sono grandi?
4. Quanto costano queste fotografie in bianco e nero e quanto sono grandi?
5. Quanto costano quelle riproduzioni a colori e quanto sono grandi?

Exercise 3

Di che cos'è? Di lana?
Di che cos'è? Di cotone?
Di che cos'è? Di ceramica?
Di che cos'è? Di terracotta?
Di che cos'è? Di legno?

Exercise 4

1. Sì, lo prenoto.
2. Sì, la ordino.
3. Sì, li guardo.
4. Sì, la regalo.
5. Sì, le prendo.
6. Sì, la ascolto.

Exercise 5

1. No, non mi piace.
2. No, non mi piacciono.
3. No, non mi piace.
4. No, non mi piacciono.
5. No, non mi piacciono.

Exercise 6
C'è un albergo non lontano?
C'è una camera matrimoniale libera senza bagno?
La camera è rumorosa?
Da lunedì prossimo.
Per una settimana.
Quant'è?
Dov'è l'albergo? A destra o a sinistra?

B

Exercise 7
1. È in un negozio di artigianato.
2. Sì, li hanno.
3. Sì, li hanno.
4. No, non li hanno.
5. No, non li hanno.
6. Quello rosso e grigio chiaro.
7. È grande due metri per un metro e dieci centimetri.
8. No, non le compra.
9. No, non le compra.

Exercise 8
1. È un po' caro. Mi mostri dei vasi meno cari.
2. Sono prodotti dell'artigianato locale?
3. Di che cosa sono fatti?
4. Ma questo è caro come quello bianco.
5. L'ultimo prezzo?
6. È proprio l'ultimo prezzo?
7. Niente di meno?
8. Bene, lo prendo.
9. Levi il prezzo e lo incarti.

Exercise 9
1. Da quanto tempo lo conosci?
2. Da due mesi?
3. La sua ragazza è bella?
4. La conosci?
5. Sono fidanzati?
6. Parla italiano?
7. Lo capisce un po'?
8. Ha tre auto?
9. Lei le guida?
10. Quella blu?

CHAPTER 13 GIVING ORDERS; THE POST OFFICE SYSTEM

A

Exercise 1
1. Devo scrivere il biglietto?
2. Devo andare in tabaccheria?
3. Devo comprare una busta?
4. Devo chiedere quant'è per l'Inghilterra?
5. Devo prendere anche una cartolina?
6. Devo andare alla posta?
7. Devo spedire il biglietto espresso?

Exercise 2
1. Posso aprire quella bottiglia?
2. Posso ascoltare quel disco?
3. Posso cercare il mio collega?
4. Posso fumare il mio Toscano?
5. Posso bere un Martini?
6. Posso prendere una birra dal frigo?

Exercise 3
1. Cerco un notes basso. Il più basso è questo?
2. Cerco della carta sottile. La più sottile è questa?
3. Cerco delle cartoline interessanti. Le più interessanti sono queste?
4. Cerco una rivista recente. La più recente è questa?
5. Cerco un biglietto grande. Il più grande è questo?
6. Cerco della carta da pacco robusta. La più robusta è questa?
7. Cerco una biro a buon prezzo. La più a buon prezzo è questa?

Exercise 4
1. Non abbiamo (delle) patatine.
2. Che cosa faccio?
3. Nel frigo ci sono solo alcuni pomodori.
4. I negozi sono ancora aperti?
5. A che ora chiudono?
6. Alla una?
7. Ma come faccio a arrivare là?
8. L'auto?
9. Non ce l'ho.

Exercise 5
Portiere: Buongiorno. Come va?
McKenzie: Molto bene, grazie, e lei?
Portiere: C'è un messaggio per lei.
McKenzie: Scusi? Non capisco.
Portiere: C'è un messaggio per lei.
McKenzie: Ah! Grazie. Devo andare alla Banca Centrale. Mi scusi, per andare a questa banca, che cosa devo prendere?
Portiere: Deve prendere il sette.
McKenzie: Dov'è la fermata? Ogni quanto c'è l'autobus?

Portiere: È dietro l'angolo. C'è ogni quarto d'ora.
McKenzie: La metropolitana è più veloce?

Exercise 6
— Prego.
— Quant'è un francobollo per una cartolina?
— Per l'estero o per l'Italia?
— Per l'Inghilterra.
— Quattrocento.
— Vorrei spedire una lettera via aerea per l'Inghilterra. Quant'è?

Exercise 7
1. Porti il giornale di oggi, per favore.
2. Compili questi moduli.
3. Non firmi quelle lettere.
4. Scriva alla ditta Pradella.
5. Telefoni alla Camera di Commercio; vado là tra mezz'ora.
6. Per favore, ordini due caffè, con latte e con zucchero.
7. Quando va a casa, vada alla banca e cambi questi soldi.
8. Prepari queste ricevute.
9. Spedisca questi pacchi espresso.

Exercise 8
Cerco delle cartoline della città e dei dintorni. Queste sono le più interessanti. Prendo dieci cartoline e una biro. No, non ho i francobolli. Devo comprare dieci francobolli per l'Inghilterra. Compro anche della carta da lettere e delle buste. Sì, chiedo le più forti. Sono senza, ma ripasso più tardi. Sono aperti fino alle sette.

Exercise 9
Aspetto fino alle due e mezzo. Ho bisogno di carta da pacchi e di spago perchè spedisco un pacco in Scozia. È fragile. È un vaso. Ma la cartoleria è chiusa. . . . Ha della carta da pacco robusta e dello spago? Quanto è grande il pacco? È un metro e venti centimetri per quindici centimetri. Molte grazie. Molto gentile. Posso offrire un aperitivo?

CHAPTER 14 FINDING OUT ABOUT ENTERTAINMENTS; REFUSING INVITATIONS

A

Exercise 1
1. Signorina, ché cosa fa questo pomeriggio?
2. Signor Bianchi, che cosa fa domenica?
3. Signor direttore, che cosa fa dopo?
4. Tim, che cosa fai venerdì?
5. Carla, che cosa fai mercoledì?

Exercise 2

Impiegata: Prego?
Tim: Due biglietti.
Impiegata: Per quando?
Tim: Per adesso.
Impiegata: Che posti?
Tim: I più a buon prezzo.
Impiegata: Duemila lire.
Tim: A che ora comincia il film? (lo spettacolo)

Exercise 3

(a)
1. Signori Bianchi, venite a teatro?
2. Laura, vieni in una discoteca fantastica?
3. Signora Pardi, viene in ufficio alle quattro?
4. Laura e Lucio, venite in gelateria stasera?
5. Tim, vieni a scuola in auto?

(b)
1. Non possiamo questa volta. Veniamo la prossima.
2. Non posso questa volta. Vengo la prossima.
3. Non posso questa volta. Vengo la prossima.
4. Non possiamo questa volta. Veniamo la prossima.
5. Non posso questa volta. Vengo la prossima.

Exercise 4

1. Sì, per me è lo spettacolo più divertente.
2. Sì, per me, sono i cantanti più bravi.
3. Sì, per me è il musical più comico.
4. Sì, per me è l'attrice più romantica.
5. Sì, per me sono le canzoni più drammatiche.
6. Sì, per me è il concerto più classico.
7. Sì, per me è il complesso più famoso.

Exercise 5

McKenzie: Buonasera.
Impiegata: Desidera?
McKenzie: Che cosa danno stasera nei cinema locali?
Impiegata: Ecco la pagina degli spettacoli sul giornale locale.
McKenzie: Devo prenotare?
Impiegata: No! Non deve prenotare. C'è sempre posto.
McKenzie: Ci sono altri spettacoli in città o nei dintorni?
Impiegata: Sì, c'è uno spettacolo vicino al lago. È molto bello, dicono.
McKenzie: È divertente? A che ora comincia?
Impiegata: Guardi questo opuscolo. Ci sono tutte le informazioni.

Exercise 6

Mi chiamo . . . di nome e . . . di cognome.
Sono di . . .
Sì, lo so un po'.

Sì, lo parlo.
Sono impiegato/a.
Lavoro per una ditta grande.
Si chiama . . .
Resto in Italia per un anno.
Sì, conosco il signor Bruni e la sua famiglia.

B

Exercise 7
Che cosa fate stasera? Perchè non andiamo al cinema? Danno un film interessante con Robert de Niro. Il regista è Martin Scorsese. Allora prenoto quattro posti al cinema Astra. Domenica? No, non faccio niente di speciale. Vengo volentieri a un concerto di Claudio Abbado. Posso invitare anche un collega inglese? A lui piace molto la musica classica.

Exercise 8
A lei piace molto la musica classica? Sì. A me piace molto. Ho dischi di Mozart e Bach . . . A me piace la musica drammatica. Mia moglie preferisce la musica classica più allegra. Le piace la musica di Vivaldi e di Monteverdi. Di solito, io la ascolto di mattina presto, quando vado in ufficio in auto o di sera tardi. Vado spesso ai concerti. A noi non piace andare alle feste perchè la musica rock non mi va. La musica leggera mi va ma non quella rumorosa. A me piace la musica leggera come il valzer. Non vado mai con mia moglie o con amici a una discoteca. Le discoteche? Non so dove sono. Mio figlio e mia figlia ballano spesso nelle discoteche. A mio figlio piace molto il rock. Noi preferiamo l'opera lirica o una buona risata con un musical.

Exercise 9
— Vieni a teatro con noi stasera?
— Mi dispiace. Non posso venire con voi stasera. Un'altra volta.
— Non puoi venire domani sera?
— No, non posso. Devo finire del lavoro.
— Abbiamo dei biglietti per un musical divertentissimo!
— Grazie. Ma proprio non posso venire. Se non finisco queste lettere non posso partire domani.
— Ma sono poltrone! E viene anche Laura . . .
— A che ora comincia lo spettacolo?
— Alle nove in punto.
— E a che ora finisce?
— Alle undici e un quarto, circa.
— È molto tardi . . . è divertente, dicono? Va bene! Vado in ufficio quando lo spettacolo finisce . . . e voi venite tutti con me!

CHAPTER 15 SAYING WHAT YOU DID SOME TIME BEFORE; TALKING OF THE WEATHER

A

Exercise 1
1. No, grazie. Ho già assaggiato. Un'altra volta.
2. No, grazie. Ho già bevuto. Un'altra volta.

3. No, grazie. Ho già fumato. Un'altra volta.
4. No, grazie. Ho già ordinato. Un'altra volta.
5. No, grazie. Ho già preso. Un'altra volta.

Exercise 2
1. L'ho spedita questa mattina.
2. Li ho comprati lunedì scorso.
3. L'ho fatto qualche ora fa.
4. Li ho preparati la notte scorsa.
5. Li ho prenotati qualche settimana fa.

Exercise 3
1. No, il mese scorso. Che tempo ha avuto?
2. No, l'anno scorso. Che tempo ha avuto?
3. No, l'estate scorsa. Che tempo hai avuto?
4. No, l'autunno scorso. Che tempo ha avuto?
5. No, la settimana scorsa. Che tempo ha avuto?

Exercise 4
1. Ho abitato (ho vissuto, irr.) a Londra per tre anni.
2. Ho cominciato alla Banca Internazionale.
3. Ho lavorato come cameriere per cinque mesi in campagna.
4. Ho cambiato lavoro l'estate scorsa.
5. Ho incontrato il mio ragazzo qualche mese dopo (alcuni mesi dopo).

Exercise 5
Cameriere: Prego?
Cliente: Ho già ordinato un'ora fa.
Cameriere: Mi dispiace, può ordinare ancora?
Cliente: Non prendo il primo (non prendo niente di primo). Di secondo, prendo pollo arrosto e zucchine. Poi prendo della zuppa inglese.
Cameriere: Quale vino ha ordinato?
Cliente: Mezza bottiglia di vino rosso sciolto. . . . Non sono quelli i nostri amici? . . . Venite qui.
Amici: È buona la cucina qui, vero? Prendiamo il pollo.
Cliente: Avete ragione. L'ho preso anch'io. Mi porti il conto.

Exercise 6 (revision ch. 5)
1. Come si dice 'passport' in italiano?
2. La banca è aperta?
3. Quando apre?
4. Ce l'ho.
5. Posso cambiare il denaro senza il passaporto?
6. Mi dispiace, ho solo un pezzo da mille lire.

B

Exercise 7
1. L'estate scorsa ho avuto bel tempo solo per tre settimane.
2. L'autunno scorso, ho avuto molta pioggia, ogni giorno.
3. Il maggio scorso, non ho avuto molto sole, la prima settimana.
4. In montagna, la settimana scorsa, ho avuto brutto tempo, tutto il giorno.

5. Ieri, qui in città, ho avuto bel tempo di mattina, ma brutto tempo, di pomeriggio.

Exercise 8
1. Provali anche tu. Li ho provati anch'io.
2. Bevilo anche tu. L'ho bevuto anch'io.
3. Assaggiale anche tu. Le ho assaggiate anch'io.
4. Ordina del pane. L'ho ordinato anch'io.
5. Prendi della carne. L'ho presa anch'io.

Exercise 9
1. Ho avuto un accendino in regalo tre giorni fa.
2. Ho avuto una scatola grande di cioccolatini in regalo tre giorni fa.
3. Ho avuto una borsa di pelle in regalo tre giorni fa.
4. Ho avuto della carta da lettere elegante in regalo tre giorni fa.
5. Ho avuto due biglietti per il teatro in regalo tre giorni fa.

Exercise 10
1. Abbiamo cominciato alle quattro e abbiamo finito alle sette. Abbiamo lavorato tre ore.
2. Abbiamo cominciato a mezzogiorno e abbiamo finito alle sei. Abbiamo lavorato sei ore.
3. Abbiamo cominciato alle nove e abbiamo finito alle dieci. Abbiamo lavorato un'ora.
4. Abbiamo cominciato alle quattro e mezza e abbiamo finito alle cinque. Abbiamo lavorato mezz'ora.

CHAPTER 16 TALKING OF WHERE YOU HAVE BEEN; DRESSING UP

A

Exercise 1
1. Dovrei vederlo anch'io.
2. Dovrei provarla anch'io.
3. Dovrei farlo anch'io.
4. Dovrei prenderlo anch'io.
5. Dovrei cambiarlo anch'io.

Exercise 2
— Perchè sei ritornato senza rivista?
— Ma, Lucio, sei stato dal giornalaio?
— Hai comprato quella rivista che ti ho chiesta?
— Non l'hai trovata?
— Perchè non sei andato all'edicola?
— Hanno venduto tutte le riviste?
— Hai comprato un altro giornale?

Exercise 3
Tim: Ciao! Non ti vedo da molto! Dove sei stato?
Amico: Sono stato all'università di Torino.

Tim: E Giulia, la tua amica?
Amico: La mia amica è stata in vacanza in Francia.
Tim: È andata da sola?
Amico: È andata con degli amici.
Tim: Quando ritorna?
Amico: È già ritornata.

Exercise 4
1. Ma! Mi trucco o non mi trucco?
2. Ma! Mi riposo o non mi riposo?
3. Ma! Mi rilasso o non mi rilasso?
4. Ma! Mi faccio o non mi faccio la barba?
5. Ma! Mi metto o non mi metto il vestito rosso?

Exercise 5
1. No, mi sembra un po' chiara.
2. No, mi sembrano un po' eleganti.
3. No, mi sembrano un po' care.
4. No, mi sembra un po' grande.
5. No, mi sembra un po' lungo.
6. No, mi sembra un po' scuro.

Exercise 6 (revision ch. 6)
Libraio: Prego?
McKenzie: Vorrei un vocabolario italiano-inglese.
Libraio: Un'edizione tascabile o un vocabolario più grande?
McKenzie: Vorrei un'edizione buona, ma non molto cara.
Libraio: I vocabolari sono su questo scaffale.
McKenzie: Vorrei anche vedere alcuni libri in italiano ma facili . . . racconti o un romanzo breve.

B

Exercise 7
1. Io li ho fatti ieri.
2. Io le ho fatte ieri.
3. Io l'ho fatta ieri.
4. Io l'ho fatto ieri.
5. Io li ho fatti ieri.

Exercise 8
1. No, grazie, sono andato/a ieri.
2. No, grazie, li ho comprati ieri.
3. No, grazie, l'ho guardata ieri.
4. No, grazie, sono ritornato/a ieri.
5. No, sono andato/a ieri.
6. No, grazie, l'ho preso ieri.

Exercise 9
Amici: Come va?
McKenzie: Molto bene, grazie. E voi? Che cosa fate qui?
Amici: Siamo appena ritornati dalla Sicilia.

McKenzie: Quando siete partiti?
Amici: Siamo partiti quindici giorni fa.
McKenzie: Siete andati in auto?
Amici: Sì, siamo andati in auto.
McKenzie: Vostro figlio è venuto con voi?
Amici: Sì, nostro figlio è venuto con noi.
McKenzie: Anche vostra figlia è venuta con voi?
Amici: No, nostra figlia è restata a casa.

Exercise 10

1. Mi vesto subito!
2. Mi faccio la barba subito!
3. Mi metto la giacca subito!
4. Mi trucco subito!
5. Mi vesto subito!

Exercise 11

1. Non siete mai state in Inghilterra?
2. Quando siete state a Londra?
3. Il vostro amico è venuto con voi?
4. Quando siete ritornate?
5. Siete restate per molto in Inghilterra?

CHAPTER 17 DESCRIBING WHAT YOU USED TO DO; TALKING OF A MISADVENTURE

A

Exercise 1

Dottore: Buongiorno. Che cosa si sente, signora?
McKenzie: Non mi sento bene. Ho mal di testa.
Dottore: Ha febbre?
McKenzie: Ho una leggera febbre, mi sembra.
Dottore: Ha mangiato molto a pranzo?
McKenzie: Ho mangiato un pranzo leggero.
Dottore: È stata sulla spiaggia questa mattina?
McKenzie: Sono stata sulla spiaggia tutta la mattina.
Dottore: Ha preso il sole tutta la mattina?
McKenzie: Sì, ho preso il sole per quattro ore.
Dottore: Ha preso troppo sole. Adesso deve riposarsi.

Exercise 2

Tim: Buongiorno. Il pieno, per favore.
Benzinaio: Ecco. Tutto bene i freni? L'olio?
Tim: Controlli i freni e l'olio, per favore.
Benzinaio: Tutto a posto.
Tim: Ha controllato anche l'acqua, per favore?
Benzinaio: Sì, ho controllato anche l'acqua.
Tim: Quant'è?
Benzinaio: Cinquemila lire in tutto.
Tim: Grazie e buongiorno.

Exercise 3
1. La signora McKenzie si è trovata molto bene.
2. Il cielo era sempre sereno e il mare era sempre calmo.
3. La spiaggia non era molto affollata e gli alberghi non erano esauriti.
4. La gente in albergo era simpatica.
5. Faceva delle gite in compagnia tutti i giorni.
6. Faceva il bagno ogni mattina alle otto, prima della colazione.
7. Sì, aveva la spiaggia privata.

Exercise 4
Ogni giorno mi fermavo al caffè dove prendevo un gelato al cioccolato. Poi andavo alla spiaggia, prendevo il sole tutto il giorno. Nel pomeriggio, facevo il bagno. Poi ritornavo all'albergo. E ogni sera, dopo (la) cena, uscivo con amici a ballare in una discoteca. Sì, la gente era molto simpatica. E il tempo era bello.

Exercise 5
1. Ti telefono subito.
2. Le scrivo subito.
3. Ti dico subito sì.
4. Le mostro subito il catalogo.

Exercise 6 (revision ch. 7)
1. A colazione beviamo di solito tè con il latte, senza zucchero.
2. Sì, preferiamo una colazione inglese.
3. No, non capiamo molto l'italiano.
4. A colazione mangiamo di solito due fette di pane tostato, della marmellata, del burro e del miele.
5. Le patatine sono buone?
6. Abbiamo voglia di prendere un bicchiere di birra alla spina.
7. Le bottiglie sono grandi? Sono care?

B

Exercise 7
1. No, lo prendevo tutti i giorni.
2. No, lo facevo tutti i giorni.
3. No, andavo a ballare tutti i giorni.
4. No, uscivo tutti i giorni.
5. No, entravo tutti i giorni.

Exercise 8
Ci siamo fermate a bere un caffè. Ci siamo sedute fuori e abbiamo guardato la gente. La signora McKenzie mi ha detto che si è trovata bene l'anno scorso al mare in Liguria. Il cielo era azzurro e il mare era calmo. Ogni giorno faceva una gita da qualche parte in compagnia di altra gente. Quella gente era molto simpatica. Ma un giorno ha avuto una disavventura. Niente di serio. Una mattina aveva mal di testa e aveva la febbre. È andata dal farmacista. Il farmacista le ha domandato come si sentiva, se aveva febbre: 'Un pomeriggio sono uscita in motoscafo, senza cappello, senza niente . . . '. E il farmacista mi ha detto: 'Signora, deve riposarsi un giorno o due; ha preso un colpo di sole'.

Exercise 9

Mamma: (to Lucio) Come si è trovato Tim l'anno scorso?
Lucio: In campeggio? Si è divertito molto.
Mamma: Com'era il campeggio?
Lucio: Il campeggio era attrezzato bene con tutte le comodità e tutti i servizi.
Mamma: Era pulito?
Lucio: Sì, era molto pulito.
Mamma: Dove mangiavano ogni giorno?
Lucio: Ogni giorno cucinavano a turno. Compravano mezzo chilo di pane, due etti di salame, uova . . .
Mamma: Tutti i giorni?
Lucio: Tranne un giorno. Un lunedì, sono andati in una trattoria locale vicino alla spiaggia. Hanno mangiato vitello arrosto, pomodori, melanzane . . .
Mamma: Non hanno ordinato il primo?
Lucio: No, tutti hanno preso un antipasto.

Exercise 10

1. No, è prima dell'albergo Firenze.
2. No, vengo prima delle due.
3. No, è prima dell'edicola.
4. No, è prima della cartoleria.
5. No, vengo prima di Carla.

CHAPTER 18 TALKING OF YOUR YOUTH; TALKING OF WHAT YOU WERE DOING ONE DAY

A

Exercise 1

1. Giocavo a cricket una volta. Non gioco più.
2. Giocavo a golf una volta. Non gioco più.
3. Giocavo a rugby una volta. Non gioco più.
4. Nuotavo una volta. Non nuoto più.
5. Suonavo musica classica una volta. Non suono più.
6. Recitavo una volta. Non recito più.
7. Parlavo francese una volta. Non parlo più (non lo parlo più).

Exercise 2

Carla: Hai degli animali a casa in Francia?
Julie: Sì, ho un gatto e un cane.
Carla: Sono vecchi o giovani?
Julie: Il gatto è giovane, il cane è vecchio. Ha quindici anni. E tu, Carla, non hai nessun gatto? Nessun cane?
Carla: Non ho nessun gatto, adesso. Avevo due gatti fino a due anni fa.
Julie: Come erano?
Carla: Erano belli. Avevano il pelo lungo. E i tuoi animali?
Julie: Il cane è marrone, con occhi affettuosi marrone scuro. Il pelo del gatto è nero, lungo. Gli occhi sono verdi.

Carla: Come si chiamano?
Julie: Si chiamano Mimi e Mumu.

Exercise 3
— Buongiorno, desidera?
McKenzie: Volevo far pulire questa camicia.
— Per quando?
McKenzie: Per domani. Ho premura.
— Che macchia è?
McKenzie: Non lo so. Facevo dei panini. Forse era burro . . .
— o mentre mi vestivo e mi truccavo.

Exercise 4
McKenzie: Buongiorno. Ho perso la borsa.
Vigile: Quando l'ha persa?
McKenzie: L'ho persa un'ora fa.
Vigile: Dove?
McKenzie: Al grande magazzino di via Milano. Provavo delle scarpe con un'amica. Quando ho finito, la borsa non era più là.
Vigile: Che cosa aveva dentro?
McKenzie: Avevo circa cinquanta sterline.
Vigile: Il suo nome, prego.

Exercise 5
1. Avevi molti studenti nella tua scuola?
2. C'erano molti professori?
3. Studiavi molte ore alla settimana?
4. Ti sei fermato molti giorni a Milano?
5. Avevi molte amiche a Milano?

Exercise 6
1. Per me, dell'altra mozzarella, per favore. È buonissima.
2. Per me, dell'altro prosciutto crudo, per favore. È buonissimo.
3. Per me, dell'altro formaggio tenero, per favore. È buonissimo.
4. Per me, dell'altro vino rosso, per favore. È buonissimo.
5. Per me, dell'altra macedonia, per favore. È buonissima.
6. Per me, dell'altra insalata condita, per favore. È buonissima.
7. Per me, dell'altro sugo, per favore. È buonissimo.
8. Per me, dell'altra acqua minerale, per favore. È buonissima.
9. Per me, dell'altro gelato alla frutta, per favore. È buonissimo.
10. Per me degli altri frullati, per favore. Sono buonissimi.
11. Per me delle altre pizze ai funghi, sono buonissime.

B

Exercise 7
1. Queste scarpe sono le tue?
2. Questi calzoni sono i tuoi?
3. Queste camicie sono le sue?
4. Queste giacche sono le sue?
5. Questi soldi sono i tuoi?

6. Questi documenti sono i suoi?
7. Queste riviste sono le tue?

Exercise 8

1. Quando ero un bambino (da bambino) abitavo in una casa grande in campagna.
2. Mi piaceva giocare nel giardino o in casa con delle automobili piccole.
3. Avevo due cani grossi. Si chiamavano Black e White. Avevano un pelo lungo e lucente. Gli occhi erano marroni.
4. Mi piaceva andare a scuola perchè mi piaceva il mio maestro, ma non mi piaceva che cosa mangiavamo.
5. Quando avevo dodici anni, ho cominciato a giocare a tennis. Mi piaceva anche nuotare. Mia sorella era più tranquilla. Lei leggeva, suonava la musica. Era sempre molto elegante perchè mia madre (la mamma) faceva i suoi vestiti (le faceva i vestiti: made the dresses for her).

Exercise 9

Questa mattina sono uscito dall'albergo Torino verso le otto (circa alle otto). Avevo la mia cartella con me. L'ho messa in auto. Mentre guidavo verso l'ufficio, mi sono fermato di fronte a un'edicola. Sono sceso e sono andato a comprare un giornale. Mentre lo compravo e lo pagavo, un uomo è entrato nella mia auto e ha preso la mia cartella. Che cosa devo fare?

Exercise 10

1. Mentre guardavo le vetrine di un negozio di scarpe . . .
2. Mentre facevo il pieno di benzina . . .
3. Mentre parlavo a un mio conoscente . . .
4. Mentre ero seduto/a al bar con un mio amico . . .
5. Mentre prendevo il tram con una mia collega . . .
6. Mentre scendevo dalla metropolitana con molti pacchi . . .

Exercise 11

1. Mi dispiace, non ho nessun rotocalco nuovo.
2. Mi dispiace, non ho nessuna cartolina di Milano.
3. Mi dispiace, non ho nessun gettone del telefono.
4. Mi dispiace, non ho nessun foglio e nessuna busta.
5. Mi dispiace, non ho nessuna biro.

Exercise 12

1. Sa giocare a tennis?
2. Perchè non giochiamo a tennis questo pomeriggio?
3. Dove la incontro?
4. Benissimo (benone), la incontro fuori dal suo ufficio, alle tre e mezzo.
5. No, giocavo a rugby quando avevo vent'anni. Adesso gioco a golf. Sì, mi piacevano tutti gli sport.

CHAPTER 19 ORGANISING DEPARTURES; FAREWELLS

A

Exercise 1

Dani: Quando partirà per Amalfi?
McKenzie: Partirò tra una quindicina di giorni.
Dani: Quanto tempo ci vuole da Roma a Napoli?
McKenzie: Ci vogliono circa tre ore.
Dani: Ci sarà subito la coincidenza?
McKenzie: Se ci sarà subito la coincidenza, proseguirò.
Dani: Quanto tempo starà a Amalfi?
McKenzie: Starò quindici giorni. Ma se ci sarà bel tempo, starò di più.

Exercise 2

1. Sì, mi è piaciuto molto. Grazie di tutto.
2. Sì, mi è piaciuta molto. Grazie di tutto.
3. Sì, mi sono piaciuti molto. Grazie di tutto.
4. Sì, mi è piaciuto molto. Grazie di tutto.
5. Sì, mi è piaciuto molto. Grazie di tutto.
6. Sì, mi è piaciuta molto, grazie di tutto.

Exercise 3

1. Se ci sarà un posto, partirò subito.
2. Se ci sarà la coincidenza, proseguirò.
3. Se ci sarà uno sciopero, non prenderò il treno. Andrò in auto.
4. Se ci sarà bel tempo, starò di più.
5. Se avrò tempo, scriverò.
6. Se avrò tempo, andrò a trovare la signora Bianchi.

Exercise 4

1. Arriverò tra venti giorni.
2. Sarò a casa tra due ore.
3. Partirò tra un'ora.
4. Telefonerò tra una settimana?
5. Ritornerò tra un mese.

Exercise 5

1. No, ci vogliono più di nove ore.
2. No, ci vogliono più di otto ore.
3. No, ci vogliono più di undici ore.
4. No, ci vogliono più di quattro ore.
5. No, ci vogliono più di sei ore.

Exercise 6

1. Dove posso comprare della birra?
2. Dov'è quel negozio?
3. Quanto dista?
4. Ci dia un pacchetto di sigarette da venti.
5. Quelle con il filtro, per favore.
6. Ci dia anche dei gettoni.

7. Quanto costa un gettone?
8. Mi dispiace, non ho moneta.

B

Exercise 7
1. Quanti chilometri ci sono da qui a Amalfi?
2. Quante ore ci vogliono?
3. Quanti panini compro?
4. Quanti chili di frutta compro?
5. Quanti giorni starai via?
6. Quante valigie hai?

Exercise 8
1. Chi sono? Sono le tue amiche?
2. Chi è? È il tuo professore?
3. Chi sono? Sono i tuoi ospiti?
4. Chi sono? Sono le tue compagne?
5. Chi sono? Sono i tuoi colleghi?
6. Chi è? È il tuo direttore?
7. Chi sono? Sono i tuoi clienti?
8. Chi sono? Sono le tue figlie?

Exercise 9
1. Se avrò bisogno, chiederò un tuo consiglio.
2. Se avrò premura, prenderò un taxi.
3. Se avrò sete, prenderò la birra nel frigo.
4. Se avrò la coincidenza, arriverò prima.
5. Se avrò un posto in treno, farò un viaggio più comodo.
6. Se avrò un appuntamento, sarò contenta.
7. Se avrò bel tempo, mi fermerò di più.

Exercise 10
1. Ti è piaciuto il mese a Milano?
2. Ti ringrazio di tutto.
3. Ti ringrazio tanto.
4. Sei stata molto gentile.
5. Tua moglie è stata molto ospitale.
6. Salutami i tuoi figli.
7. Salutami gli amici.
8. Ti scriverò senz'altro.
9. Non dimenticarti di noi.

Exercise 11
1. Volevo fare un viaggio a Amalfi con mia moglie. Che treni ci sono?
2. Volevo partire di mattina.
3. C'è un rapido così non devo cambiare?
4. Quanto costa il biglietto?
5. Quanto tempo prima devo prenotare?
6. Con questo espresso quando arriviamo a Roma?
7. C'è una coincidenza, subito?
8. Questo treno è di solito in orario?

CHAPTER 20 PRIVATE LETTERS; BUSINESS LETTERS

A

Exercise 1

Egregio direttore,

gradirei prenotare una camera matrimoniale con bagno per quattordici giorni. Gradirei sapere quanto costa.

Distinti saluti

Exercise 2

Cara . . . ,

ti ringrazio della compagnia, a nome mio e del mio ragazzo. Abbiamo fatto buon viaggio e spero di rivederti in Inghilterra.

Cari saluti a te e a tua madre

Exercise 3

Gentile signora . . . ,

arriverò all'aeroporto di Milano martedì prossimo alle dodici. Prenderò il pullman per l'air-terminal. Poi telefonerò. Il tempo in Inghilterra è brutto. So che è bello in Italia.

Distinti saluti

Exercise 4

1. Sto telefonando.
2. Sto andando.
3. Lo sto cercando.
4. Le sto scrivendo.
5. La sto preparando.

Exercise 5

I miei fiori! Le mie piante! I miei dischi! I miei manifesti! Le mie amiche! I miei colleghi! I miei genitori! I miei gatti!

Exercise 6

McKenzie: Pronto? Signora Pardi? Sono la signora McKenzie.

Pardi: Telefona dall'Inghilterra?

McKenzie: Sì. Le telefono perchè la voglio ringraziare del piacevole soggiorno a Milano e della sua compagnia.

Pardi: Ha fatto buon viaggio?

McKenzie: Sì, grazie.

Pardi: Io ho trovato due belle stampe di Milano e Lucio gliele porterà.

McKenzie: La ringrazio di nuovo di tutto. Saluti a tutti. Arriverderci.

Pardi: Mi saluti la sua famiglia. Arriverderci.

Exercise 7

1. Noi partiamo alle due, loro partono alle due e mezzo.
2. Noi prendiamo il pullman delle due, loro prendono il pullman delle tre.
3. Noi arriviamo alle quattro, loro arrivano alle otto.
4. Noi ritorniamo alle dieci, loro ritornano alle dieci e mezzo.
5. Noi leggiamo un romanzo di Alberto Moravia, loro leggono un racconto di Italo Calvino.
6. Noi restiamo in montagna un mese, loro restano un mese e dieci giorni.

B

Exercise 8

1. C'è nessuno lì?
2. Non avete nessun dizionario russo?
3. Non c'è nessun cioccolatino?
4. Non c'è nessuno che parla inglese?
5. Non c'è nessun treno per Roma?
6. Il negozio non apre mai alle due?

Exercise 9

1. Le mie foto sono qui. Te le porto subito.
2. I miei bicchieri sono qui. Te li porto subito.
3. La mia cartella è qui. Te la porto subito.
4. La mia penna è qui. Te la porto subito.
5. I miei libri sono qui. Te li porto subito.
6. Le mie giacche sono qui. Te le porto subito.
7. Le mie camicie sono qui. Te le porto subito.

1. Vuole le mie foto? Gliele do adesso.
2. Vuole i miei bicchieri? Glieli do adesso.
3. Vuole la mia cartella? Gliela do adesso.
4. Vuole la mia penna? Gliela do adesso.
5. Vuole i miei libri? Glieli do adesso.
6. Vuole la mia giacca? Gliela do adesso.
7. Vuole le mie camicie? Gliele do adesso.

Exercise 10

Gentile signora,

scrivo in risposta al suo annuncio dell'8 gennaio sul *Giornale di Como* per un posto alla pari. Ho vent'anni. Ho lavorato con una famiglia italiana a Roma l'estate scorsa. Adesso lavoro come commessa in un grande magazzino a Londra. Gradirei (vorrei) passare l'estate prossima in Italia nella sua città. Gradirei avere ulteriori informazioni sul lavoro. Mi piacciono i bambini e le posso spedire delle lettere di referenze se necessario.

In attesa di una gentile risposta,
distinti saluti

Exercise 11

Cara Laura,

sono in Italia da una settimana. Mi piace il mio lavoro. (il mio lavoro mi piace). La famiglia è simpatica. C'è la madre, il padre e due bambini piccoli. Il bambino ha otto anni, la ragazza cinque. Dalla mia camera posso vedere tutta la città e il lago. L'Italia è un paese molto interessante: i francobolli si comprano dai tabaccai. E i biglietti dell'autobus si vendono dal giornalaio. I posti per i pullman non si possono prenotare. Si mangia l'insalata con l'olio e l'aceto e si beve il caffè tutto il tempo. Si mangia tra la una e le due, e tra le otto e le nove di sera. Poi si va al cinema o al teatro. Sono le due di notte. Anch'io sono stata al cinema.

KEY TO THE REVISION AND SELF-ASSESSMENT TESTS

CHAPTERS 1–5

Exercise 1
1. Tutto bene in viaggio?
2. Scusi, è la signora Pardi?
3. Scusa, sei Lucio?
4. Scusa, sei Julie?
5. È la chiesa di San Babila?

Exercise 2
1. Scusi, di dov'è?
2. C'è una camera libera?
3. Dov'è?
4. È lontano?

Exercise 3
Dov'è via Verdi quattro?
Dov'è via Verdi uno?
Dov'è via Verdi cinque?
Dov'è via Verdi otto?
Dov'è via Verdi sette?
Dov'è via Verdi sei?
Dov'è via Verdi dieci?

Exercise 4
1. Ogni quanto c'è il dodici?
2. La metro va fino a San Siro?
3. Dov'è la fermata?
4. È vicino al semaforo?
5. Molte grazie.

Exercise 5
Quant'è? Settemila? – Quant'è? Cinquemila? – Quant'è? Duemila? – Quant'è? Tremila? – Quant'è? Mille? – Quant'è? Seimila?

Exercise 6
È più comoda la pensione Firenze o la pensione Venezia? È più grande l'università di Milano o l'università di Torino? È più lontana la filiale di via Roma o di via Verezia? È più piccola Venezia o Verona? È più vicino piazzale Garibaldi o piazzale Mazzini?

Exercise 7
Dov'è il mio assegno da viaggio? Non lo so dov'è il tuo. Il mio è qui.
Dov'è il mio biglietto? Non lo so dov'è il tuo. Il mio è qui.
Dov'è la mia cartella? Non lo so dov'è la tua. La mia è qui.
Dov'è il mio pezzo da diecimila? Non lo so dov'è il tuo. Il mio è qui.
Dov'è la mia penna? Non lo so dov'è la tua. La mia è qui.

Exercise 8
Lavoro a Londra.
No, non abito a Londra.
Sono in Italia per lavoro.
Resto in Italia per una settimana.
Capisco l'italiano ma non parlo italiano molto bene.

Exercise 9
1. Come si chiama la signora?
2. Come si chiama?
3. Come si dice in italiano 'a first class hotel'?
4. Sa dov'è piazza Roma?
5. Può arrivare tra un quarto d'ora?
6. Di dov'è?

Exercise 10
1. Sì, via Pasubio è vicino a via Crespi.
2. Via Lovani è a destra di corso Garibaldi.
3. No, via Della Moscova non è in fondo a corso Garibaldi.
4. No, via Della Moscova non è dopo via Statuto.
5. No, non c'è Largo La Foppa in fondo a corso Garibaldi.

CHAPTERS 6–10

A

Exercise 1
1. Vorrei comprare una scatola di cioccolatini.
2. Vorrei vedere un vocabolario di italiano.
3. Vorrei ascoltare dei dischi di musica leggera.
4. Vorrei un altro gelato e una sola aranciata.

Exercise 2
Signora, che cosa prende? E tu? E lei? Cameriere! Per tutti . . . Pago io questa volta! La prossima volta . . . Cin . . . cin!

Exercise 3

Per me . . . Per noi . . . (or per me e mia moglie) Del formaggio, per favore. Quello tenero, non quello bianco. Il formaggio è molto leggero e tutto è buonissimo. . . . Grazie.

Exercise 4

1. Non capisco. (c) Può ripetere?
2. Ho bisogno di un'altra camera. (f) Può cercare due camere?
3. Ho voglia di un altro panino. (b) Può portare un panino al formaggio?
4. Non ho moneta. (e) Può cambiare mille lire?
5. Il treno parte alle sette. (d) Può ordinare un taxi?
6. Ecco la firma. (a) Può verificare?

Exercise 5

1. No, non mangiamo mai prosciutto con lo zucchero.
2. No, non prendiamo mai l'insalata condita.
3. No, non beviamo mai aperitivi amari.
4. No, non ordiniamo mai le pizze fredde.
5. No, non beviamo mai birra ghiacciata.

Exercise 6

lighter; bread; nothing else; meanwhile; draught (beer); cover; pop group; made; fridge; best; short; yesterday; ice-cream parlour.

Exercise 7

1. Dei bicchieri di vino anche per noi e per loro, allora.
2. Delle uova sode anche per noi e per loro, allora.
3. Delle fette di pane tostato anche per noi e per loro, allora.
4. Delle trote piccole anche per noi e per loro, allora.
5. Dei settimanali italiani anche per noi e per loro, allora.

Exercise 8

1. Io cambio gli assegni, loro pagano con le sterline.
2. Io telefono alla libreria, loro vanno in discoteca.
3. Io lavoro, loro studiano.
4. Io ritorno a mezzogiorno, loro mangiano alla tavola calda.
5. Io incontro il professore, loro parlano con il dottor Segni.

Exercise 9

1. Quell' autobus va in via Venezia?
2. L'assicurazione è inclusa in quel prezzo?
3. La benzina è inclusa in quelle tariffe?
4. Quelle camere hanno il bagno?
5. Quella ragazza è la tua amica italiana?
6. Quell'auto rossa è tua?
7. Quella gita sul Lago di Como costa molto?

CHAPTERS 11–15

A

Exercise 1
1. Mi porti un giornale locale.
2. Mi prepari due uova sode.
3. Mi porti dell'altro tè.
4. Mi metta la mia borsa in auto.
5. Mi prepari il conto.

Exercise 2
1. Ha dei figli?
2. Ha delle figlie?
3. Dove lavora la figlia più giovane?
4. Suo marito è qui in Italia?
5. Riceve posta dall'Italia?

Exercise 3
1. Il biglietto è un po'caro.
2. La gita è un po' corta.
3. Il pullman non è molto comodo.
4. Cerco una gita meno cara.
5. Il pullman parte troppo presto.

Exercise 4
1. Le posso presentare . . .
2. È l'ultimo prezzo?
3. Offro io.
4. Che cosa danno?

B

Exercise 5
Negoziante: Desideri?
Tim: Cerco qualche cartolina a colori *or* (delle cartoline).
Negoziante: Ecco qualche cartolina a colori. Va bene?
Tim: Ci sono altri soggetti? Con una gondola e il mare?
Negoziante: Sì, abbiamo queste con il mare e la gondola.
Tim: È proprio l'ultimo prezzo?
Negoziante: Sì, è proprio l'ultimo prezzo.
Tim: Le prendo e le incarti.

Exercise 6
1. Mi può fare uno sconto? Mi dispiace, ma abbiamo prezzi fissi.
2. Mi può presentare a quella signorina? Mi dispiace, ma non conosco quella signorina.
3. Mi può riportare a casa? Mi dispiace, ma non ho l'automobile.
4. Mi può telefonare? Mi dispiace, ma non ho il suo numero.
5. Mi può comprare quella rivista? No, non posso perchè l'edicola è chiusa.

Exercise 7

1. Mi piace questo formaggio perchè è molle.
2. Studio il tedesco ma non è facile.
3. McKenzie ha un appuntamento con la sua collega.
4. McKenzie noleggia un auto perchè è tardi.
5. Non è inglese perchè è nata a Milano.

Exercise 8

1. Che cosa fai stasera? Ritorni a Roma?
2. Che cosa fai ora? Vai fuori a bere qualcosa?
3. Che cosa fai fra mezz'ora? Telefoni a tua madre?
4. Che cosa fai alla banca? Cambi i soldi?
5. Che cosa fai? Lo compri?

Exercise 9

1. Non l'abbiamo mai presa in affitto. Prendiamola!
2. Non l'abbiamo mai comprato. Compriamolo!
3. Non li abbiamo mai prenotati. Prenotiamoli.
4. Non li abbiamo mai ascoltati. Ascoltiamoli.
5. Non l'abbriamo mai suonata. Suoniamola.

Exercise 10

1. Sì, la so cominciare.
2. Sì, lo so chiedere.
3. Sì, li so cercare.
4. Sì, li so prenotare.
5. Sì, lo so parlare.
6. Sì, la so guidare.

Exercise 11

1. I nostri? Li abbiamo venduti l'anno scorso.
2. La nostra? L'abbiamo pagata due giorni fa.
3. Il nostro? L'abbiamo avuto un'ora fa.
4. I nostri? Li abbiamo preparati una settimana fa.
5. I nostri? Li abbiamo assaggiati un momento fa.

CHAPTERS 16–20

Exercise 1

Tim: Venite spesso in questa trattoria?

Carla: Veniamo qualche volta. La volta scorsa ho ordinato lasagne con i funghi. Le ho gustate moltissimo.

Tim: (to Julie) La mamma di Lucio le ha fatte la settimana scorsa. Le ho mangiate a pranzo e a cena!

Julie: Che vino avete bevuto con le lasagne?

Lucio: Non hai mai assaggiato i nostri vini? Li fa mio papà ogni autunno.

Carla: (to Julie) Ti piace cucinare?

Julie: Sì. Stamattina ho sperimentato una nuova ricetta: la zuppa inglese.

Exercise 2

1. Dove trovo delle camicie?
2. Vorrei vedere una camicia.
3. Sì, è per me.
4. Di cotone non di nylon.
5. La mia taglia è . . .
6. La posso provare?
7. È un po'troppo piccola.
8. Posso provare un'altra camicia? *or* Ne posso provare un'altra?
9. Questa va bene.
10. Avete una camicia rossa come questa?
11. Quant'è *or* quanto costa?
12. Va bene. La prendo.
13. Grazie. Buonasera *or* buongiorno.

Exercise 3

Mrs McKenzie: Non mi sento bene, dottore.
Dottore: Che cosa si sente?
Mrs McKenzie: Ho mal di testa.
Dottore: Ha febbre? Ha mangiato molto a pranzo?
Mrs McKenzie: Non ho febbre. No, non ho mangiato molto a pranzo.
Dottore: Ha bevuto della birra molto fredda?
Mrs McKenzie: No, non ho bevuto della birra molto fredda.
Dottore: Che cosa ha fatto ieri pomeriggio?
Mrs McKenzie: Ieri pomeriggio sono andata fuori in motoscafo.
Dottore: Ha preso molto sole?
Mrs McKenzie: Sì, ho preso molto sole.

Exercise 4

1. È sempre sereno?
2. Il mare è sempre calmo?
3. La spiaggia è molto affollata?
4. Gli alberghi sono esauriti?
5. C'è gente simpatica in albergo?
6. Fa il bagno tutti i giorni?

Exercise 5

1. C'era un mio amico alla stazione.
2. Ero stanco e volevo rilassarmi.
3. Il mio amico mi ha accompagnato a un piccolo albergo vicino alla stazione.
4. La città sembrava rumorosa ma interessante.
5. L'albergo era pulito.
6. La mattina dopo sono andato-a a scuola dove ho incontrato la mia professoressa di italiano. Si chiamava Paola Marazzelli.

Exercise 6

1. Scusi, da che marciapiede parte il treno delle nove e venticinque?
2. Scusi, da che marciapiede parte il treno delle dieci e dieci?
3. Scusi, da che marciapiede parte il treno delle cinque e dieci?
4. Scusi, da che marciapiede parte il treno delle sei e trentacinque?

5. Scusi, da che marciapiede parte il treno delle dodici e quaranta?
6. Scusi, da che marciapiede parte il treno delle sette e dieci?
7. Scusi, da che marciapiede parte il treno delle due e venti?
8. Scusi, da che marciapiede parte il treno delle sei e venti?

Exercise 7

1. Dove si prenotano i posti per il teatro?
2. Scusi, dove si comprano delle cartoline?
3. Dove si può trovare un albergo a buon prezzo?
4. Dove si può prendere un autobus per viale Venezia?
5. Dove si può comprare del vino rosso buono?

SUPPLEMENTARY VOCABULARY LISTS

CONTENTS

1 Greetings; nationalities

a presto	see you soon
arrivederci per ora	goodbye for now
molto lieto-a	glad to have met you
spero di rivederla	I hope to see you again (formal)
spero di rivederti	I hope to see you again (informal)
americano-a	American
austriaco-a (pl. -ci, -che)	Austrian
gallese-e	Welsh
irlandese-e	Irish
pachistano-a	Pakistani

2 Accommodation

ammobiliato-a	furnished
l'aria condizionata (f)	air-conditioning
la camera a due letti (f)	room with two beds
con vista su ...	with view on ...
la mezza pensione (f)	half board
il motel (m)	motel
la pensione completa (f)	full board
il pianterreno (m)	ground floor
il riscaldamento (m)	heating
il servizio di lavanderia (m)	laundry service

3 Towns; transport

la cattedrale (f)	cathedral
il consolato (m)	consulate
il museo (m)	museum
l'ospedale (m)	hospital
il parcheggio (m)	car park
il viale (m)	avenue
l'abbonamento (m)	season ticket
la biglietteria (f)	ticket office
la fermata a richiesta (f)	request stop
la fermata obbligatoria (f)	regular stop
valido-a	valid

4 Jobs

l'agricoltore (m)	farmer
avere un lavoro	to have a job
il capo (m)	head, boss
disoccupato-a	unemployed
la fabbrica (f) (pl. -che)	factory
fare (irr.) il/la ...	to work as ...
la fattoria (f)	farm
l'industria (f)	industry
il manager (m)	manager
l'operaio (m)	worker; working class person
in pensione	retired

5 Money; telephones

il dollaro (m)	dollar
l'operazione bancaria (f)	bank transaction
il resto (m)	rest
riscuotere	to cash
la sterlina (f)	pound

la valuta (f)	currency
il centralino (m)	operator
fare (irr.) un numero	to dial a number
le pagine gialle (f pl.)	yellow pages
fare una telefonata	to make a telephone call
il prefisso (m)	code number
la teleselezione (f)	trunk call

6 Ice-cream parlour

il cappuccino (m)	white coffee
la cioccolata (f)	chocolate drink
il cono (m)	cone
la panna (f)	cream
la pasta (f)	small cake

6 Book/record shop

la cassetta (f)	cassette
esaurito-a	out of print
lo scrittore (m)	writer
tascabile-e	pocket size

7 Drinks; cutlery

l'acqua tonica (f) (pl. toniche)	tonic water
la bibita (f)	drink (non-alcoholic)
il caffè corretto (m)	coffee with brandy
la limonata (f)	lemonade
il coltello (m)	knife
il cucchiaio (m)	spoon
la forchetta (f)	fork
il piattino (m)	saucepan
la tazza (f)	cup
il cognac, lo whisky, la vodka	remain the same in Italian

8 Snacks

l'aceto (m)	vinagre
il boccale (m)	tankard
condire	to dress (salad)
la maionese (f)	mayonnaise
il pepe (m)	pepper
il piatto freddo (m)	cold plate
la pizza alla marinara (f)	pizza with seafood
la pizza alle quattro stagioni (f)	(lit. four seasons) four different slices

la tartina (f)	savoury cake
il self service (m)	self-service

9 Tobacconist; newsagent

accendere	to light
formato lungo (m)	king size
la stecca (f) (pl. -che)	carton
le Esportazioni (f pl.)	brand of cigarette
le Nazionali (f pl.)	brand of cigarette
l'abbonamento (m)	subscription
il giornale della sera (m)	evening paper
il giornale sportivo (m)	sport paper
la stampa (f)	press
l'ultimo numero (m)	last number

10 Months

gennaio (m)	January
febbraio (m)	February
marzo (m)	March
aprile (m)	April
maggio (m)	May
giugno (m)	June
luglio (m)	July
agosto (m)	August
settembre (m)	September
ottobre (m)	October
novembre (m)	November
dicembre (m)	December

11 Family

il cognato (m) la cognata (f)	brother/sister in law
il cugino (m) la cugina (f)	cousin
il fidanzato (m) la fidanzata (f)	fiancé, fiancée
il nipote (m) la nipote (f)	nephew, niece
il nonno (m) la nonna (f)	grandparent
i parenti (m pl.)	relatives
il suocero (m) la suocera (f)	father/mother in law
stretto-a	close
il vicino (m) la vicina (f) di casa	neighbour
lo zio (m) la zia (f) (pl. zii, zie)	uncle, aunt

12 Materials; souvenirs

l'anello (m)	ring
l'argento (m)	silver

il braccialetto	bracelet
la collana (f)	necklace
l'oro (m)	gold
l'orologio (m)	watch; clock
il piatto (m)	decorative plate
la porcellana (f)	porcelain
il quadro (m)	picture
il vetro (m)	glass

13 Post office

assicurato-a	insured
la consegna (f)	delivery
la corrispondenza (f)	correspondence
a domicilio	at one's own residence
il postino (m) la postina (f)	postman
il sovrappeso (m)	overweight
lo sportello (m)	counter, window
il telegramma (m)	telegram
il telex (m)	telex

14 Entertainments

l'attore (f)	actor
la fila (f)	row
l'intervallo (m)	interval
la maschera (f)	usherette
il posto (m)	seat
la prenotazione (f)	reservation
il programma (m)	programme
il protagonista (m)	main character
la protagonista (f)	
il vestito da sera (evening dress)	evening dress

15(a) Fruit

la fragola (f)	strawberry
la mela (f)	apple
la pera (f)	pear
la pesca (f) (pl. -che)	peach
l'uva (f sing.)	grapes

(b) Weather

nuvoloso-a	cloudy
piovere	to rain
la primavera (f)	spring
tiepido-a	warm
il vento (m); c'è –	wind; it's windy

16 Clothes

la biancheria (f)	linen
i calzini (m pl.)	socks
la camicetta (f)	blouse
il collant (m)	tights
il fazzoletto (m)	scarf; handkerchief
il golf (m)	cardigan
il maglione (m)	jumper
la manica (f); con le . . .; senza maniche	sleeve; with . . . ; sleeveless
i sandali (m pl.)	sandals
scollato-a	low neck (dress, shoes)

17 Health problems

la bocca (f) (-che)	mouth
il cerotto (m)	sticking plaster
il dente (m); mal di denti	tooth; toothache
ferito-a	wounded
l'incidente (m)	accident
il naso (m); sangue da –	nose; nose bleed
la pastiglia (f)	pill
la ricetta (f)	prescription
scottarsi	to burn oneself
tagliarsi	to cut oneself

18 Sports; hobbies

l'atletica (f)	athletics
il calcio (m); giocare a –	football; to play –
il cavallo (m); andare a –	horse; riding
dipingere	to paint
disegnare	to draw
fare fotografie	to take pictures
la gara (f); fare una –	competition; to take part in –
il giardinaggio (m)	gardening
la ginnastica (f)	gymnastics
interessarsi a	to be interested in
la barca a vela (f); fare della vela	sailing boat; to go sailing

19 Trains

la biglietteria (f)	ticket office
il binario (m)	platform
la carrozza ristorante (f)	dining car
il deposito bagagli (m)	left luggage office
il gabinetto (m)	toilet

occupato-a	engaged; taken
prenotato-a	booked
lo scompartimento (m)	compartment
seconda classe (f); biglietto di –	second class; – ticket
l'ufficio informazioni (m)	information office

20 Airport

addio	farewell
l'abbraccio (m)	hug
l'arrivo (m); in –	arrival; on arrival
il bacio (m)	kiss
i bagagli (m pl.)	luggage
il check-in (m)	check-in
la mancia (f)	tip
la partenza (f); in –	departure; leaving
il portabagagli (m)	porter
la sala d'attesa (f)	waiting room

21 Conversion table: temperatures

Centigrade – Fahrenheit
10 – 50; 15 – 59; 20 – 68; 25 – 77; 38 – 89

Weight
The figure in the middle can be read as either a metric or an imperial measurement.

lb		*kg*	*kg*		*lb*
2.2	1	0.45	15.4	7	3.2
6.6	3	1.4	17.6	8	3.6
1.1	5	2.2	22	10	4.5

Litres – gallons
5 = 1.1; 10 = 2.2; 15 = 3.3; 20 = 4.4; 30 = 6.6; 40 = 8.8

USEFUL BOOKS AND ADDRESSES

BOOKS

Italy. Travellers' Handbook (1982–83). Available from the Italian State Tourist Office, 1 Princes Street, London W1R 7RA. An excellent and comprehensive book with a mine of information and addresses and a bibliography of guidebooks.

Holme Timothy (ed.), *Penguin Italian Reader* (Penguin, 1974). Very short reading passages from newspapers and contemporary writers.

Lazzarino Graziana, *Da capo. A review grammar* (Holt, Rinehart & Winston, 1979). An intermediate detailed reference grammar.

Lepschy, Anna Laura e Giulio, *The Italian Language Today* (Hutchinson, 1979). An advanced reference grammar text.

McCormick Colin, Colaciechi Julie, *Life in an Italian Town* (Harrap, 1978). English passages about Italy.

Smith Herbert W., *A First Italian Reader for Adults* (University of London Press, 1971).

Trevelyan Raleigh, *Italian Short Stories-Racconti italiani, Penguin Parallel Text* (Penguin Books Ltd, 1965).

Waldman Guido, *The Penguin Book of Italian Short Stories* (Penguin, 1969). A bird's eye view of Italian literature in translation.

DICTIONARIES

Collins Sansoni, *Italian–English, English–Italian Dictionary*, Sansoni Editore, 1981.

The Concise Cambridge Italian Dictionary, compiled by Barbara Reynolds, Penguin Books, 1975.

Dizionario Garzanti della lingua italiana, Garzanti editore, Milano.

Pietro Elia, *I verbi italiani per gli stranieri*, Edizioni Scolastiche Mondadori, 1980.

ADDRESSES

CILT (The Centre for Information on Language Teaching and Research), Regent's College, Inner Circle, Regent's Park, London NW1 4NS. The centre offers an information service on all aspects of language learning and course materials. It also has an extensive library where books and audio materials may be consulted.

GRAMMAR SUMMARY

CONTENTS

NOUNS: GENDER AND PLURALS

1 The gender: all nouns are either masculine or feminine (even the angels! They are masculine). The ending of a noun does not reveal the gender; it is therefore indispensable to learn the gender when you learn the noun.

2 Professions: some words describing professions are masculine or feminine according to the sex of the person referred to. The article, the adjectives or the pronoun related to the noun must vary accordingly. These nouns have been indicated in the vocabulary lists in the following way: il/la barista (m and f).

Questo è un barista simpatico. This is a friendly barman.
Questa è una barista simpatica. This is a friendly barmaid.

3 How to form the plural: most nouns are made plural by changing the ending of the singular form. Here is a chart of the changes:

MASCULINE NOUNS		FEMININE NOUNS	
singular	*plural*	*singular*	*plural*
un libr – o	due libr – i	una donn – a	due donn – e
uno student – e	due student – i	una nott – e	due nott – i
un turist – a	due turist – i		

4 Nouns which do not change in the plural:
a) nouns ending with a consonant:

un bar, due bar; un film, due film.

b) nouns ending with an accented vowel:
un tè (tea); due tè; una città (town), due città.

c) abbreviations:
un'auto (one car); due auto (two cars); una foto (photo); due foto (photos)

5 Plurals depending on the stress:
a) nouns ending in -io drop the -o when -io is not stressed: negozio, negozi; viaggio, (journey) viaggi.

b) nouns ending in -cia and -gia drop the -i in the plural, when it is not stressed: un'arancia (orange) due arance.

6 Changes of spelling: most nouns ending in -co, -ca, -go, -ga, insert an h in the plural to maintain the hard sound of the singular: la giacca (jacket) le giacche; il collega (colleague) i colleghi. Masculine nouns ending in -**o**logo change in -**o**logi: soci**o**logo, soci**o**logi.

Notice: all plurals which differ from the chart in (3) above are written next to their singular form in the vocabulary lists.

INDEFINITE ARTICLES

7 The indefinite article (a, an) varies according to the gender of the noun referred to, as well as according to the first letter of the word following the article: una camera antica but un'antica camera (an ancient room).

	MASCULINE	FEMININE
before a consonant	un francese (Frenchman)	una banca (a bank)
before a vowel	un italiano (Italian)	un'altra banca (another bank)
before s + consonant, z, ps, gn, w, j	uno spagnolo (Spaniard)	

8 The indefinite article used as a number – one – varies as indicated above if it is followed by a noun:

un caffè e un' aranciata, per favore (one coffee and one orange squash, please)

If it is not followed by a noun, one is uno (m sing.) and una (f sing.).

9 Uno, una followed by an adjective convey the English sentence a . . . one:

ne prendo una grande (I take a large one).

10 Omissions: Sometimes expressions requiring 'a' in English, do not require it in Italian:
(a) before nouns indicating professions, social, political, religious or temporary status: è qui come turista (he is here as a tourist): è dottore (he is a doctor).

(b) with the exclamation form CHE: che brutto film! (what an awful film!).

(c) when 'a' stands for each: due ore al giorno (two hours a day).

CARDINAL AND ORDINAL NUMBERS; AGE

11(a) Cardinal numbers

1 – 10: Uno (1)
Due (2)
Tre (3)
Quattro (4)
Cinque (5)
Sei (6)
Sette (7)
Otto (8)
Nove (9)
Dieci (19).

11 – 22: Undici (11)
Dodici (12)
Tredici (13)
Quattordici (14)
Quindici (15)
Sedici (16)
Diciassette (17)
Diciotto (18)
Diciannove (19)
Venti (20)
Ventuno (21)
Ventidue (22)
Notice that 20, 30, 40 etc. drop the -o before adding -uno.

30–100: Trenta (30)
Quaranta (40)
Cinquanta (50)
Sessanta (60)
Settanta (70)
Ottanta (80)
Novanta (90)
Cento (100)

200–3000: Duecento (200)
Trecento (300)
Quattrocento (400)
Mille (1000)
Duemila (2000)
Tremila (3000)

Notice: the plural of mille is mila. Multiples of cento and mille are written in one word.

11(b) Ordinal numbers

Primo-a (1st)
secondo-a (2nd)
terzo-a (3rd)
quarto-a (4th)
quinto-a (5th)
sesto-a (6th)
settimo-a (7th)
ottavo-a (8th)
nono-a (9th)
decimo-a (10th)
undicesimo-a (11th)
dodicesimo-a (12th)
ventesimo-a (20th) etc.

From eleventh onwards, ordinal numbers are formed dropping the last vowel of the cardinal number and adding–esimo to it.
Ordinal numbers agree in gender and number with the nouns they refer to:

La seconda strada a sinistra e il secondo viale a destra.	The second road on the left and the second avenue on the right.

12 Age
To express your age you use the verb avere:
ho dieci anni. (lit. I have ten years.)

The word anni must always be stated.

THE DEFINITE ARTICLE

13 As with the indefinite article, it is the noun which indicates the gender and it is the word immediately following the article that determines which form of the definite article to use:

	SINGULAR		PLURAL	
	masculine	*feminine*	*masculine*	*feminine*
before a consonant	il libro	la scarpa	i libri	le scarpe
before a vowel	l' amico	l' amica	gli amici	le amiche
before s + cons., z, gn, ps, w, y	lo sconto		gli sconti	

The definite article when followed by an adjective conveys the English expression, the ... one:

Delle scarpe? *Le* grandi o *le* piccole? Some shoes? The large ones or the small ones?

14 Unlike English, the definite article is also used in the following cases, in Italian:
a) before titles followed by proper names: la signora Rossi (Mrs Rossi). It is omitted, however, when speaking directly: Scusi, signora Rossi. (Excuse me, Mrs Rossi.)

b) before names of languages: L'italiano è facile. (Italian is easy) but: Parlo/studio italiano. (I speak/study Italian).

c) before countries and regions: l'Italia (Italy). But: in Italia (in Italy).

d) with nouns used in a general sense: Mi piace il tè. (I like tea.); Da dove partono i pullman? (Where do coaches leave from?).

e) with abstract nouns and topics: Mi piace la storia. (I like history).

f) with dates: il 26 ottobre del 1982.

g) to say the time: sono le due (It's 2 o'clock).

15 Omissions of the definite article: some expressions of direction, locations, means of transport do not require the article, unlike English: a destra (on the right); in campagna (in the countryside); in auto (in the car).

PREPOSITIONS AND THE DEFINITE ARTICLE

16 Prepositions combine with the definite article to form new words as in the chart below:

	IL	LO	LA	L'	I	GLI	LE	
A	al	allo	alla	all'	ai	agli	alle	at, in, to
DA	dal	dallo	dalla	dall'	dai	dagli	dalle	from, by
IN	nel	nello	nella	nell'	nei	negli	nelle	in, into
DI	del	dello	della	dell'	dei	degli	delle	of
SU	sul	sullo	sulla	sull'	sui	sugli	sulle	on

a is used to indicate:
places: Vado a Roma. (I go to Rome) Telefono a Firenze (I ring up Florence.) Sono a casa. (I am at home)
time: Parto alle due. (I leave at 2 o'clock.) alla mattina (in the morning) due volte all'anno (twice a year)
unit cost: £.2.000 al chilo, al litro (. . . to the kilo, to the lire)
ways of cooking: spaghetti alla bolognese (spaghetti with 'bolognese' sauce)
as indirect object: Scrivi alla mamma? (Do you write to mother?).

di is used to indicate:
possession: il Duomo di Milano (Milan's cathedral)
origin: è di Londra (he is from London)
comparisons: è più grande di quello (it's larger than that); è la più grande città del mondo (it's the largest town in the world)
to be specific: una camicia di cotone (a cotton shirt), il posteggio dei taxi (taxi rank).

da is used to indicate:
from where: arriva da Venezia (is arriving from Venice)
usage: una racchetta da tennis (a tennis racket)
since when: sono qui da due ore (I have been here for two hours)
at someone's place: abita da Maria (she lives at Maria's house)
value: un francobollo da cento (a one hundred liras stamp)
+ *infinitive*: qualcosa da bere (something to drink).

in is used to indicate:
places: abito in Inghilterra (I live in England) Vado in centro. (I go to the city centre.)
means of transport: in treno (by train) in auto (by car).

DEMONSTRATIVE ADJECTIVES AND PRONOUNS

17 Questo

	SINGULAR (this)	PLURAL (these)
masculine	questo libro	questi libri
feminine	questa casa	queste case

In front of a noun starting with a vowel, in the singular, you may use quest': quest'auto (this car).

18 Quel, quello follow a pattern similar to that of the definite article:

SINGULAR		PLURAL	
masculine	*feminine*	*masculine*	*feminine*
(il) quel	(la) quella	(i) quei	(le) quelle
(l') quell'	(l') quell'	(gli) quegli	
(lo) quello			

19 Questo quello (pronouns): when they are not immediately followed by a noun, questo and quello follow a regular pattern:

	this (one)	*these (ones)*	*that (one)*	*those (ones)*
masculine	questo	questi	quello	quelli
feminine	questa	queste	quella	quelle

To point to something near, you say questo-a qui (this one here), to point at something distant, you say: quello-a là (that one there).

When referring to a whole sentence, you use the masc. form

non dico questo — I am not saying this.

20 Indicating possession quello di (that of):

la foto? è quella di Maria — the photo? it's Maria's.

21 The expressions this, that ... **of mine** is translated as follows:

questo/quel mio collega. — this/that colleague of mine.

22 Questo (sing. and pl.) and quello (sing. and pl.) followed by an adjective convey the English expression 'this ... one', 'that ... one'; these ... ones', 'those ... ones'; prendo questo rosso (I take this red one); prendo quella lunga (I take that (the) long one).

EXPRESSIONS OF QUANTITY. PARTITIVES

23 Quanto-i (how much, how many) follows the regular pattern:

quanto latte? quanti metri? quanta carne? quante ore?

24 Molto-i (a lot, much, many) follows the regular pattern:

molto pane molti libri molta frutta molte lezioni

Tanto may replace molto.

25 Poco, pochi (a little, a few, few) follows the regular pattern:

poco sale pochi soldi poca acqua poche parole

Poco is frequently used in expressions of *time*: ho poco tempo (I have little time); and in expressions of *space*: c'è poco spazio (there is little space).

26 Alcuni-e (some, pl.) is mostly used with plural nouns and omitted in negative sentences.

alcuni ragazzi alcune cartoline

27 Summary

These words may refer to people or things. They may be used on their own (as pronouns) or followed by a noun (as adjectives). When they are used on their own, the word ne is inserted before the verb:

hai molte lezioni? (have you got many lessons?) Sì, ne ho molte (yes, I have many) NE = of the lessons, of them.

28 Del (di + def. article) (some, any, no . . .)
For the various forms of this partitive article see chart, ref. 16. These forms occur frequently. They are used with sing. and pl. nouns, in questions and negative sentences:

C'è del pane?	Is there any bread?
No, non c'è del pane.	There is no bread.

(a) NE. The partitive article del is always used when followed by a noun. If the statement (usually a reply, or a reference to a previous sentence) does not repeat the noun, the word ne must be inserted before the verb:

Scusi, avete dei gettoni? – Sì, *ne* abbiamo. No, non *ne* abbiamo.

See also 27; 52

29 Qualche (m and f, sing.) (some, a few) is followed only by sing. nouns: qualche città. It cannot be used with nouns which do not have a plural form or in negative sentences. A common expression is qualche volta (sometimes).

30 Un poco di, un po' di (a bit of, a little of):
Un po' di vino (a little wine) Un po' di burro (a little butter).

31 Di più, di meno (more, less)
are used after a verb uttered or implied: ne vuoi di più? (do you want some more?) No, di meno (no, less).

POSSESSIVE ADJECTIVES AND PRONOUNS

32(a) Unlike English, possessive adjectives (my, your etc.) and possessive pronouns (mine, yours) have identical forms;
(b) they generally require the definite article in front;
(c) they agree in gender and number with what is possessed.

	MASCULINE		FEMININE	
	singular	*plural*	*singular*	*plural*
my, mine	il mio	i miei	la mia	le mie
your, yours (familiar)	il tuo	i tuoi	la tua	le tue
your, yours (formal)	il suo	i suoi	la sua	le sue
his, her, hers, its	il suo	i suoi	la sua	le sue
our, ours	il nostro	i nostri	la nostra	le nostre
your, yours (plural)	il vostro	i vostri	la vostra	le vostre
their, theirs	il loro	i loro	la loro	le loro

33 Remember that 'his' and 'her' describe the possessor, while il suo, la sua etc. are determined by the gender and number of what is possessed: il suo libro (m) = his book, her book. In case of possible misunderstandings – very rare because the context usually makes the meaning clear – one says: i genitori di lui (of him) e di lei (of her).

34 Omission of the definite articles:
(a) the definite article is not compulsory in the following expressions:
è suo? is it yours? sono tuoi? are they yours?
(b) it is not required when the possessive refers to *one* member of the family: mia madre;

35 Possessives with indefinite articles: there is no Italian expression grammatically equivalent to the English *a* (friend) of mine. In Italian it is more simple: un mio amico. Equally, you say: due mie amiche (two friends of mine); dei tuoi amici (some friends of yours); qualche suo collega (some colleague of his) etc.

36 Possessives after the noun: notice the following expressions: a casa mia (at my house, at home); da parte sua (on his/her behalf); mamma mia! (good gracious!).

ADJECTIVES: COMPARATIVE AND SUPERLATIVE FORMS

37 Adjectives agree with the noun they describe. They vary as follows in relation to masc. sing. and pl. or fem. sing. and pl. nouns. Adjectives may end in -o, -e, -a in the masc. sing.

MASCULINE	*singular*	piccol-o	grand-e	laburist-a
	plural	piccol-i	grand-i	laburist-i
FEMININE	*singular*	piccol-a	grand-e	laburist-a
	plural	piccol-e	grand-i	laburist-e

Notice that when an adjective agrees with a noun, the ending of the two words may be different: una casa (f sing.) grande (f sing.).

Most adjectives ending in -a (m sing.) refer to political or artistic positions. But there is belga (Belgian); cipriota (Cypriot); keniota (Kenyan).

38 Adjectives changing their spelling: spelling variations and irregularities applying to nouns (ref. 6) also apply to adjectives: uno stivale lungo (a long boot), stivali lunghi (long boots); una ragazza belga (a Belgian girl) delle ragazze belghe (Belgian girls). These variations are indicated in the vocabulary lists.

39 Adjectives of colour: most colours follow the regular pattern (n. 37). A few are invariable: rosa (pink), arancione (orange-like), viola (purple), blu (blue).

40 Position:
(i) most adjectives can precede or follow the noun they refer to. In most cases, the difference is in the style, not in the meaning.

(ii) Some adjectives have one meaning if they precede the noun, and a different one if they follow it: eg. un grande romanzo (a great novel); una città grande (a large city); una semplice lettera (just a letter); una lettera semplice (a simple letter); il ragazzo stesso (the boy himself); lo stesso ragazzo (the same boy).

41 Bello, buono, grande: these adjectives have an irregular pattern if they precede the noun. Buono and grande become buon and gran before a sing. masc. noun starting with a consonant (except s + consonant, gn etc.): un buon tè (a good tea); un gran caffè. Bello follows a pattern similar to that of the definite article (il etc.): un bel ragazzo; un bello sconto; un bell'autunno; una bell' estate; una bella stagione; dei bei fiori.

42 Altering adjectives:
As in English, adjectives may be changed by placing additional words before them: eg. molto (very); tanto (very); poco (a little); abbastanza (rather, quite, enough); troppo (too). a) These words don't change their endings in front of adjectives. b) adjectives modified by these words always follow the noun: è una casa molto bella (it's a very pretty house).

43 Reinforcing adjectives: a frequent technique is that of repeating the adjective twice: è caro, caro (it's very dear). Or you replace the last vowel of the masc. plur. form of the adjective with the ending -issimo-a-i-e: ricco (rich) s., ricchi pl., ricchissimo (very rich).

44 Endings added to adjectives: the following endings may be added to nouns or adjectives to convey the meaning of bello (nice), grande (big), piccolo (small), brutto (ugly, bad): una cas + etta (a pretty house); and un libr + one (a huge book); un giornal + accio (a bad paper). If an adjective is modified, the ending follows this pattern: -o, -a, -i, -e: una casa bell + ina.

45 Adjectives as nouns:
(a) adjectives may be used as nouns by placing a definite or indefinite article in front of them. This is common with names of nationalities – gli inglesi (the English); un inglese (an Englishman); and with social status: un ricco (a rich man); i ricchi (the rich).

46 Comparisons: these are the most frequent forms of comparison:

più . . . di	(more . . . than)
è più caro di questo	It's dearer than this.
meno . . . di	(less . . . than)
è meno bello del primo	It's less nice than the first.
. . . come	(as . . . as)
È bello come il tuo.	It's as nice as yours.

When the comparison is made between two nouns or two adjectives, than is translated by che:

È più caro che bello.	It's more expensive than nice.

Remember that di in the sense of 'than' combines with the definite article following it in the usual forms:

È più brutta della mia.	It's more ugly than mine.

Il più . . . il meno . . . (the most . . . the least): the article before più or meno depends on the noun it refers to: il (m s.), la (f s.), i (m pl.), le (f pl.): questo vino è il più leggero (this is the lightest wine); questa birra é la più leggera (this is the lightest beer).

Position: notice the two possible positions of this comparative form:

è la borsa più bella; è la più bella borsa	It's the most beautiful bag

This latter form may be used without the noun and is equivalent to the English expression:

è la più lunga.	It's the longest one.

PERSONAL PRONOUNS: SUBJECT AND OBJECT

47 Pronouns used after a preposition: parlo con lui (I talk with him).

		SINGULAR		PLURAL
1st person	me	me	noi	us
2nd person	te	you (familiar)	voi	you (plural)
	lei	you (formal)		
3rd person	lui	him	loro	them
	lei	her		

(a) The word di is required between one of these prepositions and a pronoun: dietro di (behind); dopo di (after); prima di (before); senza di (without); sopra di (above); sotto di (under); verso di (towards): prima di me (before me).
(b) Notice these expressions:
secondo me (according to me) and da me (at my house).

48 Subject pronouns: unless there is a need for clarity or emphasis, these pronouns are usually omitted: arrivo domani (I arrive tomorrow). For emphasis the pronoun may be put after the verb: pago io! (*I* shall pay).

		SINGULAR		PLURAL
1st person	io	I	noi	we
2nd person	tu	you (familiar)	voi	you (plural)
	lei	you (formal)		
3rd person	lui	he	loro	they
	lei	she		

(a) Tu is the familiar form of address.
Lei is the formal form of address.
Voi is used to address more than one person.
Loro is used to address a group of people on *very* formal occasions.

(b) The subject pronouns are also used when there is no verb (the verb is implied):

io prendo del vino e tu?	I take some wine, and you?

(c) Unlike English, they are used in these expressions:

anche tu	you too;
solo io	only me;
neanche lei	not even her.

(d) Unlike English they are used after all forms of the verb **essere**:

Sei tu, Maria?	Is it you, Maria?
Sì, sono io	Yes, it's me, or it's I.

49 Object pronouns (direct and indirect): unlike English, they are placed before the verb in most cases: mi telefoni? (do you ring me up?).

		SINGULAR		PLURAL
1st person	mi	me, to me	ci	us, to us
2nd person	ti	you, to you (familiar)	vi	you, to you (plural)
addressing people	la	you (formal)		
	le	to you (formal)		
3rd person	lo	him, it (m)	li	them (m)
	la	her, it (f)	le	them (f)
	gli	to him	gli, loro	to them
	le	to her	ne	of it, of them

50 Combined forms of pronouns: when *two* pronouns are related to a verb, they undergo some changes as shown in this chart and are placed in a set order before the verb: (dia expresses polite requests; it is a gentle imperative).

me lo dia; me la dia; me li dia; me le dia	give it/them to me
te lo dà; te la dà; te li dà; te le dà	he gives it/them to you
glielo dà; gliela dà; glieli dà; gliele dà	he gives it/them to you (formal)
glielo dia; gliela dia; glieli dia; gliele dia	give it/them to him, to her, to them
ce lo dia; ce la dia; ce li dia; ce le dia	give it/them to us
ve lo dia; ve la dia; ve li dia; ve le dia	give it/them to you

(a) Lo and la (49–50) become l' before all forms of the verb avere (to have): l'ho (I have got it); ce l'abbiamo (we have it).

(b) ecco (here it is, here there are) is often reinforced with a pronoun: eccolo (here it is m.s.); eccoci (here we are).

51 Pronouns after the verb:

(a) loro (*see 49*) is mostly used in writing and always follows the verb:

Scrivo loro.	I write to them.

(b) apart from loro, all object pronouns (*49–50*) are added to the infinitive form after dropping the last vowel of the verb:

Vado a portarlo.	I go and take it.

(c) similarly, they are combined with the imperative form:
prendila pure (do take it, please);
non prenderlo (don't take it). (*For negative commands see 65.*)

(d) with any form of these verbs dovere (must), potere (can), volere (to want) – object pronouns (*49–50*, except loro) can be placed before these verbs or after the infinitive following them:

Ti devo telefonare. or devo telefonarti	I must telephone you.

52 Ne (of it, of them) follows the same rules as the object pronouns for its position. (*for its use see 28*) It combines with other pronouns in the following way:
me ne dia ... gliene, te ne ... ce ne ... ve ne ...

53 The following verbs require a direct pronoun object in Italian: aspettare la aspetto (lit. I await you); il aspetto (lit. I await them). Ascoltare (to listen) to), cercare (to look for), guardare (to look at).

The following require an indirect personal pronoun object:
gli dico (lit. I tell to him); le chiedo (lit. I ask to you). Chiedere (to ask), dare (to give); dire (to say); domandare (to ask); illustrare (to show); offrire (to offer); ordinare (to order); portare (to bring, to take); raccontare (to tell); ripetere (to repeat); rispondere (to answer); scrivere (to write); spedire (to send).

REFLEXIVE PRONOUNS AND VERBS

54 Verbs ending in -si in the infinitive are preceded by the following pronouns when conjugated: divertirsi = mi diverto (I enjoy myself); cambiarsi = mi cambio (I change myself); accorgeresi = mi accorgo (I realize). *See also 51(b).*

		SINGULAR		PLURAL
1st person	mi	myself	ci	ourselves
2nd person	ti	yourself (familiar)	vi	yourselves
	si	yourself (formal)	si	themselves
3rd person	si	himself, herself		

Notice that not all verbs which are reflexive in Italian are reflexive in English and viceversa. Check with the dictionary: mi ricordo (I remember).

The plural forms of the reflexive pronouns can have a reciprocal meaning: ci incontriamo (we meet each other).

RELATIVE PRONOUNS

55
(a) Che; (who, whom, that, which) is used for people and things.
(b) Chi: (those who). It requires a sing. verb: chi studia ... those who study ...
(c) Cui: it is used after a preposition: con cui ... (with whom, with which).
(d) Quello che: non capisco quello che vuole (I don't understand what he wants).

INDEFINITE PRONOUNS

56 The following words are often used as subject pronouns and require a plural verb:
pochi (a few people); molti (a lot of people); alcuni (some people); altri (other people), tutti (everybody). The following ones require a verb in the singular: ognuno (everyone); chiunque (anyone); qualcuno (someone); qualcosa (something).

When some of the above words are used as object pronouns – molti-e, pochi-e, alcuni-e, altri-e – , they require NE before the verb: ne compro molti (I buy a lot); ne cerco altri (I am looking for others). *But* li/le compro tutti/e (I buy all of them).

57 Tutto: has various translations in English, when not followed by a noun. Tutti sono qui (everybody is here). È tutto (that is all). Prendo tutto (I take everything). Lo prendo tutto (I take it all).

VERBS: PRESENT TENSE

58 The formal form of address and the 3rd person sing. (he, she) have the same ending with all verbs, and with all the tenses.

There are three types of regular verbs. One with the infinitive ending in -are (1st conjugation); one in -ere (2nd conj.) and one in -ire (3rd conj.). They follow the pattern below. Essere and avere are irregular in most tenses and forms.

	ESSERE	AVERE	1ST CONJ.	2ND CONJ.	3RD CONJ.
SINGULAR					
1st person	io sono	ho	parlo	prendo	parto
2nd person	tu sei	hai	parli	prendi	parti
3rd person	lui, lei è	ha	parla	prende	parte
(*you formal*)					
PLURAL					
1st person	noi siamo	abbiamo	parliamo	prendiamo	partiamo
2nd person	voi siete	avete	parlate	prendete	partite
3rd person	loro sono	hanno	parlano	prendono	partono

59 Verb of the 3rd conj. with an irregular pattern: a group of verbs indicated in the vocabulary lists with *, have the following pattern: capire
cap-isco
cap-isci
cap-isce
capiamo
capite
cap-iscono.
They are regular in the past tense and future.

60 Spelling changes: in order to preserve the original hard g or c sound of the infinitive, verbs ending in -care or -gare require an h before the endings of the 2nd person sing. and 1st person plur.: pagare = paghi, paghiamo.

All verbs ending in -iare, drop the i of the stem before endings starting with -i: studiare – studi + iamo = studiamo.

61 Uses of the present tense:
(a) as in English it describes *a state of affairs*:
Ho pochi soldi. I have little money.

(b) it is used to express the English *present continuous*:
Lavori a Londra adesso? Are you working in London now?

(c) to express an *intention* or a *suggestion*:
Le prendo. I'll take them.
Andiamo? Shall we go?

(d) to express an action that has started in the past and is still continuing at the moment of speaking:
Aspetto da tre ore. I have been waiting for three hours.
Sono qui da lunedì. I have been here since Monday.

(e) to express an action in the *immediate future*:
Quanto tempo resti? How long are you going to stay?

62 C'è (there is) and ci sono (there are) change if ne is inserted in this way:
C'è frutta? sì, ce n'è. There is some of it.
Ci sono dei fiori? sì, ce ne sono. Yes, there are some.

63 Expressions with the verb avere: unlike English, some important expressions relating to the senses, require avere:
ho caldo (I am hot); ho freddo (I am cold); ho fame (I am hungry); ho sete (I am thirsty); ho paura (I am afraid); ho sonno (I am sleepy); ho premura (I am in a hurry).

64 Irregular verbs may differ from the standard patterns only in some forms and some tenses. They are pointed out in the vocabulary lists as irr.. Only the most common are given here. For the rest, see dictionaries or reference grammars.

1ST CONJ.

andare	*dare*	*fare*	*stare*
vado	do	faccio	sto
vai	dai	fai	stai
va	dà	fa	sta
andiamo	diamo	facciamo	stiamo
andate	date	fate	state
vanno	danno	fanno	stanno

2ND CONJ.

bere	*dovere*	*potere*	*sapere*
bevo	devo	posso	so
bevi	devi	puoi	sai
beve	deve	può	sa
beviamo	dobbiamo	possiamo	sappiamo
bevete	dovete	potete	sapete
bevono	devono	possono	sanno

2ND CONJ.	3RD CONJ.		
volere	*dire*	*uscire*	*venire*
voglio	dico	esco	vengo
vuoi	dici	esci	vieni
vuole	dice	esce	viene
vogliamo	diciamo	usciamo	veniamo
volete	dite	uscite	venite
vogliono	dicono	escono	vengono

65 IMPERATIVE: REQUESTS AND SUGGESTIONS

guardare	*prendere*	*sentire*	*andare*	(irr.)
guarda	prendi	senti	vai	(familiar)
guardi	prenda	senta	vada	(formal)
guardate	prendete	sentite	andate	(plural)

(a) The irregular verbs of chart 64 are regular in the familiar and the plural form of the imperative (except dire = di', say!). The formal form is irregular: vada (andare); dia (dare); stia (stare); faccia (fare); beva (bere); esca (uscire); venga (venire).

(b) The English form 'let's' is expressed with the 1st person plur. of the present tense:
andiamo! let's go!

(c) To give negative commands the word non is placed in front of the verb, except for the familiar sing. form. In this case the negative command is expressed with non + the infinitive: Tim, non andare là (Tim, don't go there).

(d) Indirect and direct object pronouns follow and combine with the 2nd person sing. and 2nd person pl. of the imperative: ascoltala (listen to it); ascoltatela (listen to it). Here are two useful anomalies: dammi (give me); dimmi (tell me).

THE PRESENT PERFECT—THE SIMPLE PAST

66 The tense in the chart below (passato prossimo) is used to express both the Present Perfect and the Simple Past:
Ho prenotato due posti. I've booked two seats.
Ho incontrato tua madre ieri. I met your mother yesterday.

essere	*avere*	*comprare*	*vendere*	*sentire*
sono stato-a	ho avuto	ho comprato	ho venduto	ho sentito

67 Most verbs form the perfect tense with *avere*. Some use *essere*:

(a) the verb essere itself, stare, restare: sono restato a casa (I remained at home);

(b) with reflexive and reciprocal verbs ci siamo incontrati ieri. (We've met yesterday).

(c) with verbs describing a movement and not followed by a direct object: Sono ripartita ieri. (I left yesterday.)

(d) in the passive form: è invitato da me. (He is invited by me).

68 With verbs using essere, the past participle agrees in gender and number with the subject: Tim è arrivato; Lucia è partita.

69 The past participle of a verb which requires *avere* in the past tense may agree in gender and number with the direct object pronoun preceding the verb: ci ha salutati (he has greeted us, men) ci ha salutate (he has greeted us, women). If a relative pronoun precedes the verb, the past participle may agree: la frutta che ho comprata (the fruit I bought)

70 For some of the verbs requiring essere, *see 16.3(f)*. Remember, also: piacere—mi è piaciuto (I liked it) and mi è sembrato (it seemed to me).

THE IMPERFECT

71 The vast majority of verbs are regular in this tense.

essere	*avere*	*andare*	*leggere*	*uscire*
ero	avevo	andavo	leggevo	uscivo

eri	avevi	andavi	leggevi	uscivi
era	aveva	andava	leggeva	usciva
eravamo	avevamo	andavamo	leggevamo	uscivamo
eravate	avevate	andavate	leggevate	uscivate
erano	avevano	andavano	leggevano	uscivano

72 To form the imperfect of fare and dire, add the regular endings of the imperfect to the old infinitive forms:
fac-ere and dic-ere: facevo . . . (I used to make . . .); dicevo (I used to say . . .).

Uses: this tense is used:
(a) to describe an action which was in progress in the past:
leggevo quando . . . (I was reading when . . .).
(b) to describe habitual actions in the past:
uscivo tutti i giorni (I used to go out every day).
(c) to describe past situations (age, social and moral conditions, physical situations).
Avevo due anni. (I was two years old); Abitavo a Londra. (I lived in London); Ero allegro. (I was cheerful).

THE FUTURE

73

essere	*avere*	*comprare*	*scrivere*	*partire*
sarò	avrò	comprerò	scriverò	partirò
sarai	avrai	comprerai	scriverai	partirai
sarà	avrà	comprerà	scriverà	partirà
saremo	avremo	compreremo	scriveremo	partiremo
sarete	avrete	comprerete	scriverete	partirete
saranno	avranno	compreranno	scriveranno	partiranno

To form the future of the irregular verbs (*64*), add these endings: (-ò; -ai; -à; -emo; -ete; -anno) to these stems: andare- andr-; dare- dar-; fare- far-; stare- star-; bere- ber-; dovere- dovr-; potere- potr-; sapere- sapr-; volere- vorr-; dire- dir-; venire- verr-.

Spelling changes: verbs ending in -iare drop the -i of the stem before the endings of the future: cominc(i)-are = cominc-erò; verbs ending in -care and -gare insert an h before the endings of the future: pagare = pag + h-erò = pagherò.

Uses: (a) the future expresses an action expected to take place in the future described in English with shall, will, to be going to.

(b) unlike English it is used in sentences with quando (when), finchè (until), se (if): se verrò, porterò il mio cane (If I come, I will take my dog).

74 Stare per + infinitive: to express an action on the point of being done, one uses the present form of stare followed by per and the infinitive of the verb expressing the action: sto per uscire, I am going out.

QUESTIONS

75 Questions are very simply formed by giving the voice the intonation of a question (the tone rises at the end of the sentence). The subject may be put before the verb or at the end of the sentence: Franca arriva oggi? Arriva oggi Franca? (Does Franca arrive today?)

76 Questions are also formed with these words:
(a) dove? come? come mai? quando? perchè? dove lavora Lucio? (where does Lucio work?); come va il tuo lavoro? (how is your work going?); come mai non sei partita? (why ever didn't you leave?) quando parte il treno? (when does the train leave?); perchè telefoni? (why do you ring up?). With these interrogative adverbs the subject may be placed at the end of the sentence or at the beginning: dove va Franco? Franco dove va? (where is Franco going?)

(b) **Interrogative adjectives:** che (what), quanto-a-i-e (how much, how many), quale . . . ?(s.) quali? (pl.) (which . . . ?) agree in gender and number with the nouns they refer to, except che . . . (invar.): che birra prendi? (what beer do you take?); quale attore preferisci? (what actor do you prefer?); quanti chili vuole? (how many kilos do you want?). Che etc. may be used with a preposition in front: in che città abita? (in what town do you live?).

(c) **Interrogative pronouns:** chi? (who?) che cosa? (what?) quanto-a-i-e? (how much, how many?) quale-i? (which one?) chi è? (who is it?); che cosa desidera? (what do you wish?) quanti sono? (how many are they?) quali compra? (which ones do you buy?) Chi may be used with prepositions: con chi è? (with whom is he?) Di chi means whose: di chi è questa borsa? (whose bag is this?) Che cosa may be shortened to cosa?; che?

(d) Interrogatives may be reinforced with words such as vero? davvero? which are equivalent to the English expressions is it? don't they?

NEGATIVE SENTENCES

77 Negative sentences are made by placing non before the verb: non vado oggi (I'm not going today); non capisce? (don't you understand?) Non is placed **before object pronouns:** non lo vedo (I don't see him); non mi piace (I don't like it).

78 Unlike English non is not dropped in a sentence where there is mai (never), niente (nothing), nessuno (nobody), nessun + *a noun* (no . . .), nè . . . nè (neither . . . nor): non ho mai visitato Londra (I have never visited London); non ho comprato niente (I haven't bought anything). But non is not required if any of these words start the sentence: nessuno è venuto (no one has come).

THE IMPERSONAL FORM SI; THE PASSIVE

79 The word *SI* (without accent) is used in Italian to convey the English pronouns one + verb: